British Social Attitudes

Attitudes

The 26th
REPORT

The **National Centre for Social Research** (NatCen) is an independent, non-profit social research organisation. It has a large professional staff together with its own interviewing and coding resources. Some of NatCen's work – such as the survey reported in this book – is initiated by NatCen itself and grant-funded by research councils or charitable foundations. Other work is initiated by government departments or quasi-government organisations to provide information on aspects of social or economic policy. NatCen also works frequently with other institutes and academics. Founded in 1969 and now Britain's largest social research organisation, NatCen has a high reputation for the standard of its work in both qualitative and quantitative research.

The contributors

Rossy Bailey
Senior Researcher at NatCen and Co-Director of the *British Social Attitudes* survey series

Matt Barnes
Research Director (analyst) at NatCen

Sarah Butt
Senior Researcher at NatCen and Co-Director of the *British Social Attitudes* survey series

Elizabeth Clery
Research Director at NatCen and Co-Director of the *British Social Attitudes* survey series

John Curtice
Research Consultant at the *Scottish Centre for Social Research*, part of NatCen, and Professor of Politics at Strathclyde University

Rory Fitzgerald
Deputy Director of the Centre for Comparative Social Surveys, City University London

Elizabeth Fuller
Research Director at NatCen

Eric Harrison
Senior Research Fellow at the Centre for Comparative Social Surveys, City University London

Robert Johns
Lecturer in Politics, University of Strathclyde

Rodney Ling
Research Assistant at the Institute for Social Change, University of Manchester

Siobhan McAndrew
Research Associate at the Institute for Social Change, University of Manchester

Stephen McKay
Professor of Social Research in the School of Social Policy, University of Birmingham

Rachel Ormston
Research Director at the *Scottish Centre for Social Research*

Stephen Padgett
Professor of Politics, University of Strathclyde

Alison Park
Research Group Director at NatCen and Co-Director of the *British Social Attitudes* survey series

Miranda Phillips
Research Director at NatCen and Co-Director of the *British Social Attitudes* survey series

Andy Ross
Senior Researcher at NatCen

Amanda Sacker
Research Professor at the Institute for Social and Economic Change, University of Essex

Katarina Thomson
Formerly Research Director at NatCen and Co-Director of the *British Social Attitudes* survey series

Wojtek Tomaszweski
Senior Researcher (analyst) at NatCen

David Voas
Simon Professor of Population Studies at the Institute for Social Change, University of Manchester

Los Angeles | London | New Delhi
Singapore | Washington DC

British
Social
Attitudes

work   diversity
FAMILY
smoking food
taxation
WORK   government
DRUGS work COHABITATION
attitude change LONE PARENTS
COHABITATION food
food ELECTIONS
WORK   drinking
smoking ageing
FAMILY EUROPE smoking
spending   family   DIVERSITY
turnout FAMILY
attitude change GOVERNMENT
food RETIREMENT
welfare DRUGS WORK VOTING
taxation attitude change
work voting europe
cohabitation
WORK DIVERSITY
food SPENDING
governments diversity
taxation family WORK
RELIGION FOOD
food welfare taxation Europe lone parent
government cohabitation work
FOOD
drugs attitude change taxation food work
COHABITATION Spending WORK DRUGS
family
RELIGION DIVERSITY turnout GOVERNMENT
FOOD AGEING FAMILY attitude change work
smoking RELIGION COHABITATION
drugs FAMILY taxation WORK ageing
turnout attitude change LONE PARENTS
retirement governments COHABITATION
turnout WORK attitude change work spending
VOTING food RELIGION FOOD drugs
drinking Europe
voting
DRUGS

British Social
Attitudes

The 26th REPORT

Editors

Alison Park, John Curtice, Katarina Thomson,
Miranda Phillips, Elizabeth Clery and Sarah Butt

SAGE Publications Ltd
1 Oliver's Yard
55 City Road
London EC1Y 1SP

SAGE Publications Inc.
2455 Teller Road
Thousand Oaks, California 91320

SAGE Publications India Pvt Ltd
B 1/I 1 Mohan Cooperative Industrial Area
Mathura Road
New Delhi 110 044

SAGE Publications Asia-Pacific Pte Ltd
33 Pekin Street #02-01
Far East Square
Singapore 048763

Library of Congress Control Number: 2009941310

British Library Cataloguing in Publication data

A catalogue record for this book is available from the British Library

ISBN 978-1-84920-387-6

Printed by MPG Books Group, Bodmin, Cornwall
Printed on paper from sustainable resources

Mixed Sources
Product group from well-managed forests and other controlled sources
www.fsc.org Cert no. SA-COC-1565
© 1996 Forest Stewardship Council
FSC

Contents

Appendix I: Technical details of the survey   269

Subject index   291

List of tables and figures

Chapter 4

Chapter 5

Chapter 6

Chapter 7

Chapter 8

Chapter 9

Chapter 10

Chapter 11

Appendix I

Table conventions

1. Figures in the tables are from the 2008 *British Social Attitudes* survey unless otherwise indicated.
2. Tables are percentaged as indicated by the percentage signs.
3. In tables, '*' indicates less than 0.5 per cent but greater than zero, and '–' indicates zero.
4. When findings based on the responses of fewer than 100 respondents are reported in the text, reference is made to the small base size.
5. Percentages equal to or greater than 0.5 have been rounded up (e.g. 0.5 per cent = one per cent; 36.5 per cent = 37 per cent).
6. In many tables the proportions of respondents answering "Don't know" or not giving an answer are not shown. This, together with the effects of rounding and weighting, means that percentages will not always add to 100 per cent.
7. The self-completion questionnaire was not completed by all respondents to the main questionnaire (see Appendix I). Percentage responses to the self-completion questionnaire are based on all those who completed it.
8. The bases shown in the tables (the number of respondents who answered the question) are printed in small italics. The bases are unweighted, unless otherwise stated.

Introduction

The first *British Social Attitudes* survey took place in 1983 and, since then, nearly 80,000 people have taken part in what has become an annual study. Their generosity has helped make *British Social Attitudes* the authoritative guide to public opinion in modern Britain, and to the ways in which our attitudes and values are shifting over time. Our aim is that these robust and impartial survey findings give a voice to the general public, and paint a picture of what Britain *really* thinks and feels, in all its richness and diversity.

The report begins with three chapters of particular relevance to the 2010 general election. In Chapter 1 we examine people's views about voting and whether it is seen to be a civic 'duty'. Chapters 2 and 3 then explore public opinion about government and policy, focusing on the ways in which public attitudes are related to the ideological positions taken by different political parties. Chapter 2 focuses on Britain, and its reaction to two terms of New Labour, while Chapter 3 looks at the British experience in a European context, and examines the extent to which political parties are able to influence attitudes and values within different countries.

Chapters 4 and 5 focus on religion. Chapter 4 examines the similarities and differences between Britain and the US in terms of religious faith, practice and attitudes towards religion. And Chapter 5 looks at the extent to which religious faith in Britain is linked to people's views about bio-ethical debates (such as abortion and assisted dying), gender relations and politics.

Chapters 6 and 7 both consider attitudes towards a range of lifestyle choices and behaviours. In Chapter 6 we explore the role that ageing plays in shaping people's attitudes, while Chapter 7 examines how British views about family and fertility compare with those held in other European countries.

The final chapters bring our attention back to Britain, and focus on a number of policy areas that are often in the spotlight. Chapter 8 describes views about older workers, retirement and extended working, while Chapter 9 assesses public opinion about lone parents and whether there is support for the government's increasing requirement that this group be expected to look for work in some circumstances, as a pre-requisite for benefit receipt. Chapter 10 explores public attitudes towards innovative food technologies (for instance, technologies that seek to make a product healthier or longer lasting), including genetically modified foods. Finally, in Chapter 11, we focus on attitudes towards three legal and illegal drugs – alcohol, tobacco and cannabis – and consider public attitudes towards increasingly restrictive legislation about their use.

Most of the tables in the report are based on *British Social Attitudes* data from 2008 and earlier years. Conventions for reading the tables can be found at the start of the report. Full details of all the questions included in the 2008 survey can be found at www.natcen.ac.uk/bsaquestionnaires.

A number of chapters make use of data from other surveys than *British Social Attitudes*. Two, both cross-national, are worthy of particular mention; the *International Social Survey Programme* (results from which are discussed in Chapters 3, 4 and 5) and the *European Social Survey* (Chapters 7 and 8).

Our thanks

British Social Attitudes could not take place without its many generous funders. The Gatsby Charitable Foundation (one of the Sainsbury Family Charitable Trusts) has provided core funding on a continuous basis since the survey's inception and in doing so has ensured the survey's security and independence. A number of government departments have regularly funded modules of interest to them, while respecting the independence of the study. In 2008 we gratefully acknowledge the support of the Departments for Health, Transport, and Work and Pensions. We also thank the Department for Children, Schools and Families, the Department for Business, Enterprise and Regulatory Reform (now the Department for Business, Innovation and Skills), and the Food Standards Agency. Our thanks are also due to the Hera Trust.

The Economic and Social Research Council (ESRC) continued to support the participation of Britain in the *International Social Survey Programme* (ISSP), a collaboration whereby surveys in over 40 countries administer an identical module of questions in order to facilitate comparative research. Some of the results are described in Chapters 3, 4 and 5. Thanks are also due to the John Templeton Foundation and NORFACE, who funded additional questions about religion, to supplement those being included as part of the ISSP. Finally, we would like to thank The Leverhulme Trust, who funded a series of questions about national identity, that we will describe in our next report.

We are also grateful to Professor Richard Topf of London Metropolitan University for all his work in creating and maintaining access to an easy to use website that provides a fully searchable database of all the questions that have ever been carried on a *British Social Attitudes* survey, together with details of the pattern of responses to every question. This site provides an invaluable resource for those who want to know more than can be found in this report. It is located at www.britsocat.com.

The *British Social Attitudes* survey is a team effort. The research group that designs, directs and reports on the study is supported by complementary teams who implement the survey's sampling strategy and carry out data processing.

The researchers in turn depend on fieldwork controllers, area managers and field interviewers who are responsible for all the interviewing, and without whose efforts the survey would not happen at all. The survey is heavily dependent too on staff who organise and monitor fieldwork and compile and distribute the survey's extensive documentation, for which we would pay particular thanks to Pauline Burge and her colleagues in NatCen's administrative office in Brentwood. We are also grateful to Sandra Beeson in our computing department who expertly translates our questions into a computer assisted questionnaire, and to Roger Stafford who has the unenviable task of editing, checking and documenting the data. Meanwhile the raw data have to be transformed into a workable SPSS system file – a task that has for many years been performed with great care and efficiency by Ann Mair at the Social Statistics Laboratory at the University of Strathclyde. Many thanks are also due to David Mainwaring and Imogen Roome at our publishers, Sage.

Finally, we must praise the people who anonymously gave up their time to take part in our 2008 survey. They are the cornerstone of this enterprise. We hope that some of them might come across this volume and read about themselves and the story they tell of modern Britain with interest.

The Editors

1 Duty in decline? Trends in attitudes to voting

*Sarah Butt and John Curtice**

Recent British general elections have been notable for low levels of turnout. Between 1922 and 1997 the officially recorded level of turnout had never fallen below 70 per cent. But in 2001 it dropped to just 59 per cent, while in 2005 it recovered only slightly to 61 per cent. It seemed as though the electorate had suddenly become 'disengaged' from those who wished to lead their country.

The causes and consequences of this development have been the subject of considerable debate and analysis. In particular, there is ongoing discussion about whether the recent decline in turnout marks the start of a longer-term trend towards lower turnout, brought about by long-term changes in the character of the electorate. In support of this argument, a number of possible reasons as to why the electorate may generally have become less interested in and more cynical about conventional politics have been put forward. One such suggestion is that because voters are better educated nowadays they also have higher expectations. At the same time, thanks to the impact of globalisation and an increasingly interdependent world, the ability of national governments to effect change has been curtailed. The resulting mismatch between voters' expectations and governments' capacity to deliver has, it is suggested, rendered people more cynical about and thus less willing to get involved in conventional politics (Dalton, 2004).

A second such line of argument focuses on the role of the media. Long before the expenses scandal engulfed MPs in 2009, it was claimed that the media had come to adopt a more critical tone in its coverage of politics, and had developed an unhealthy obsession with personal scandal in particular (Deacon, 2004). Such coverage, it was suggested, encouraged cynicism about politics (Patterson, 1993; Blumler, 1997; Barnett, 2002). Others, meanwhile, have suggested that the large amount of time spent in front of the television nowadays is time not spent engaging in social activities with others. Because people do not interact

* Sarah Butt is a Senior Researcher at the *National Centre for Social Research* and is Co-Director of the *British Social Attitudes* survey series. John Curtice is Research Consultant at the *Scottish Centre for Social Research*, part of NatCen, and Professor of Politics at Strathclyde University.

with each other they are less likely to trust each other and thus feel the sense of connection with the wider society that might encourage them to vote in elections alongside their fellow citizens (Putnam, 2000).

A third body of theory, meanwhile, focuses on changes in the social psychology of voters. Long-term social changes, it is suggested, have served to make people think of themselves more as individuals and less as members of a social group with whom they identify. For example, people are supposedly less likely nowadays to think of themselves as either middle or working class, thanks both to the decline of heavy industry and the homogenous class communities that they generated (Clark and Lipset 1991; Pakulski and Waters 1996) and to the development of competitive labour markets where workers are encouraged to seek individual rather than collective advancement (Beck, 1992; Beck and Beck-Gernsheim, 2001). Similarly, it has often been argued that voters are less likely nowadays to feel a sense of attachment to a political party, both as a result of the alleged decline in class identities and because voters now see and hear about politics *via* the relatively neutral tones of television rather than through partisan sources such as political parties or family (Butler and Stokes, 1974; Rose and McAllister, 1986; Wattenberg, 2000).

Such identities and attachments matter at election time because they can provide voters with the motivation to turn out and vote even when it is not clear that bothering to vote will make much difference. It has long been pointed out that, given there is little chance that one vote will ever make a difference to the outcome of an election, it is arguably irrational for any individual voter to go to the trouble of casting a ballot (Downs, 1957; Riker and Ordeshook, 1968). But if casting a vote is an 'expressive' act, undertaken because voters wishes to register their sense of attachment to a particular social group or a party, then voters can be expected to turn out and vote regardless of whether they think their vote is likely to make a difference. So if voters are now less likely to have such attachments, this could well result in lower turnout.

The sense of attachment that might help bring voters to the polls need not necessarily be a sense of attachment to a particular section of society, but rather to a society – or nation – as a whole. A voter may feel that as someone who enjoys the rights and freedoms of being a British citizen they have an obligation to their fellow citizens at election time to exercise the right to vote that comes with citizenship. Doing so expresses their sense of commitment to their country and its democracy. Certainly those who say that they feel that people have a duty to vote have repeatedly been shown to be more likely actually to participate at election time (Jones and Hudson, 2000; Bromley and Curtice, 2002; Curtice *et al.*, 2007). Indeed, in extensive multivariate analyses of turnout, a sense of duty to vote emerges as one of the most important predictors of whether someone votes or not, and so any explanation of who does and does not vote is likely to be incomplete without taking its role into account (Clarke *et al.*, 2004). Evidently, if that sense of duty to vote were to become less commonly felt, turnout would be expected to fall.

Others have argued that the principal explanation of the low turnout at recent British elections lies not in a change in the character of the electorate but, rather, in that of elections (Heath and Taylor, 1999; Bromley and Curtice, 2002; Clarke *et al.*, 2004, Curtice *et al.*, 2007). The 2001 and 2005 elections in particular had two characteristics that served to depress turnout. First, there was little difference between the policy stances adopted by the political parties, largely as a result of a shift to the centre by the Labour Party (Bara and Budge, 2001; Bara, 2006). Second, the opinion polls suggested that the incumbent government was almost certain to win. As a result, voters might easily have come to the conclusion that it was obvious who would win and that who won would not make much difference anyway. In such circumstances we should not be surprised if voters who did not feel a duty to vote decided to stay at home (Blais, 2000). But equally, if and when those circumstances change, turnout might be expected to return to its previous levels once more.

Even if recent low levels of turnout have been the product of short-term circumstance rather than long-term social change, however, they may still have left a permanent mark on the electorate. It is often argued that social psychological attachments such as those that might foster a duty to vote are in part developed and reinforced by being expressed (Butler and Stokes, 1974). In other words, a sense of duty is fostered if voters do actually go to the polls and, conversely, is likely to wither if they do not. This is often thought to be particularly true of younger people who have only recently acquired the right to vote. If those who have recently become adults do not vote when they first have the opportunity to do so, they seem less likely to develop the sense of duty that would help ensure they vote on a regular basis throughout their lives (Clarke *et al.*, 2004). So, even if voters were initially dissuaded from voting because of the particular circumstances surrounding recent elections in Britain, we might still find that fewer people now feel that they have an obligation to vote, and that as a result turnout may well remain low even if circumstances change.

In this chapter we chart long-term trends in duty to vote, taking advantage of the only long-term time-series of data on this subject in Britain. Thereafter we examine some possible explanations of the trends we identify with reference to the arguments we have just outlined. We conclude by assessing the implications of our findings for the level of turnout in future British general elections and for the degree to which general elections can be relied upon to provide a reasonable reflection of the preferences of the electorate.

Why duty to vote matters

We begin, however, by demonstrating just how much more likely it is that someone who feels a duty to vote will actually cast a ballot. We ascertain duty to vote by asking respondents the following question:

> *Which of these statements comes <u>closest</u> to your view about general elections? In a general election ...*
> *... it's not really worth voting*
> *... people should vote only if they care who wins*
> *... it's everyone's duty to vote*

Data are available not only for the two most recent general election years, but also for the 1987 election. Those who gave the last response are regarded as feeling a duty to vote (or 'civic duty'). And, as Table 1.1 shows, this group is consistently more likely to report having voted at the most recent general election. Moreover, this was particularly true in 2001 and 2005 when the overall level of turnout was low. Turnout among those who felt a duty to vote was only seven percentage points lower in 2001 and 2005 than it had been in 1987. In contrast it was as much as 25 percentage points lower among those who said that "people should only vote if they care who wins". Among those who said "it's not really worth voting at all", turnout was as much as 13 points down, even though in 1987 only just over a third of this group had bothered to make the journey to the polling station. This pattern is consistent with the argument that feeling a sense of duty to vote matters, particularly when the circumstances in which an election is fought do not offer much incentive to participate.

Table 1.1 Turnout, by civic duty, 1987, 2001 and 2005

% who voted	1987[+]	Base	2001	Base	2005	Base	Change 1987– 2005
Civic duty							
It's not really worth voting	37	109	24	317	24	210	-13
People should only vote if they care who wins	75	697	49	644	50	379	-25
It's everyone's duty to vote	92	2586	85	1798	85	1122	-7

[+] Source: British Election Study

Indeed, the importance that civic duty plays in encouraging otherwise apparently disengaged voters to the polls is demonstrated in Table 1.2, which shows how reported turnout at the 2005 election varied on the basis of both civic duty and reported interest in politics combined.

Table 1.2 Turnout, by civic duty and interest in politics, 2005

% who voted	Civic duty			
	It's everyone's duty to vote	Base	Other	Base
How much interest in politics				
Great deal/quite a lot	87	485	58	117
Some	86	397	52	209
Not much/none at all	82	240	25	263

Among those who felt a sense of duty to vote, and hence were motivated to vote for expressive reasons, reported turnout was high regardless of their level of interest in politics. Conversely, those without such a sense of duty were unlikely to vote at all unless they had at least some interest in politics. Evidently, therefore, any marked decline in the sense of civic duty could well have important implications for the level of turnout.

The downward trend in duty to vote

But is there any evidence of a decline in civic duty? Table 1.3 shows there is. At the time of the 1987 election around three in four people acknowledged such a duty. Now, less than three in five people (56 per cent) do so. True, this comparison may overstate the decline somewhat. The 1987 figure in Table 1.3 comes from the British Election Study, a survey specifically about elections and politics. In contrast, all subsequent readings in the table come from the more wide-ranging *British Social Attitudes* survey. Given this difference of subject matter, the 1987 survey may have been less likely to secure the participation of those with little interest in politics, and thus those who do not feel a sense of civic duty (see also Heath *et al.*, 2007). But even so, the most recent figure for civic duty is still as much as 12 percentage points lower than the equivalent figure in the 1991 *British Social Attitudes* survey, and is also markedly lower than it had been as recently as the last general election.

Meanwhile, there has been a corresponding increase in the proportion of people saying that it is not really worth voting. The proportion of people giving this response now stands at nearly one in five (18 per cent) of respondents, an increase of 10 percentage points on 1991. This, as we saw in Table 1.1, is the group that is least likely to vote at all. In contrast, there has been no apparent change in the proportion who say people should only vote if they care who wins, that is, the group whose propensity to vote lies in between that of the other two groups identified by our civic duty question.

Table 1.3 Civic duty, 1987–2008

	1987[+]	1991	1994	1996	1998	2000	2001	2004	2005	2008
Civic duty	%	%	%	%	%	%	%	%	%	%
It's not really worth voting	3	8	9	8	8	11	11	12	12	18
People should only vote if they care who wins	21	24	21	26	26	24	23	27	23	23
It's everyone's duty to vote	76	68	68	64	65	64	65	60	64	56
Base		*3413*	*1224*	*970*	*989*	*1654*	*2008*	*2795*	*2609*	*1732*	*990*

[+] Source: British Election Study

Of course, we have to be wary of making too much of a change in one particular year. However, the decline in civic duty in 2008 follows on from a relatively low reading in 2004, while all readings from 1996 onwards have been lower than those before 1996. Meanwhile, there is no particular reason to anticipate that the sense of civic duty will be restored during the course of an election campaign; it certainly did not bounce back in the wake of the 2001 campaign. In short, it looks as though there has been a long-term decline in civic duty in Britain and that it could well be weaker at the time of the next election than on the occasion of any previous general election. This would not seem to augur well for a return at future elections to a higher level of turnout.

Why has civic duty declined?

So how might we account for this change? We look at three possibilities. First, we have seen that more than one attempt to explain the decline in turnout has suggested that it is the result of increasing cynicism among voters. So we look at the possibility that the decline in the sense of duty to vote could also be the result of growing distrust of politics and politicians. At the same time we look at the wider argument that the decline is the product of growing distrust across society in general.

Secondly, we have noted the argument that young adults who do not vote are unlikely to develop the feeling that they have a duty to vote. There is certainly considerable evidence that turnout was particularly low among younger people at recent elections (see also Clarke et al., 2003; Curtice, 2006). We therefore examine whether there is any evidence that those who have entered the electorate more recently have a weaker sense of civic duty than previous generations did at the same stage in their lives – and thus, perhaps, are never likely to develop as strong a sense of duty as older generations have done.

Finally, we take up the argument that the decline in turnout in recent elections has occurred primarily among those with little interest in or attachment to the world of politics. Perhaps this pattern has not just meant that such voters have been dissuaded from voting in the short term, but has also served to undermine whatever sense of civic duty they previously had. If so, this might mean that the low turnout created by the particular circumstances of the 2001 and 2005 elections may still be with us for some time to come.

Declining political trust

It clearly makes sense that people who do not trust politicians should be less likely to feel an obligation to vote for any of them at election time. Indeed, as Table 1.4 illustrates, there is a clear link between duty to vote and political trust as measured by the following question:

How much do you trust British governments of any party to place the
needs of the nation above the interests of their own political party?
    Just about always
    Most of the time
    Only some of the time
    Almost never

In 2005, seven in ten of those who said they trusted government "just about always" or "most of the time" felt a sense of civic duty compared with only just over half of those who said they "almost never" trusted government to put the country's interests first. So any decline in levels of political trust would seem potentially capable of accounting for the decline in civic duty.

Table 1.4 Civic duty, by trust in government, 2005

	Trust government ...			
	... just about always/most of the time	**... some of the time**	**... almost never**	**All**
Civic duty	%	%	%	%
It's everyone's duty to vote	70	67	53	64
Other	29	33	46	35
Base	*433*	*847*	*431*	*1732*

Indeed, a decline in political trust does appear to have occurred (see Table 1.5). In a reading taken just before the 1987 General Election 37 per cent said that they trusted government at least most of the time. By 2007 that figure had fallen to 29 per cent, while just 12 months earlier it had been even lower still at 19 per cent.

However, a closer look at the trend suggests that this decline is unlikely to have been a major cause of the decline in civic duty. First, we should note that the level of political trust is quite sensitive to the electoral cycle. It consistently increases after a general election has been held, a phenomenon not immediately apparent in the trend for civic duty shown in Table 1.3. The first readings for 1987 and 1997 were taken in the weeks immediately before the general election of that year, while the second readings were taken immediately afterwards. The readings in 2001 and 2005 were taken after the election.[1]

More importantly, however, the main decline in political trust seems to have occurred well before the more recent decline in civic duty. For example, the level of political trust reached a low of 16 per cent as early as 2000, four years before the most recent slippage in civic duty. If the decline in political trust has helped erode the decline in civic duty, then it has certainly only done so after some considerable delay.[2]

Table 1.5 Trust in government, 1987–2007[3]

	87 (1)	87[+] (2)	91	94	96	97 (1)	97[+] (2)	98	00	01	02	03	05	06	07
Trust government ...	%	%	%	%	%	%	%	%	%	%	%	%	%	%	%
... just about always/most of the time	37	47	33	24	22	25	33	28	16	28	26	18	26	19	29
... some of the time	46	43	50	53	53	48	52	52	58	50	47	49	47	46	45
... almost never	11	9	14	21	23	23	12	17	24	20	24	31	26	34	23

[+] Source: British Election Study

Declining social trust

The possibility that the decline in civic duty might be accounted for by a decline in levels of trust in society in general ('social trust') can be dismissed relatively easily. We have asked the following question measuring social trust a number of times since 1997. The same question was also asked before 1997 on the World Values Survey:[4]

> *Generally speaking, would you say that most people can be trusted or that you can't be too careful in dealing with people?*

The answers have proved to be remarkably consistent from survey to survey (see Table 1.6).

Table 1.6 Social trust, 1990–2008

	1990[+]	1997	1998	2000	2002	2005	2006	2007	2008
Social trust	%	%	%	%	%	%	%	%	%
Most people can be trusted	42	42	44	45	39	45	41	41	40
You can't be too careful	55	57	54	54	59	53	57	57	55
Base	*1484*	*1355*	*2071*	*2293*	*2287*	*3167*	*1077*	*4124*	*2236*

[+] Source: World Values Survey

Throughout the last two decades around two in five have said that most people can be trusted, while somewhat over a half have said that you cannot be too careful in dealing with people. In short, there is simply no evidence of a decline in our general willingness to trust each other and thus no reason to believe that a decline in social trust helps to explain the decline in civic duty.[5]

Generational change

What then of the argument that civic duty has declined because younger generations of voters have failed to acquire the habit of voting, not least because they entered the electorate at a time when elections seemed to offer relatively little choice? As Table 1.7 shows, younger voters are certainly less likely to feel that they have a duty to vote. Nowadays, less than half of those aged under 35 acknowledge a civic duty to vote, whereas nearly three-quarters of those aged 65 and over do so. Yet on its own this difference tells us little. Perhaps younger people have always been less likely to feel they have a duty to vote, and civic duty was something they only came to feel as they grew older. If so, then perhaps today's younger adults are no less likely to feel a sense of duty than were previous generations of young people, and like those previous generations, they will eventually become a cohort of model citizens.

Table 1.7 Civic duty, by age

Age	% who say "It's everyone's duty to vote"	Base
18–34	41	206
35–54	54	380
55–64	67	179
65+	73	224
All	56	990

Table 1.8, however, suggests that this is not the case. In this table we have divided respondents to the 1991, 2001 and 2008 surveys into cohorts of people who were all born in the same decade. Thus, for example, the third row of the table shows for each of those three years the level of civic duty among those who were born between 1961 and 1970. This group was aged between 21 and 30 in 1991, were exactly 10 years older in 2001, while they were aged between 38 and 47 in 2008. So if we look along each row we can establish how each cohort's sense of civic duty developed as it grew older. For example, in this cohort, civic duty stood at 58 per cent in 1991, rose to 60 per cent in 2001 and fell to 54 per cent in 2008.

Meanwhile, if we read diagonally upwards from left to right we can compare the level of civic duty among the same age group in each year.[6] It is this diagonal comparison for the youngest age group that is most telling. It shows that each successive cohort of young voters has entered the electorate with a weaker sense of civic identity than did its predecessor. The level of civic duty amongst those who were born between 1981 and 1990, and who thus entered the electorate between 1999 and 2008 at a time when elections provided relatively little encouragement to vote, is no less than 23 percentage points lower than it was among those who entered the electorate 20 years earlier (35 per cent compared with 58 per cent). As a result, the gap between the generations (measured as the difference between the youngest and oldest age groups in each column) is now much wider than it was in 1991.

Table 1.8 Civic duty, by birth cohort 1991, 2001 and 2008[7]

				% who say "It's everyone's duty to vote"		
				1991	2001	2008
All				68	65	56
Cohort	Age in 1991	Age in 2001	Age in 2008			
1981–1990	1–10	11–20	18–27	–	–	35
1971–1980	11–20	21–30	28–37	–	47	49
1961–1970	21–30	31–40	38–47	58	60	54
1951–1960	31–40	41–50	48–57	63	61	56
1941–1950	41–50	51–60	58–67	65	68	72
1931–1940	51–60	61–70	68–77	80	81	–
1921–1930	61–70	71–80	78–87	78	–	–
Generation gap				20	34	37

– Cohort was either too young to be interviewed in that year or no longer contained sufficient respondents to be able to report a figure

However, it seems that generational change may not be a sufficient explanation of what has happened. Table 1.8 also shows some evidence that in recent years the sense of civic duty may no longer be relied upon to grow stronger as the younger generations age. Among older generations, such as those born in the 1940s, civic duty has strengthened somewhat over time: by 2008, members of that cohort were seven percentage points more likely than they had been in 1991 to say that it is everyone's duty to vote. However, among those who were born a decade later the very opposite seems to have happened. There is little sign of civic duty strengthening over time among those born between 1961 and 1970 either. It seems that the decline in civic duty has had some impact across large parts of the electorate rather than just the youngest voters.

The uninterested

Contrary to what is often presumed but in line with the evidence that we have reported previously (see, for example, Curtice *et al.*, 2007), there is little sign that people in Britain have lost interest in politics. As Table 1.9 illustrates, the reported level of interest in politics has been remarkably stable over the last two decades. Consistently, around a third say they have "a great deal" or "quite a lot" of interest in politics, a third state that they have "some" interest, while the remaining third admit they have "not much" or "none at all". While politics may not be a passion for most people in Britain, this is hardly a new situation.

Table 1.9 Interest in politics, 1991–2008

How much interest in politics	1991	1994	1996	1998	2000	2001	2004	2005	2008
	%	%	%	%	%	%	%	%	%
Great deal/quite a lot	32	32	31	29	32	31	31	34	35
Some	31	35	33	36	35	35	34	34	33
Not much/none at all	36	33	37	35	35	34	36	32	32
Base	1445	2302	3620	3146	2293	3287	3199	4268	1128

Our interest, however, is in whether the relationship between interest in politics and civic duty has changed. In particular, following on from previous research that has found that turnout fell most at recent elections among those who were less interested in politics, do we observe that civic duty has also declined most heavily among this group?

Table 1.10 suggests that this is indeed what has happened. Among those who have a great deal or quite a lot of interest in politics, the percentage who say that everyone has a duty to vote has fallen by seven percentage points since 1991. In contrast, among those who have little or no interest in politics at all it has dropped over the same period by as much as 18 percentage points. Feeling a sense of civic duty is apparently now more likely to be the preserve of the politically interested.

We need to be careful about presuming that a difference seen at the beginning and end of a period reflects a consistent trend across the whole of that period. However, if we look at the pattern of results across the first three years for which we have relevant data (that is, for 1994 and 1996 as well as 1991), together with the last three (2004 and 2005 as well as 2008), it would seem that the difference between 1991 and 2008 is indicative of a broader pattern. So, for example, between 1991 and 1996 civic duty fell by just as much (indeed by rather more) among the politically interested as it did among the uninterested. In contrast, if we compare the position in 1996 with that in 2004 the difference between the interested and the uninterested in their level of civic duty was considerably wider on the latter occasion.

Table 1.10 Civic duty, by interest in politics, 1991–2008[8]

How much interest in politics	% who say "It's everyone's duty to vote"						
	1991	1994	1996	2004	2005	2008	Change 1991–2008
Great deal/quite a lot	80	81	74	75	79	73	-7
Some	73	68	67	63	65	59	-14
Not much/none at all	52	55	52	42	46	34	-18

We can use a technique known as log-linear analysis to study the interrelationship between interest and civic duty over time to see if there is a statistically significant difference in the strength of this relationship in different years. The evidence from Table 1.10 suggests that for this analysis we might reasonably gather together the data available to us for the period between 1991 and 1996 and compare it with the combined data for 2004 to 2008. Combining the data in this way has the advantage of providing us with a larger number of cases for analysis, and, indeed, in doing so we find that the relationship between interest in politics and duty to vote is significantly different in the two periods.[9] It seems, therefore, that we can reasonably conclude that feeling a duty to vote has indeed declined most among those less interested in politics. If so, then the circumstances created in the 2001 and 2005 elections did not simply discourage those with less interest in politics to vote at that time, but, seemingly, also served to undermine their longer-term disposition to participate in the electoral process.

Civic duty and political preference

Such an underlying shift in people's attitudes towards voting means that, even if future elections appear to offer the electorate greater choice, it is quite possible that lower turnouts may nevertheless become the norm in British elections. If so, doubts might well be raised as to whether the outcomes of those elections will reflect the views of the public as a whole. We have already seen that civic duty has fallen disproportionately among the young and those who are disengaged from conventional politics. Perhaps now that the sense of civic duty is no longer more or less ubiquitous, those who feel that sense of duty, and hence are more likely to vote, are unrepresentative in their political views.

Here, at least, there seems to be rather better news for Britain's democracy. In Table 1.11 we show how the incidence of civic duty varies among the supporters of each of the three main parties. It seems that those who identify with the Labour Party are a little less likely to feel a sense of civic duty, but that this is no more the case now than at the beginning of the 1990s. The decline in civic duty has occurred at the same rate amongst all three groups of party supporters.

Table 1.11 Civic duty, by party identification, 1991, 2005 and 2008

	% who say "It's everyone's duty to vote"						
Party identification	1991	Base	2005	Base	2008	Base	Change 1991–2008
Conservative	75	448	77	430	67	331	-8
Labour	71	425	67	699	64	286	-7
Liberal Democrat	73	150	74	226	66	84	-7

Equally, those with a sense of civic duty have not become more distinctive in the values that they bring to the issues that are typically central in election campaigns in Britain. In Table 1.12 we show where those with a sense of civic duty and those without stand on average on a scale of left–right values that is designed to tap people's perspective on the merits of equality and of governmental efforts to promote it (for further details see Appendix I of this report). The lower someone's score on this scale the more they value greater equality – and the more to the 'left' they are in their politics. So the figures in the table indicate that those with a sense of civic duty are evidently somewhat to the 'right' of those without civic duty, but that the gap has not become any wider in recent years.

Table 1.12 Mean position on left–right scale, by civic duty, 1991, 2005 and 2008

	1991		2005		2008	
Civic duty	Mean position	Base	Mean position	Base	Mean position	Base
People have a duty to vote	2.58	787	2.73	1099	2.63	574
Other	2.40	346	2.58	579	2.50	386
Gap between those with civic duty and those without	0.18		0.16		0.13	

Nevertheless, even if it does not seem to be undermining how good a job elections do in representing the views of the wider electorate, declining civic duty, and hence turnout, remains a cause for concern. Elections are not just occasions to elect MPs who reflect the balance of public opinion; they also provide an opportunity to express a common sense of community and support for the political system. Their ability to perform that role does depend on a high turnout and that role, at least, is apparently in danger of being undermined.

Conclusions

A widespread sense of civic duty among voters is arguably one of the crucial foundations upon which democracy rests. It helps ensure that voters participate at election time even if there does not seem to be much difference between the options on offer or if it seems fairly obvious who is going to win. Meanwhile, a high level of turnout helps confer legitimacy on those who emerge victorious from the electoral process as well as on the democratic institutions within which they operate.

It seems, however, that fewer citizens in Britain now feel a sense of civic duty than was the case two decades ago. The low level of turnout in 2001 and 2005 may have primarily been occasioned by the particular circumstances that surrounded those elections. But, even if that is the case, it seems those contests may still have left a longer-term mark. Certainly, the decline in duty to vote has occurred primarily in those groups – the politically uninterested and younger people – among whom turnout fell most heavily on those occasions. It thus seems quite likely that in discouraging these groups from voting in 2001 and 2005, the circumstances in which those elections were fought may have also served to undermine those groups' longer-term commitment to voting. These are groups, moreover, for whom a sense of civic duty was particularly important in bringing them to the polls.

It remains to be seen whether our politicians can still persuade those for whom politics is no more than a passing interest that voting at election time is still worth their time and attention. However, it is more than possible that, regardless of whether future elections provide the electorate with a greater choice or a more closely fought contest, large sections of the population will choose to remain at home on election day. While this may not necessarily impact upon which party wins that particular election, it would ultimately be a loss for democracy.

Notes

1. Much of the fieldwork for the 2007 survey was conducted after Tony Blair was replaced as Prime Minister by Gordon Brown and it is possible that that may help to account for the increase in political trust between 2006 and 2007.

2. Our scepticism is reinforced by the results of a comparison of the relationship between political trust and civic duty in 1987 (that is, in the post-election survey of that year) and again in 2005. If the decline in civic duty between those two dates was accounted for by the decline in political trust, then the level of civic duty among those who trust government always or most of the time should be much the same in both years. In fact, civic duty was 11 points higher among this group in 1987 than it was in 2005. Equally, the equivalent figure among those who only trust government some of the time was seven points higher in 1987, while among those who never trust government it was four points higher. Thus it seems that civic duty has declined independently of people's level of political trust. Unfortunately, our question on trust in government was not asked in 2008 so we cannot undertake the equivalent analysis for that year.

3. Bases for Table 1.5 are as follows:

87 (1)	87 (2)	91	94	96	97 (1)	97 (2)	98
1410	3413	1445	1137	1180	1355	3615	2071
00	**01**	**02**	**03**	**05**	**06**	**07**	
2293	1099	2287	3299	3167	1077	992	

4. The question was asked slightly differently in the 2008 *British Social Attitudes* survey compared with previous years. In 2008 a random half of respondents were asked the question with the answer options reversed i.e. "Generally speaking, would you say that you can't be too careful in dealing with people or that most people can be trusted?" In addition, any spontaneous "it depends" answers were recorded separately. However, these differences do not appear to have influenced the distribution of responses.

5. This is not to deny that there is a link between social trust and civic duty. In 2005, among those who said that most people can be trusted, 71 per cent felt a sense of civic duty, whereas this was only true of 57 per cent of those who said that you cannot be too careful dealing with people. Evidently, civic duty has declined despite the fact that social trust has not.

6. Though, as the 2001 and 2008 surveys are only seven years apart, the age groups in 2008 are not exactly the same as in 1991 and 2001.

7. Bases for Table 1.8 are as follows:

				Base 1991	Base 2001	Base 2008
All				1224	2795	990
Cohort	**Age in 1991**	**Age in 2001**	**Age in 2008**			
1981–1990	1–10	11–20	18–27	–	–	100
1971–1980	11–20	21–30	28–37	–	358	172
1961–1970	21–30	31–40	38–47	225	635	211
1951–1960	31–40	41–50	48–57	219	473	142
1941–1950	41–50	51–60	58–67	223	479	181
1931–1940	51–60	61–70	68–77	196	385	–
1921–1930	61–70	71–80	78–87	179	–	–

8. Bases for Table 1.10 are as follows:

	1991	1994	1996	2004	2005	2008
How much interest in politics						
Great deal/quite a lot	404	321	316	831	604	354
Some	390	338	330	882	616	329
Not much/none at all	425	311	343	895	512	306

9. We undertook a log-linear analysis of interest in politics, duty to vote and year in which the three-way interaction between interest, duty and year was not fitted. If the likelihood chi-square for the residuals from this model suggests that adding this further term would significantly improve the fit of the model, we can conclude that the relationship between interest and duty differs significantly over time. Running a model which compared 1991 and 2008 (and which combined those with some interest in politics with those who have a great deal or quite a lot), the likelihood chi-square for the residuals was 0.93 which, with 1 degree of freedom, has a p value of 0.33. However, if we increase the number of cases available for analysis and compare the period 1991–1996 with 2004–2006 the likelihood chi-square for this model is 4.06 which, with one degree of freedom, has a p value of 0.04. Note that much the same result is obtained if we undertake an analysis of the relationship between strength of party identification and civic duty. This suggests that civic duty has declined significantly more amongt those who do not identify with a party at all than it has among those with a very or fairly strong identity. The relevant chi-square is 10.84 which, with 2 degrees of freedom, has a p value of 0.00.

References

Bara, J. (2006), 'The 2005 Manifestos: A Sense of *Déja Vu?*', *Journal of Elections, Public Opinion and Parties*, **16**: 265–281

Bara, J. and Budge, I. (2001), 'Party Policy and Ideology: Still New Labour?', in Norris, P. (ed.), *Britain Votes 2001*, Oxford: Oxford University Press

Barnett, S. (2002), 'Will a crisis of journalism provoke a crisis of democracy?', *Political Quarterly*, **73**: 400–408

Beck, U. (1992), *Risk Society: Towards a New Modernity*, London: Sage

Beck, U. and Beck-Gernsheim, E. (2001), *Individualization: institutionalized individualism and its social and political consequences*, London: Sage

Blais, A. (2000), *To vote or not to vote? The limits of rational choice theory*, Pittsburgh, Pa.: University of Pittsburgh Press

Blumler, J. (1997), 'Origins of the crisis of communication for citizenship', *Political Communication*, **14**: 395–404

Bromley, C. and Curtice, J. (2002), 'Where have all the voters gone?', in Park A., Curtice, J., Thomson, K., Jarvis, L. and Bromley, C. (eds.), *British Social Attitudes: the 19th Report*, London: Sage

Butler, D. and Stokes, D. (1974), *Political Change in Britain*, 2nd edition, London: Macmillan

Clark, T.N. and Lipset, S.M. (1991), 'Are social classes dying?', *International Sociology*, **6**: 397–410

Clarke, H., Sanders, D., Stewart, M. and Whiteley, P. (2003), 'Britain (not) at the polls 2001', *PS*, **36**: 59–64

Clarke, H., Sanders, D., Stewart, M. and Whiteley, P. (2004), *Political Choice in Britain*, Oxford: Oxford University Press

Curtice, J. (2006), 'Losing the Voting Habit', in Gough, R. (ed.), *2056: What future for Maggie's Children?*, London: Policy Exchange

Curtice, J., Fisher, S. and Lessard-Phillips, L. (2007), 'Proportional voting and the disappearing voter', in Park, A., Curtice, J., Thomson, K., Phillips, M. and Johnson, M. (eds.), *British Social Attitudes: the 23rd Report – Perspectives on a changing society*, London: Sage

Dalton, R. (2004), *Democratic Challenges, Democratic Choices*, Oxford: Oxford University Press

Deacon, D. (2004), 'Politicians, Privacy and Media Intrusion in Britain', *Parliamentary Affairs*, **57**: 9–23

Downs, A. (1957), *An Economic Theory of Democracy*, New York: Harper and Row

Heath, A., Martin, J. and Elgenius, G. (2007), 'Who do we think we are? The decline of traditional social identities', in Park, A., Curtice, J., Thomson, K., Phillips, M. and Johnson, M. (eds.), *British Social Attitudes: the 23rd Report – Perspectives on a changing society*, London: Sage

Heath, A. and Taylor, B. (1999), 'New Sources of Abstention?', in Evans, G. and Norris, P. (eds.), *Critical Elections: British Parties and Elections in Long-Term Perspective*, London: Sage

Jones, P. and Hudson, J. (2000), 'Civic Duty and Expressive Voting: Is Virtue its own Reward?', *Kyklos*, **53**: 3–16

Pakulski, J and Waters, M. (1996), *The Death of Class*, London: Sage

Patterson, T. (1993), *Out of Order*, New York: Knopf

Putnam, R. (2000), *Bowling Alone: The collapse and revival of American community*, New York: Simon and Schuster

Riker, W. and Ordeshook, P. (1968), 'A Theory of the Calculus of Voting', *American Political Science Review*, **62**: 25–42

Rose, R. and McAllister, I. (1986), *Voters Begin to Choose: From Closed-Class to Open Elections in Britain*, London: Sage

Wattenberg, M. (2000), 'The Decline of Party Mobilization', in Dalton, R. and Wattenberg, M. (eds.), *Parties without Partisans: Political change in advanced industrial democracies*, Oxford: Oxford University Press

2 Thermostat or weathervane? Public reactions to spending and redistribution under New Labour

John Curtice[*]

The domestic policy of the Labour government first elected in 1997 has been distinguished by two notable characteristics. The first is a marked shift to the right in its approach towards the market economy. Prior to gaining office Tony Blair persuaded his party to ditch Clause IV of its constitution, which committed the party to "the common ownership of the means of production, distribution and exchange". The party was also rebranded as 'New Labour', a designation intended to signify that the party had left its 'socialist' past behind it (Gould, 1998). Analysis of the content of the 1997 election manifesto indicated that never before in the post-war period had the party contested an election on so centrist a manifesto programme, an ideological stance that changed little at the time of the 2001 or 2005 elections (Budge, 1999; Bara and Budge, 2001; Bara, 2006; see also the chapter by Padgett and Johns in this report).

If this first characteristic constituted a sharp break with the party's past, the second was a more familiar tune for a party traditionally associated with a belief in government action – a sharp increase in public spending on health and education. True, there was little sign of this in the Labour government's early years as it stuck to a manifesto commitment to keep to the previous Conservative government's spending plans during its first two years in office. But between 1999/2000 and 2007/2008 public spending on health rose from 5.2 per cent to 7.2 per cent of the country's (then continuously growing) GDP. Spending on education increased over the same period from 4.5 per cent to 5.8 per cent of GDP (HM Treasury, 2009a). Meanwhile, although the tax burden varied somewhat from year to year, by 2007/2008 it represented 36.3 per cent of GDP compared with the level of 34.0 per cent inherited from the previous Conservative government (HM Treasury, 2009b).

In this chapter we assess how the public has reacted to these contrasting features of New Labour government and the implications their response might have for the future of British politics. Have they, like a thermostat, been inclined to react against the policy direction set by the government and

---

[*] John Curtice is Research Consultant at the *Scottish Centre for Social Research*, part of NatCen, and Professor of Politics at Strathclyde University

increasingly indicated that they wanted it to go no further? Or have they, like a weathervane, been persuaded of the merits of the government's actions and aligned their views with the direction set by its policies? We begin by considering how and why we might expect the public to have reacted to these two different aspects of Labour's policy stance, before examining some of the relevant long-term trends in public attitudes as revealed by the *British Social Attitudes* survey series.

A tale of two reactions?

It is, perhaps, fairly obvious why we might expect the public to act as a thermostat. Say that a voter thinks that a little more money should be spent on health and rather less on defence. Or that perhaps more money should be spent on schools, and taxes increased in order to pay for this. As a result, when asked in a survey whether they think health or education spending should rise, fall or stay the same, they indicate they believe it should increase. They may even be willing to say that taxes should go up to pay for some of this increased spending.

Subsequently, the government makes these changes. Policy is now closer to what our hypothetical voter wanted. Indeed it may have even moved rather further in that direction than they wanted. So when interviewed now about their attitudes they might well say that health and education policy spending should remain much as it is – or, perhaps, even feel that it should be reduced somewhat. They may even be beginning to grumble about the taxes they are now having to pay.

According to this perspective, voters have relatively fixed preferences so far as the direction of public policy is concerned. Changes in attitudes expressed in surveys reflect informed reactions to changes in the *status quo* rather than volatility in what voters actually prefer. Previous analyses of public reactions to shifts in public spending suggest that voters do indeed tend to behave in this way (Wlezien, 1995; Soroka and Wlezien, 2005).

Decisions about public spending are, however, decisions about 'more' or 'less', about trade-offs between purposes that might all be considered desirable. Not all issues of public policy have this character (Stokes, 1963). Some are arguments about the kind of society that is thought to be desirable, and about the values that should underpin government policy. For example, the political debate between 'left' and 'right' in Britain is primarily an argument about the relative merits of a more equal society *versus* one in which individuals and organisations have the freedom to pursue economic advantage (Heath *et al.*, 1994). People differ in the degree to which they value equality and economic freedom.

Such debates about values are relatively abstract and complex. Voters may be unwilling or unable to devote much time to unravelling them. They thus might look for cues to help them decide what they should think, such as what they see and hear in the media or directly from politicians themselves (Zaller, 1992). The stances taken by the political parties might be thought to be particularly influential. If voters regard themselves as supporters of a party and have come to regard it as a source of information that they can trust, they can be expected to replicate its position when asked about their own political views (Butler and Stokes, 1974).

Such processes might be thought to be particularly important when a major political party adopts a new ideological stance on one or more issues, either because new issues have erupted on to the political landscape (Carmines and Stimson, 1989) or simply because, as in the case of New Labour, it feels it has to respond to a changed political environment. As a result of the party's repositioning, its former stance is less likely to be promoted in the media; indeed, such arguments may disappear from the air waves entirely if the repositioning means that no major party at all now advocates that stance. Consequently, the centre of gravity of public debate is shifted, and public opinion in general can be expected to shift in the same direction. However, supporters of the party that has repositioned itself may well face a particular dilemma. They may be faced with a mismatch between their views and the position now adopted by their party. They might be expected to resolve this tension by adjusting their attitudes so that they match the new stance adopted by their party, and so exhibit a particularly marked change of opinion (see also the chapter by Padgett and Johns in this report).

So the public's reaction to Labour's ideological repositioning on the relative merits of 'socialist' equality *versus* laissez-faire freedom may not have been the same as that to its increase in spending on health and education. In pursuing the latter policy, Labour was adopting a stance with which it was traditionally associated and was doing so on an issue that is primarily about 'how much' of a widely supported activity a government should do. Here there is little reason to anticipate that voters' underlying preferences should have changed and as a result they can be expected to have acted like a thermostat, gradually losing their enthusiasm for more health and education spending as actual expenditure increased. In the case of the former development, however, the party adopted a new stance on issues that were at the heart of a contested debate about what kind of society Britain should be. Voters, and especially Labour voters, might be expected to have responded to this new message by aligning their views with the party's revised stance, pointing like a weathervane to the new direction set by the party.

The public as thermostat? Attitudes to taxation and spending

The increase in health and education spending under New Labour, coupled with an increase in taxation, has been in marked contrast to what happened during much of the previous period of Conservative rule. The late 1980s in particular were a time of spending restraint. Spending on health as a proportion of GDP fell from 5.0 per cent in 1983/1984 to 4.7 per cent in 1988/1989, while that on education fell even more heavily over the same period from 5.2 per cent to 4.6 per cent (HM Treasury, 1999).[1] Taxes fell too from 38.2 per cent in 1983/1984 to 36.1 per cent in 1988/1989 (HM Treasury, 2009b). True, thereafter spending on health and education returned to their former levels, but taxation continued to fall, reaching a low of 31.8 per cent in 1993/1994.

So if the public has reacted like a thermostat to this issue over the years, we should have seen a marked rise and a subsequent fall in support for more spending in the period since 1983. In particular, support should have increased during the 1980s in response to the cutbacks under the Conservatives, and subsequently fallen away again during the course of the new century as Labour's increased spending eventually sated the public's appetite. Figure 2.1 shows what has happened in practice. It is based on the answers to a question that has been included on every *British Social Attitudes* survey since the series' foundation in 1983:[2]

> *Suppose the government had to choose between the three options on this card. Which do you think it should choose?*
>
> > *Reduce taxes and spend less on health, education and social benefits*
> >
> > *Keep taxes and spending on these services at the same level as now*
> >
> > *Increase taxes and spend more on health, education and social benefits*

Note that the question explicitly invites people to compare their preferred balance of taxation and spending with the *status quo*. So if their preferred balance does not change, there is every reason to anticipate that the proportion saying they want higher taxation and spending should vary inversely with the current level of taxation and spending.

Figure 2.1 Attitudes towards taxation and spending, 1983–2008

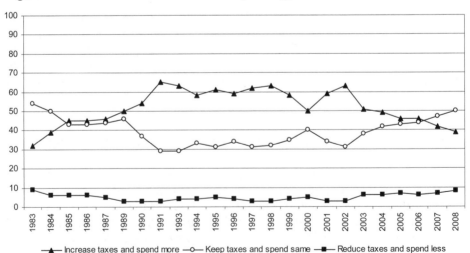

The data on which Figure 2.1 is based can be found in the appendix to this chapter

This seems to be very much what has happened. When our question on taxation and spending was first asked in 1983, a little under a third of respondents (32 per cent) said they wanted spending to increase. But during the remainder of the 1980s support for this option gradually increased, such that by 1991 it was double what it had been just eight years earlier (65 per cent). Thereafter it remained at the 60 per cent mark or so for the remainder of the Conservatives' time in office. Indeed, apart from a perhaps surprising drop (to 49 per cent) in 2000,[3] support for more spending remained at around the 60 per cent level until 2002. But thereafter it has gradually but persistently slipped away. Now according to our most recent reading, just 39 per cent would like to see yet further increases in support for taxation and spending, no more than were of the same view during the heyday of the last Conservative government in 1984. While few respondents appear to be willing to say that spending should actually be cut, for the time being, at least, the public seems to be saying, just like a thermostat, that it is time for the increases to stop.

The public as weathervane? Left–right attitudes

But how has the public reacted to Labour's ideological repositioning? We have available to us three measures that between them provide an indication of long-term trends in left–right attitudes, that is, attitudes towards the relative merits of equality (together with attempts by government to secure greater equality) and economic freedom. The first of these is a question on attitudes towards one of the principal mechanisms by which government protects citizens from the untrammelled consequences of the market and in so doing redistributes income from the better off to those who are less well off, that is, the payment of unemployment benefit. Respondents are asked which of the following options comes closest to their views:

> *Benefits for unemployed people are too low and cause hardship, or, benefits for unemployed people are too high and discourage them from finding jobs*

We also have a direct measure of people's attitudes towards attempts by government to secure greater equality through income distribution. People are asked how much they agree or disagree that:

> *Government should redistribute income from the better off to those who are less well off*

This question is actually one of five items that between them are designed to provide a scale of left–right attitudes. Further details about this scale are provided in Appendix I of this report, but, as can be seen there, all of the component items tap attitudes towards possible inequalities between different groups in society. It thus provides us with a general indication of where the public stands on the principal attitudinal dimension in British politics.

Using these three measures, Figure 2.2 charts the long-term trends in the expression of left-wing attitudes. It shows the proportion in each year who say that unemployment benefits are too low, who agree that government should redistribute income, and the total proportion who might be regarded as left-of-centre on our overall left–right scale.[4]

Figure 2.2 Incidence of left-wing attitudes, 1983–2008

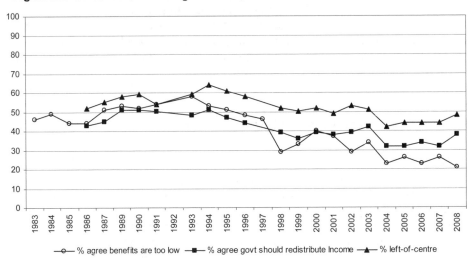

The data on which Figure 2.2 is based can be found in the appendix to this chapter

Margaret Thatcher, the Conservative prime minister between 1979 and 1990, declared that she wanted to persuade the public that government could and should do less than it had done in much of the post-war period (Curtice and Fisher, 2003). However, she appears to have had relatively little success in achieving her objective. If anything, the public drifted somewhat to the left under her tenure together with that of her successor, John Major. So, for example, whereas in 1983, 46 per cent said that unemployment benefits were too low, 10 years later 58 per cent expressed that view. Support for the redistribution of income edged up from 43 per cent in 1986 to 51 per cent a few years later, while the overall proportion who appeared to be left-of-centre increased from 52 per cent in 1986 to 59 per cent in 1993 and the year after even reached 64 per cent.

In exhibiting these trends the public would seem to have been reacting more like a thermostat than a weathervane. But we should bear in mind that Margaret Thatcher's message of smaller government could be regarded as, at most, a more radical version of the right-of-centre position with which the Conservative party had always been associated. It did not represent a marked change of direction or a major break with her party's past. In those circumstances there is little reason to anticipate that large sections of the public should have looked at their own attitudes afresh.

The position since the emergence of New Labour has, however, been very different. On all three measures the public has taken a decisive turn to the right, and indeed now appears to be more inclined towards that view than it was at any time during the period of Conservative rule for which we have data. Just 21 per cent now think that unemployment benefits are too low, less than half the 46 per cent figure that pertained in the last months of the previous Conservative government.[5] In recent years support for redistribution has been as low as 32 per cent, well down on the 51 per cent who took that view when Tony Blair became Labour leader in 1994. Meanwhile, it seems that now consistently a little under half (48 per cent) of all adults are left-of-centre, in contrast to the 60 per cent or so who adopted that outlook in the early 1990s.

So it seems that, since the advent of New Labour, public attitudes have switched towards the new direction mapped out by the party. Attitudes apparently began to shift on Tony Blair becoming leader in 1994. Then, as evidenced by the readings for 1998, there seems to have been a particularly marked change of mood once the public had begun to experience New Labour rule in practice. Thereafter, there seems to have been further signs of slippage in support for a left-wing outlook, most notably in 2004.

This pattern is very clearly replicated if we look at attitudes towards two questions on social security or welfare benefits in general, that is, payments made by government that for the most part have the effect of transferring income from those who are relatively well off to those that are better off. One of the ways in which Labour's distinctive new ideological stance has revealed itself in practical terms has been the introduction of measures that discouraged people from relying any more than necessary on social security payments and encouraged them instead to secure employment in the labour market (Hewitt, 2002; Walker and Wiseman, 2003).

To illustrate the trends in attitudes towards such payments, Figure 2.3 shows for the period since 1987 how many people have *disagreed* with two statements that express concern about social security benefits, including on the grounds often voiced by New Labour that it encouraged 'dependency'. These statements read:

> *Many people who get social security don't really deserve any help*

> *If welfare benefits weren't so generous people would learn to stand on their own two feet*

Between 1987 and 1994 typically around 50 per cent or so said that they disagreed with these views and thus might be regarded as supportive of social security payments. In both cases this figure had already slipped a little by 1996 to 42 per cent. But after just a year or so of New Labour being in power less than a third (32 per cent) expressly rejected the view that welfare benefits encouraged dependency, while since 2004 no more than one in four has held that opinion. An equally clear, if somewhat less sharp, drop has also occurred in the proportion who disagree that many recipients of social security do not deserve help.[6]

Figure 2.3 Attitudes towards welfare recipients, 1987–2008

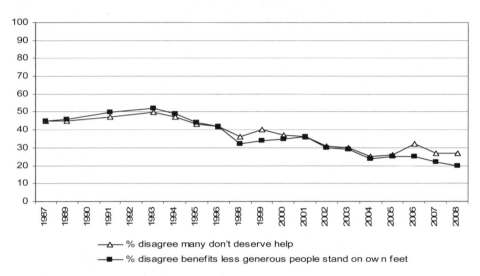

The data on which Figure 2.3 is based can be found in the appendix to this chapter

It seems, then, that the public has reacted like a weathervane to Labour's repositioning on the left–right spectrum, pointing more in the direction in which New Labour has tried to take the country (see also the chapter by Padgett and Johns in this report). In so doing it has reacted very differently from the way it has responded to the increases in health and education spending that Labour introduced. Evidently the public can be both a weathervane and a thermostat at the same time.

Whose supporters have reacted?

If this analysis is correct, however, we should not only see these two very different patterns among the public as a whole but also if we look in particular at the trends among different parties' supporters. We argued above that when a party changes its policy position, it is its own body of supporters who are particularly likely to change their views. While voters in general might be influenced by the impact of this change of position on the media's coverage of politics, it is a party's own supporters who are most likely to be relying on it for a cue as to what opinion they should themselves adopt. So, if indeed voters have reacted like a weathervane in response to New Labour's change of ideological position, the trend away from left-wing attitudes should have been particularly marked among its own supporters. In contrast, where the electorate is responding thermostatically to changes in levels of public spending, there is no particular reason why one party's supporters should react more strongly than any others. Conservative supporters, who in 1997 felt that more should be spent on health and education, may well have been no more or no less likely than Labour supporters to have felt by 2007 that enough was enough (Soroka and Wlezien, 2008).

First, though, we need to consider what we mean by a Conservative or Labour 'supporter'. We could just mean those who say they would vote for the Conservatives or Labour in an immediate general election. However, such an inclination may not be sufficient to impel a voter to regard the Conservatives or Labour as a suitable cue for their own views. This is more likely to be the case if they have a long-term sense of loyalty or affective attachment to a party, such that they actually regard themselves as 'a Conservative' or as a 'Labour' person. Such voters are often known as 'party identifiers' (Butler and Stokes, 1974).

Table 2.1 shows for every *British Social Attitudes* survey since 1983 the proportion of people who can be regarded as identifying with one of the parties. The figures are based on the answers to a sequence of questions designed to establish who might be a party identifier (see Appendix I of this report for further details).

Table 2.1 Party identification, 1983–2008[7]

	83	84	85	86	87	89	90	91	93	94	95	96
	%	%	%	%	%	%	%	%	%	%	%	%
Conservative	39	39	31	34	38	39	35	35	33	29	26	28
Labour	33	35	36	35	29	34	39	35	38	40	44	42
Lib Dem	15	13	18	17	19	11	8	12	13	14	12	11
Other	1	2	1	2	1	3	5	4	3	4	3	3
None/DK	13	11	14	13	13	12	14	13	13	13	14	16

	97	98	99	00	01	02	03	04	05	06	07	08
	%	%	%	%	%	%	%	%	%	%	%	%
Conservative	28	26	25	28	23	25	25	26	24	25	25	32
Labour	42	45	43	40	45	41	37	32	40	33	34	27
Lib Dem	11	10	10	10	13	11	11	13	13	12	9	9
Other	3	3	4	3	4	4	4	7	5	7	7	6
None/DK	16	16	18	19	15	19	23	23	18	23	25	25

Given that party identification is meant to be a long-term sense of loyalty, we might anticipate that the proportion that identify with a particular political party is much the same from one year to the next (although, see Clarke et al., 2004). However, it seems that in practice there is evidence of both cyclical and secular change. So, for example, before 1990, the proportion of Labour identifiers was never higher than 36 per cent, then between 1994 and 2002 it was never below 40 per cent, while most recently it has slumped to just 27 per cent, a figure that leaves the party trailing the Conservatives for the first time in nearly 20 years. Meanwhile, in line with long-standing claims that party identification is in decline (Crewe et al., 1977; Crewe and Thomson, 1999; Clarke et al., 2004), the proportion who do not identify with any party has gradually increased, almost doubling from 13 per cent in 1983 to no less than 25 per cent now.

This apparent volatility in who supports a party potentially poses a problem for the analysis that we wish to undertake here. If voters can change the party with which they identify, then we cannot presume that any change in the attitudes of a party's identifiers is necessarily evidence that those identifiers have changed their mind. It could, instead, be an indication that a party has managed to attract into its ranks those with a rather different set of attitudes from those upheld by its previous supporters. So if we find that the attitudes of Labour identifiers have shifted to the right, this may be because fewer left-wing voters and more right-wing voters were attracted to its ranks by the party's rebranding as New Labour. That, after all, is what the rebranding was designed to achieve.

Ultimately which process has occurred can only be determined by analysing panel data in which the same voters are interviewed on more than one occasion. (For an example of such analysis which supports the interpretation offered here, see Curtice and Fisher, 2003.) However, by looking closely at Table 2.1 we can identify an important distinction. It shows that the main increase in Labour support, from 35 per cent to 44 per cent, occurred between 1991 and 1995. So if any distinctive drift to the right occurred as a result of changes in the kind of person who supported the party, that drift should have occurred primarily during that period. If, on the other hand, we find that Labour identifiers only moved distinctively to the right thereafter, it is more plausible that the change is a result of a shift of attitudes among the party's existing supporters.

Attitudes to taxation and spending

With those considerations in mind, let us first of all examine the long-term trend among Conservative and Labour identifiers in attitudes towards taxation and spending. While we might expect Conservative supporters always to be less keen on higher taxes and more spending than their Labour counterparts, our expectation is that the rises and falls in support for more spending we uncovered in Figure 2.1 should have been more or less the same among the two groups. This is precisely what Table 2.2 reveals.

Between 1983 and 1991, during which period support for higher taxes and spending rose, the proportion of Conservative identifiers who backed that view increased by 28 percentage points. At the same time, the increase in support among Labour identifiers was much the same, at 31 points. Attitudes for the population as a whole then remained fairly stable over the next decade or so. This was found to be the case for both Labour and Conservative supporters; in 2002, attitudes among the two groups were still much the same as they had been just over a decade earlier (despite the marked change in the size of the two groups). Thereafter, as in the rest of the population, support for more taxes and spending has declined. Support for this view has fallen 24 percentage points since 1991 among Conservative supporters, and by 22 points among Labour supporters. Partisanship has apparently made little difference to the effectiveness of the thermostat.

Table 2.2 Attitudes towards taxation and spending, by party identification, 1983–2008

% who support increased taxation and spending	1983	Base	1991	Base	2002	Base	2008	Base
Conservative identifiers	24	676	56	1053	55	856	32	740
Labour identifiers	42	584	73	1010	69	1400	51	619
Con–Lab gap	-18		-17		-14		-18	

Left–right attitudes

But what about the trends in left–right attitudes, where our expectations are very different? In Table 2.3 we show for key dates between 1983 and 2008 responses to the set of items in Figure 2.2 among our two groups of party identifiers. Let us first of all focus on attitudes towards redistribution, displayed in the middle rows of the table. In 1994 both sets of party supporters were slightly more likely to support redistribution than they had been in 1986, largely in line with the trend among the public as a whole. But by 1998 the attitudes of Labour identifiers looked very different from what they had been four years earlier. Support for redistribution had fallen by no less than 20 points. In contrast it fell by less than three points among Conservative supporters.[8] Thereafter, support seems to have changed more or less in parallel in the two groups, but the gap between Conservative and Labour supporters never returns to what it had been before 1998.

Much the same pattern is evident when we examine the proportion that can be regarded as left-of-centre on our left–right scale. This figure increased among both Conservative and Labour supporters between 1986 and 1994, in line with the mood among the public as a whole. But between 1994 and 1998, the proportion of Labour supporters who were to the left-of-centre dropped by as much as 17 points, compared with only four points among Conservative identifiers. Indeed, there was no less than a 12-point fall between 1996 and 1998 alone among Labour supporters, while there was practically no decline among Conservative identifiers.[9] Thereafter, it seems that once again any rises and falls have largely occurred in parallel.

The position with respect to attitudes towards the dole is only a little different. Here, too, there was a large drop in the proportion of Labour supporters adopting the left-wing perspective as New Labour came to power. Indeed, this figure fell by no less than 25 points between 1996 and 1998 alone. But there was also a decline of 14 points among Conservative supporters during the same period, a quite notable fall given that far fewer Conservatives were of that view in the first place. However, belief that the dole is too low continued, thereafter, to edge down further among Labour identifiers, while remaining relatively steady among Conservative supporters. It seems as though here, too, Labour supporters were on the whole rather more likely to register the new direction on which their party had embarked.[10]

Table 2.3 Incidence of left-wing attitudes, by party identification, 1983–2008[11]

	1983	1986	1994	1996	1998	2002	2005	2008
% agree unemployment benefits too low								
Conservative identifiers	30	24	34	29	15	17	13	12
Labour identifiers	64	63	67	62	37	36	32	28
Con–Lab gap	-34	-39	-32	-33	-23	-19	-19	-16
% agree government should redistribute income								
Conservative identifiers	n/a	22	26	22	23	21	16	24
Labour identifiers	n/a	64	68	58	48	49	39	49
Con–Lab gap		-42	-42	-36	-25	-28	-23	-25
% left-of-centre								
Conservative identifiers	n/a	29	37	32	35	33	26	36
Labour identifiers	n/a	76	81	76	64	62	51	56
Con–Lab gap		-47	-44	-44	-29	-29	-25	-20

n/a = not asked

Equally, the equivalent analysis of attitudes towards welfare benefits in Table 2.4 suggests that while Conservative supporters were not wholly immune to the new mood it again was registered more sharply among Labour identifiers. Between 1996 and 2002 there was only a five percentage point fall in the proportion of Conservative supporters who disagreed that many social security recipients do not deserve help, but as much as a 16-point drop among Labour identifiers. Meanwhile, over the same period the proportion of Conservatives who disagreed that less generous welfare benefits would reduce dependency fell by just two points, while it dropped by no less than 19 points among Labour identifiers.[12] And although Conservative identifiers have subsequently become more wary of welfare benefits, this largely matches a continuing parallel trend among Labour supporters.

Table 2.4 Attitudes to welfare recipients, by party identification, 1987–2008[13]

	1987	1994	1996	1998	2002	2005	2008
% disagree many don't deserve help							
Conservative identifiers	34	33	27	25	22	18	20
Labour identifiers	58	59	52	44	36	30	35
Con–Lab gap	-24	-25	-25	-19	-14	-12	-15
% disagree if benefits less generous, people stand on own feet							
Conservative identifiers	28	31	21	16	19	13	10
Labour identifiers	67	63	55	42	36	30	29
Con–Lab gap	-39	-32	-35	-26	-17	-17	-19

So between them Tables 2.3 and 2.4 paint a rather consistent picture. In each case it seems that the early years of New Labour, and especially its early years in power, were accompanied by a particularly marked decline in left-wing attitudes among the party's own supporters. Sometimes they were joined in their shift of outlook by Conservative supporters, but in the early years, at least, only to a lesser degree. Only thereafter do we again see the two sets of supporters largely moving in parallel. Moreover, most of the distinctive shift among Labour identifiers occurred after the period between 1991 and 1995, during which time the party's popularity grew.[14] The change of outlook is therefore unlikely simply to be the result of a change in the kind of person who supported the party.

This examination of trends among party supporters has thus been in line with our initial expectations. We suggested that if voters were reacting like a thermostat in respect of attitudes towards taxation and spending, then Conservative and Labour supporters could be expected to shift their attitudes to more or less the same extent. This is precisely what happened. But where voters were acting like a weathervane, registering a new ideological direction established by a party, we should expect that supporters of that party should change their attitudes most. This seems to have been precisely what happened in the early years of New Labour in power. There thus seems every reason to conclude that two very different processes have helped shaped the public's reaction to just over a decade of Labour rule.

Conclusions

Two processes, perhaps, but only one consequence – an electorate that is now much further away from traditional Labour attitudes than was the case little more than a decade ago. Labour's increased spending on health and education was an astute if delayed recognition of the public mood at that time. But now that spending has been increased, the public's thirst has been satisfied. True, just after our 2008 fieldwork was largely completed, Britain's economy went sharply into reverse in the wake of a banking crisis and, perhaps, this has made the public think again (Bamfield and Horton, 2009). But if not, the more conservative tune of restraint in spending on public services and keeping a lid on the tax burden would now seem to provide a closer fit to the climate of opinion. Given that it seems likely that public expenditure will have to be on a tight leash in the near future thanks to the financial crisis, this new mood might prove to be a blessing to whichever party is in power over the next few years.

At the same time the public, including Labour supporters themselves, no longer has as much belief in the importance of equality and of government action to secure it as it once did. In repositioning itself ideologically New Labour helped ensure that the ideological terrain of British public opinion acquired a more conservative character. Winning elections may not necessarily be any easier for the Conservative Party as a result – but, if and when they do secure power, they will find themselves governing a country that is more at ease with markets and economic freedom than it ever was when Margaret Thatcher was in power. The wind of change blown by New Labour has proven to be powerful indeed.

Notes

1. Spending on social security also fell from 12.0 per cent to 10.4 per cent (HM Treasury, 2009b).
2. Readers will note that the question refers to "social benefits" as well as spending on health and education. This is an area where, at least prior to the recession occasioned by the 2008 financial crisis, spending was actually rather lower under Labour. The party inherited a level of 14.2 per cent of GDP in 1996/1997 and it was no more than 13.2 per cent in 2007/2008 (HM Treasury, 2009a). Any thermostatic reaction can thus reasonably be attributed to increases in spending on health and education in particular.
3. At the beginning of that year the prime minister, Tony Blair, announced a much publicised intention to increase the proportion of GDP spent on health so that it was in line with the European Union average (Appleby and Boyle, 2000). The public may thus have been reacting to anticipated increases in spending.
4. The scale runs from a score of 1, meaning that the respondent has given the most left-wing response to all five items, to 5, indicating that the most right-wing response has been given on each occasion. We define as left-of-centre those with a score of less than 2.5.

5. Fieldwork for the 1997 survey was undertaken just before the general election of that year.
6. Of course the trends in Figure 2.3 could well reflect the impact of the economic cycle as well as Labour's repositioning; people can be expected to be more likely to be critical of welfare recipients when unemployment is falling, as was the position after 1993. However, this does not explain why, as shown in the next section, in the period between 1996 and 2002 the change of attitude occurs primarily amongst Labour identifiers.
7. Bases for Table 2.1 are as follows:

83	84	85	86	87	89	90	91	93	94	95	96
1761	1675	1804	3100	2847	3029	2797	2918	2945	3469	3633	3662

97	98	99	00	01	02	03	04	05	06	07	08
1355	3146	3143	3426	3287	3435	4432	3199	4268	4290	4124	4486

8. It will be seen that most of the narrowing of the gap between Conservative and Labour identifiers occurred between 1996 and 1998, that is, either side of Labour's victory in the 1997 General Election. Log-linear modelling confirms that the change in the relationship between 1996 and 1998 is statistically significant. We pooled the data for the two years and fitted a model that included the main effects for attitudes towards redistribution, party identification and year together with all the two-way interactions between these three variables. This meant that omitted from the model was the three-way interaction which indicates that the relationship between attitudes towards redistribution and party identification differed between the two years. The residuals from this model had a chi-square of 10.4, which, with one degree of freedom, is significant at the 1% level, indicating that the three-way interaction is required to fit the data adequately.
9. The change between 1996 and 1998 in the relationship between party identification and being on the left or not is statistically significant. Using a modelling procedure analogous to that described in the previous note, the residuals from a model that does not include the three-way interaction between being on the left, party identification and year had a chi-square of 21.8, which, with one degree of freedom, is significant at the 1% level.
10. The comments in this paragraph are supported by the results of log-linear modelling. We followed the procedure outlined in note 10 and fitted for the years 1996 and 1998 the equivalent model for the relationship between attitudes towards the dole, party identification and year. The resulting residuals had a chi-square of 1.99, which, with one degree of freedom, is not significant at the 5% level. However, if one fits the same model for the years 1996 and 2002, the residuals have a chi-square of 11.2, which, with one degree of freedom, is significant at the 1% level.

11. Bases for Table 2.3 are as follows:

	1983	1986	1994	1996	1998	2002	2005	2008
% agree unemployment benefits too low								
Conservative identifiers	676	1054	1009	1022	818	816	802	1087
Labour identifiers	584	1080	1404	1543	1398	1400	1291	934
% agree government should redistribute income								
Conservative identifiers	n/a	452	860	866	657	728	906	1331
Labour identifiers	n/a	471	1181	1336	1122	1187	1442	1118
% left-of-centre								
Conservative identifiers	n/a	449	853	855	646	712	898	1000
Labour identifiers	n/a	467	1165	1311	1093	1159	1411	832

12. Applying the log-linear modelling procedure outlined in note 10 to the data for 1996 and 2002, the resulting residuals in the case of whether welfare recipients deserve help had a chi-square of 7.52, and in the case of whether welfare benefits discourage people from standing on their own feet of 21.7. Both of these figures are significant at the 1% level. The movement during the narrower period 1996 and 1998 alone narrowly fails in both cases to reach significance at the 5% level.

13. Bases for Table 2.4 are as follows:

	1987	1994	1996	1998	2002	2005	2008
Conservative identifiers	482	860	866	657	728	696	1000
Labour identifiers	331	1181	1336	1122	1187	1089	832

14. This claim is affirmed if we look directly at the relevant data for those two years. In each case the gap between Conservative and Labour identifiers narrowed no more than a little. In the case of attitudes towards redistribution it slipped from -39 to -35 (before falling to -25 in 1998), in the case of being on the left from -46 to -40 (whereas it then slipped to -29 in 1998), while so far as attitudes towards the dole are concerned the gap actually rose slightly from -34 to -36. There was also little change in the case of our two welfare measures. The gap on whether welfare recipients deserve more help was -25 in 1991 and -23 in 1995, while in the case of whether less generous benefits would encourage people to stand on their own feet the equivalent figures were -32 and -31.

References

Appleby, J. and Boyle, S.(2000), 'Blair's billions: Where will he find the money for the NHS?', *British Medical Journal*, **320**: 865–867

Bamfield, L. and Horton, T. (2009), *Understanding attitudes to tackling inequality*, York: Joseph Rowntree Foundation

Bara, J. (2006), 'The 2005 Manifestos: A sense of déjà vu?', *Journal of Elections, Public Opinion and Parties*, **16**: 265–281

Bara, J. and Budge, I. (2001), 'Party policy and ideology: Still New Labour?', in Norris, P. (ed.), *Britain Votes 2001*, Oxford: Oxford University Press

Budge, I. (1999), 'Party policy and ideology', in Evans, G. and Norris, P. (eds.), *Critical Elections: British Parties and Voters in Long-Term Perspective*, London: Sage

Butler, D. and Stokes, D. (1974), *Political Change in Britain*, 2nd edition., Basingstoke: Macmillan

Carmines, E. and Stimson, J (1989), *Issue Evolution: Race and the Transformation of American Politics*, Princeton, NJ: Princeton University Press

Clarke, H., Sanders, D., Stewart, M. and Whiteley, P. (2004), *Political Choice in Britain*, Oxford: Oxford University Press

Crewe, I., Särlvik, B. and Alt, J. (1977), 'Partisan Dealignment in Britain 1964–74', *British Journal of Political Science*, **7**: 129–190

Crewe, I. and Thomson. K. (1999), 'Party loyalties: dealignment or realignment?, in Evans, G. and Norris, P. (eds.), *Critical Elections: British Parties and Voters in Long-Term Perspective*, London: Sage

Curtice, J. and Fisher, S. (2003), 'The power to persuade? The tale of two prime ministers', in Park, A., Curtice, J., Thomson, K., Jarvis, L. and Bromley, C. (eds.), *British Social Attitudes: the 20th Report – Continuity and change over two decades*, London: Sage

Gould, P. (1998), *The Unfinished Revolution: How the Modernisers Saved the Labour Party*, London: Little, Brown & Company

Heath, A., Evans, G. and Martin, J. (1994), 'The measurement of core beliefs and values: the development of balanced socialist/laissez-faire and libertarian/authoritarian scales', *British Journal of Political Science*, **24**: 115–158

HM Treasury (1999), *Public Expenditure: Statistical Analyses 1999–2000, Cm 4201*, London: HMSO

HM Treasury (2009a), *Public Expenditure: Statistical Analyses 2009, Cm 7630*, London: The Stationery Office

HM Treasury (2009b), *Budget 2009: Building Britain's Future, HC 407*, London: The Stationery Office

Hewitt, M. (2002), 'New Labour and the redefinition of social security', in Powell, M. (ed.), *Evaluating New Labour's Welfare Reforms*, Bristol: Policy Press

Soroka, S. and Wlezien, C. (2005), 'Opinion-Policy Dynamics: Public Preferences and Public Expenditure in the United Kingdom', *British Journal of Political Science*, **35**: 665–689

Soroka, S. and Wlezien, C. (2008), 'Homogeneity and Heterogeneity in Public Responsiveness to Policy', Paper presented at the Annual Conference of the Elections,

Public Opinion and Parties special group of the Political Studies Association,
    University of Manchester

Stokes, D. (1963), 'Spatial Models of Party Competition', *American Political Science
    Review*, **57**: 368–377

Walker, R. and Wiseman, M. (2003), 'Making welfare work: UK activation policies
    under *New* Labour', *International Social Security Review*, **56(1)**: 3–29

Wlezien, C. (1995), 'The Public as Thermostat: Dynamics of Preferences for Spending',
    American Journal of Political Science, **39**: 981–1000

Zaller, J. (1992), *The Nature and Origins of Mass Opinion*, Cambridge: Cambridge
    University Press

Acknowledgements

The *National Centre for Social Research* is grateful to the Department for Work
and Pensions for their financial support which enabled us to ask some of the
questions in this chapter. The views expressed are those of the author alone.

Appendix

The data for Figures 2.1, 2.2 and 2.3 are shown below:

Table A.1 Attitudes towards taxation and spending, 1983–2008

	83	84	85	86	87	89	90	91	93	94	95	96
	%	%	%	%	%	%	%	%	%	%	%	%
Reduce taxes/spend less	9	6	6	6	5	3	3	3	4	4	5	4
Keep taxes/spend same	54	50	43	43	44	46	37	29	29	33	31	34
Increase taxes/spend more	32	39	45	45	46	50	54	65	63	58	61	59
Base	1761	1675	1804	3100	2847	3029	2797	2918	2945	3469	3633	3662

	97	98	99	00	01	02	03	04	05	06	07	08
	%	%	%	%	%	%	%	%	%	%	%	%
Reduce taxes/spend less	3	3	4	5	3	3	6	6	7	6	7	8
Keep taxes/spend same	31	32	35	40	34	31	38	42	43	44	47	50
Increase taxes/spend more	62	63	58	50	59	63	51	49	46	46	42	39
Base	1355	3146	3143	2292	3287	3435	3272	2146	2166	3240	3094	2229

Table A.2 Incidence of left-wing attitudes, 1983–2008

	83	84	85	86	87	89	90	91	93	94	95	96
% agree benefits too low	46	49	44	44	51	53	52	54	58	53	51	48
Base	1761	1675	2797	3100	2847	3029	2797	2918	2945	3469	3633	3662
% agree govt should redistribute income	n/a	n/a	n/a	43	45	51	51	49	48	51	47	44
Base				2531	2450	2980	2795	2900	3621	2609	3135	3119
% left-of-centre	n/a	n/a	n/a	52	55	58	59	54	59	64	61	58
Base				1308	2459	2580	2407	2643	1292	2886	3070	3037

	97	98	99	00	01	02	03	04	05	06	07	08
% agree benefits too low	46	29	33	40	37	29	34	23	26	23	26	21
Base	1355	3146	3143	3426	3287	3435	3272	3199	3193	3240	3094	3358
% agree govt should redistribute income	n/a	39	36	39	38	39	42	32	32	34	32	38
Base		2531	2450	2980	2795	2900	3621	2609	3559	3748	3578	3990
% left-of-centre	n/a	52	50	52	49	53	51	42	44	44	44	48
Base		2476	2403	2947	2756	2826	3531	2551	3496	3695	3481	3902

Table A.3 Attitudes towards welfare recipients, 1987–2008

	87	89	91	93	94	95	96	98	99
% disagree many don't deserve help	45	45	47	50	47	43	42	36	40
% disagree if benefits less generous, people stand on own feet	45	46	50	52	49	44	42	32	34
Base	*1281*	*2604*	*2481*	*2567*	*2929*	*3135*	*3119*	*2531*	*2450*
	00	**01**	**02**	**03**	**04**	**05**	**06**	**07**	**08**
% disagree many don't deserve help	37	36	31	30	25	26	32	27	27
% disagree if benefits less generous, people stand on own feet	35	36	30	29	24	25	25	22	20
Base	*2980*	*2795*	*2900*	*873*	*2609*	*2699*	*2822*	*2672*	*3000*

3 How do political parties shape public opinion? Britain in a European perspective

*Stephen Padgett and Robert Johns**

The last decade has seen a deep-seated change in Britain's core ideological values – the way people think about equality, welfare and the role of government (Johns and Padgett, 2008; see also the chapter by Curtice in this report). Surveys point to declining support for government intervention in relation to income redistribution, employment and provision for the unemployed. At the same time, there is evidence of a decline in the coherence of individual belief systems. Fewer people than previously are ideologically consistent in the values to which they subscribe and citizens' opinions on particular issues are increasingly inconsistent with their more deep-rooted values. There has also been a decline in the relationship between core values and party preferences. Differences in left–right values between Labour and Conservative supporters that had been very pronounced in the 1980s had declined very significantly by 2006.

One explanation for the erosion of values and the decline in consistency of citizens' opinions might be the way issues are 'packaged' in the party system. Values, it has been argued, are formed by the party system (Knutsen and Scarbrough, 1995). Parties are a crucial reference point for citizens' learning and thinking about politics, and they influence the way citizens perceive political issues (McQuail and Windhal, 1981; Przeworski and Sprague, 1986; Bartolini and Mair, 1990; de Graaf *et al.*, 2001). In particular, there is abundant evidence that supporters tend to adopt their party's position on new or complex issues (Zaller, 1992; Rahn, 1993). The erosion of core values in Britain might therefore reflect shifts in the ideological position of the main parties.

In our earlier work (Johns and Padgett, 2008) we have found a close parallel between New Labour's retreat from its traditional message of equality and welfare, and declining public support for these values. Moreover, as the ideological distance between the two major parties narrowed, so did the differences in opinion between supporters of those parties. Those parallel trends were clear; what was less clear was the causal nature of the relationship

* Stephen Padgett is Professor of Politics and Robert Johns is Lecturer in Politics at the University of Strathclyde.

between the two trends. Were the movements of the parties driving public attitudes, or were these movements simply coincident with shifts in public opinion that would have been happening anyway, for broader social reasons? There are two social developments that might account for the changes in public opinion we found in our previous investigation. The first is 'class dealignment', a blurring of traditional socio-economic boundaries which has left more households in 'mixed' class locations (see, for example, Sarlvik and Crewe, 1983; Franklin *et al.*, 1992). This reduces the number of citizens who would stand to gain from consistently left- or right-wing policies. The second development is 'cognitive mobilisation', a process driven by the spread of education and the proliferation of the media, which equips more citizens with the resources to form opinions independently of their basic values (Dalton, 1984; Inglehart, 1990).

Does it really matter if people's attachment to core values is declining and, if so, whether political parties are partly responsible? We would argue it does, because core values play an important role in voter–party allegiances (Scarbrough, 1984; Heath *et al.*, 1985; Rose and McAllister, 1986) and have been a key instrument in party strategies for mobilising voters. Citizens with weak attachments to values and highly differentiated palettes of opinions become increasingly difficult to satisfy. Consequently, parties have to pay increasing attention to designing mixed policy packages and in so doing they lose their distinctive character. This is important, because a perception that there is no difference between the parties is one of the main drivers of alienation from politics (Bromley and Curtice, 2002). If our postulate that party messages have an influence on public opinion is correct, they may be able to reconnect with voters by reaffirming core values.

In this chapter we seek to clarify whether parties *drive* shifts in public opinion, or whether these shifts simply *reflect* social change. We approach the question using comparative analysis. Other western, European countries have experienced broadly similar social changes to Britain, so, if these developments are responsible for the value changes that we see in Britain, we would expect to see a similar pattern of change elsewhere too. If, on the other hand, values reflect packaging in the party system, we would anticipate a more variegated pattern of change reflecting the distinctive structures of the western European party systems. We will also investigate the nature of shifts in public opinion over time. Does change occur slowly and steadily, as might be expected if it is simply a result of glacial social change, or is there evidence that parties can either accelerate or act as a brake on change, depending on how they position themselves ideologically?

We begin by presenting an ideological map of the main parties in six western European countries, drawn on the basis of data from the Manifestos Project which has analysed the general election manifestos of parliamentary parties across Europe in all post-war elections (Budge *et al.*, 2001; Klingemann *et al.*, 2006). These data allow us to answer a number of key questions. Is the trend towards ideological convergence between Labour and the Conservatives in Britain mirrored across the continent? Have European social democratic parties weakened their traditional commitments to equality and welfare in the manner of New Labour, and have centre-right parties become more socially 'progressive' like the Conservatives? We then examine support for core values among the general public, using cross-national data provided by a module of questions about attitudes towards the role of government that were fielded as part of the *International Social Survey Programme* between 1985 and 2006.[1] This allows us to compare trends in Britain with those in five countries which represent the main types of western European party system. Germany and France exemplify the Christian democratic tradition, Norway and Sweden show the effects of the Nordic social democratic model, and Spain is an example of the relatively recently formed party systems of southern Europe.

The capacity for cross-national analysis over time is limited; although the relevant questions have been asked on four separate occasions (1985, 1990, 1996, 2006), only two out of our six countries – Britain and Germany – have data for all four time points. This constrains our ability to draw strong conclusions about causal relations between different trends. Nevertheless, the available data can serve the main purpose of this chapter, which is to explore the relationship between party positions and public opinion, and to investigate whether and how this differs across countries. Specifically, we will address three questions in turn. First, do overall trends in public opinion vary according to the different dynamics of the various countries' party systems? Second, is the ideological consistency of public opinion reflective of the intensity of ideological competition between the major parties in each country? Third, when parties shift along the ideological spectrum, under what circumstances do their voters follow suit?

Party systems in western Europe

In the introduction to this chapter we suggested that the character of core values in a society, and their impact on citizens' opinions, may depend on the packaging of those values in the party system. So we begin by outlining the party system configurations found in western Europe and by plotting the location of the parties on one of the main dimensions of party competition, the left–right dimension. Using data from the Manifestos Project, we calculated a party's position on a 'left–right scale' from its manifesto's emphasis on a basket of 13 policy positions associated with the right, and then subtracting the emphasis on a similar basket of policies associated with the left. Positive scores indicate that a party is towards the right; negative scores show a bias to the left (Budge *et al.*, 2001; Klingemann *et al.*, 2006). The positions of the main parties of left and right in the six countries in our analysis are shown in Table 3.1.[2] The 'distance' row indicates how far apart the parties are on the scale. High values show ideological polarisation; low values indicate convergence.

After a decade of unprecedented polarisation in the 1980s, the British party system has been characterised by a pronounced convergence of the main parties. In 1983 there was a 68-point gap between Labour and the Conservatives. By

2001 it had shrunk to just nine points, reflecting the repositioning of both parties in relation to the role of government, welfare and the market economy. New Labour accommodated some of Mrs Thatcher's liberal thinking, while Conservative leaders from John Major to David Cameron renounced their predecessor's hostility to welfare. The parties now share a broad conception of a streamlined and cost-effective welfare state. Labour has renounced old orthodoxies in relation to government intervention in the economy; the Conservatives are less aggressively oriented towards the market. The pattern of convergence shows a striking asymmetry, however, with Labour making a 45-point shift to the right between 1983 and 2001, three times the Conservative shift of 14 points in the other direction.

The British experience does not reflect a uniform European trend. As we can see from Table 3.1, there is no uniformity in the ideological development of European parties and party systems.

Table 3.1 Party positions on left–right scale in six countries, 1983–2005

	1983	1987	1992	1997	2001	2005
UK						
Labour	-39	-14	-30	8	6	-3
Conservative	29	30	28	26	15	15
Distance	68	44	58	18	9	18
France						
PS	-28	-9	-14	-23	-13	-16
RPR/UMP	15	41	24	-5	3	-9
Distance	43	50	38	18	16	7
Germany						
SPD	-7	-14	-31	-18	1	-5
CDU	30	10	-10	27	28	23
Distance	37	24	21	45	27	28
Norway						
DNA	-23	-26	-36	-20	-18	-38
Conservative	8	-8	-7	14	4	10
Distance	31	18	29	34	22	48
Spain						
PSOE	-11	-12	-22	3	2	6
PP	13	13	-3	2	1	1
Distance	24	25	19	1	1	5
Sweden						
SDP	-21	-24	-6	24	-4	-18
Moderate	60	37	44	40	37	38
Distance	81	61	50	16	41	56

Sources: Budge *et al.*, 2001; Klingemann *et al.*, 2006

Some left-wing parties have emulated New Labour in shifting to the centre, while others have retained their location on the left. The ideological trajectories of parties of the right exhibit a similar diversity. We therefore adopt a country by country approach to showing how left–right conceptions of the role of government are packaged in the European party systems, and how this has changed in the last two decades.

Germany exemplifies the Christian democratic tradition. The party system is marked by a strong tradition of political Catholicism, and the politics of religion has tended to attenuate class politics. On the right, the Christian Democratic Union (CDU) draws significant support from the Catholic working class, and has therefore combined support for the market economy with an emphasis on welfare. Since the 1990s, however, it has shifted to the right, seeking to trim Germany's extensive and generous welfare state, and emphasising market solutions to Germany's economic problems. The Social Democratic Party (SDP) retained a strong commitment to social justice and welfare until the late 1990s when it, too, shifted to the right under the 'modernising' influence of Gerhard Schröder. Germany thus has a moderately polarised party system; in four out of the last five elections, the gap between the main parties has been in the range of 21 to 28 points. Over this period the traditional centre orientation of the parties has shifted to the right.

France had a Christian democratic tradition, but this was obliterated by the success of the Gaullist party. Gaullism is defined by a strong belief in state intervention to make the market serve French interests. Aspiring to represent the nation rather than narrow class interests, it also emphasises welfare. In the late 1980s and early 1990s the Rally for the Republic (RPR) – recently re-branded as the Union for a Popular Movement (UMP) – sent a strong ideological message to voters, but in three elections thereafter it shifted to the centre. On the left, the Socialist Party (PS) has resisted the sort of social democratic modernisation found elsewhere in western Europe. It retains a strong commitment to welfare and state intervention in the economy, reflected in its consistent positioning (between -9 and -28) on the left–right scale. At least until the election of 2007, the French party system was thus characterised by convergence towards the left of centre.

In the Nordic countries, dominant social democratic parties have defined expectations about the role of government and the welfare state. Government plays a strong redistributive role, and welfare states are extensive and generous. Centre-right parties generally conformed to the welfare consensus until the 1980s when the Scandinavian party systems began to take different paths. In Norway, both main parties retained their traditional ideological positions, the Labour Party (DNA) continuing to advocate welfare values on the left, while the Conservative Party remained bound by the welfare consensus on the centre right. In Sweden, by contrast, the party system polarised in the 1980s. The conservative Moderate Party shifted to the right, articulating concerns over economic decline and public fatigue with the high taxes required to sustain the welfare state. In response, the Social Democratic Party (SDP) embraced welfare state reform, relocating to the right in the 1990s before reverting to its traditional location in 2002. So while the Norwegian party system displays a consistent bias to the left, its Swedish counterpart is characterised by polarisation between left and right, but with a strong bias to the right. As can be seen from Table 3.1, the 2001/2002 elections saw the Norwegian Labour Party some 20 points to the left of its Swedish counterpart.

The party system in Spain is marked by the experience of authoritarian dictatorships in the first three post-war decades, and the transition to democracy thereafter. Spain had a history of left–right polarisation, which was evident in the party system that emerged with democratisation. The socialist PSOE has progressively modernised its ideological profile, however, in a manner not unlike New Labour. The Popular Party (PP) has also adopted a centrist course since the late 1980s, and the party system is characterised by pronounced convergence in the centre.

If, as we suggested at the beginning of this chapter, the 'packaging' of issues in the party system helps to structure public opinion, we would expect to find the ideological positioning of the parties shown in Table 3.1 reflected in citizens' attitudes towards left–right issues in the respective countries. In Norway, for example, the consistent bias of the party system to the left should be reflected in the persistence of support for equality and welfare. By contrast, we would expect Spain to look more like Britain, with the convergence of the main parties in the centre resulting in a weakening of the core values of left and right among voters. A second set of expectations relate to the consistency of individual belief systems. In polarised party systems like that in Sweden, we would expect to find higher levels of consistency in attitudes to equality, welfare and the role of government than in France, where the main parties converged over the 1990s and early 2000s. In the remainder of the chapter we test these expectations by examining the structure of public opinion in the six countries.

Public opinion about the role of government

We turn, first, to examine whether the different types of party system outlined above are reflected in public opinion about equality, welfare and the role of government in the six countries. Do polarised party systems generate stronger opinions than centrist ones? Is ideological convergence between the main parties reflected in changing opinion and a decline in support for traditional left–right standpoints? We compare opinion on the ideologically loaded issue of government intervention in the economy with views about the role of government in providing services like education and health. These latter issues represent a different dimension of the role of government and are less strongly related to ideological values (Sefton, 2003). Hence we would not expect public attitudes to these issues to vary with the ideological positions taken by parties on the left–right scale.

We begin to answer these questions by comparing the way that citizens in the six countries think about core left–right issues relating to government intervention in the economy. Value standpoints can only be observed indirectly, so we derive them from questions asked in the *International Social Survey Programme* between 1985 and 2006. The questions ask about the role of government in income redistribution and supporting employment (core issues of the left) and about freeing business from government regulation (a core issue of the right). The response categories are designed to capture the strength of opinions by distinguishing between definite support versus more tentative support. Our previous analysis in *The 24th Report* showed that New Labour's retreat from its traditional discourse of equality and welfare was reflected in a steep decline in public support for these values, and a corresponding decline in beliefs that government should be responsible for income redistribution or employment support (Johns and Padgett, 2008). Are these trends also evident across other western European countries?

Table 3.2 shows public attitudes in response to the question:

On the whole, do you think it should or should not be the government's responsibility to reduce income differences between the rich and the poor?

Table 3.2 Attitudes towards reducing income differences in six countries, 1985–2006[3]

% saying should be government's responsibility to reduce income differences	1985	1990	1996	2006
Britain	75	74	67	67
Definitely should	48	42	33	27
Probably should	26	32	35	40
France	n/a	n/a	79	78
Definitely should			53	53
Probably should			26	25
Germany	67	68	67	70
Definitely should	28	27	29	30
Probably should	40	41	37	40
Norway	n/a	72	73	74
Definitely should		39	40	45
Probably should		33	33	29
Spain	n/a	n/a	90	86
Definitely should			57	50
Probably should			33	36
Sweden	n/a	n/a	71	68
Definitely should			43	37
Probably should			28	31

n/a = not asked

"Can't choose" and "Refusal" responses excluded[4]

Britain stands out clearly from its European comparators. It exhibits a small decline between 1985 and 2006 in the proportion of people who believed that government should be responsible for income redistribution. More strikingly, there was a marked decline from 48 to 27 per cent in definite responses, indicating a decline in the strength of opinion even among supporters of redistribution. In France, Germany and Norway, by contrast, support remained stable and there was no attenuation in the strength of opinion. Only Spain and Sweden show a similar rate of decline in commitment to income redistribution as in Britain.

We can also look at attitudes towards the government's responsibility with regard to providing jobs and/or a safety net for the unemployed. We asked whether it should or should not be the government's responsibility to "provide a job for everyone who wants one" and to "provide a decent standard of living for the unemployed". We also asked whether the respondent was in favour or against the government providing "support for declining industries to protect jobs".

While support for income distribution held up in most of the countries, there is evidence of a general decline in the belief that government should be responsible for providing jobs for all. Table 3.3 shows that overall support for job provision (that is, the proportion of people who think this "definitely" or "probably" the responsibility of government) declined in a number of other countries just as steeply as in Britain. Support for government intervention in employment was most resilient in Norway, with a decline of only five percentage points between 1990 and 2006.

Table 3.3 Attitudes towards job provision in six countries, 1985–2006[5]

% saying "definitely" or "probably" should be government's responsibility to provide a job for everyone	1985	1990	1996	2006
Britain	72	63	69	56
France	n/a	n/a	73	64
Germany	81	78	77	66
Norway	n/a	84	81	79
Spain	n/a	n/a	91	83
Sweden	n/a	n/a	75	59

n/a = not asked
"Can't choose" and "Refusal" responses excluded

Although they became less supportive of the government taking responsibility for jobs, Table 3.4 shows that citizens in continental Europe continued to believe in government responsibility for providing the unemployed with a decent standard of living. Support was strongest in Scandinavia and Spain where there was only a marginal decline over the decade to 2006. The Christian democratic countries saw some attrition in support for the principle, especially

France, where the proportion of people giving definite support halved in a decade. Once again, though, the steepest decline occurred in Britain, down from 85 per cent support in 1985 to 55 per cent in 2006. This decline was almost entirely the result of a plunge in the proportion of people thinking this was "definitely" the responsibility of government, down from almost half (45 per cent) in 1985 to around one in ten (11 per cent) in 2006.

Table 3.4 Attitudes towards providing a decent standard of living for the unemployed in six countries, 1985–2006[6]

% saying "definitely" or "probably" should be government's responsibility to provide decent standard of living for unemployed	1985	1990	1996	2006
Britain	85	81	78	55
France	n/a	n/a	83	68
Germany	85	81	83	69
Norway	n/a	91	93	88
Spain	n/a	n/a	94	93
Sweden	n/a	n/a	91	83

n/a = not asked
"Can't choose" and "Refusal" responses excluded

There is one type of government intervention in employment that did not see a sharp fall in support in Britain between 1985 and 2006; support for declining industries to protect jobs. As shown in Table 3.5, only France and Spain exceeded Britain in advocating this type of employment protection in 2006. However, support in Britain was predominantly tentative; 47 per cent were "in favour" of this, with only 14 per cent "strongly in favour".

Table 3.5 Attitudes towards support for declining industry in six countries, 1985–2006[7]

% "in favour" or "strongly in favour" of government providing support for declining industry to protect jobs	1985	1990	1996	2006
Britain	50	60	64	60
France	n/a	n/a	69	69
Germany	58	65	67	58
Norway	n/a	46	58	56
Spain	n/a	n/a	83	82
Sweden	n/a	n/a	52	51

n/a = not asked
"Can't choose" and "Refusal" responses excluded

Perhaps these findings reflect a shift in the basis of opinion about the role of government and the welfare state. The two key drivers of support for welfare are ideology and self-interest (Taylor-Gooby, 1999; Jaeger, 2006). A decline in core ideological values in society will therefore increase the role of self-interest in shaping spending priorities. So we would expect a shift away from ideologically loaded support for labour market intervention, and provision for the unemployed, towards spending on more universal public services such as health and education from which people expect to benefit personally. We therefore asked respondents about their attitudes to spending on education and health:

> *Please say whether you would like to see more or less government spending in each area. Remember that if you say "much more", it might require a tax increase to pay for it*

Tables 3.6 and 3.7 look at support for government spending on education and health respectively. In Britain – in contrast to the decline in support for government intervention in income redistribution and employment – we see an increase in support for more spending on health and education in the 1980s and 90s (although it had fallen again by 2006). In continental European countries, on the other hand, support for increased education spending was mostly stable, and the same is true of support for more spending on health, although it is notable that levels of support were generally lower in Germany and France than in other countries. These domains of government involvement seem subject to rather different patterns of change in public support, and seem less strongly related to ideological values (see also the chapter by Curtice in this report).[8]

Table 3.6 Attitudes towards government spending on education in six countries, 1985–2006[9]

% who would like to see "more" or "much more" spending on education	1985	1990	1996	2006
Britain	75	80	84	72
France	n/a	n/a	63	60
Germany	40	59	53	81
Norway	n/a	56	51	62
Spain	n/a	n/a	74	87
Sweden	n/a	n/a	59	53

n/a = not asked
"Can't choose" and "Refusal" responses excluded

Table 3.7 Attitudes towards government spending on health in six countries, 1985–2006[10]

% who would like to see "more" or "much more" spending on health	1985	1990	1996	2006
Britain	88	90	91	81
France	n/a	n/a	52	58
Germany	52	73	57	63
Norway	n/a	83	85	86
Spain	n/a	n/a	80	87
Sweden	n/a	n/a	77	80

n/a = not asked
"Can't choose" and "Refusal" responses excluded

It is worth noting that answers to the education and health questions reflect not only normative views about the role of government but also perceptions of existing spending levels and of the quality of services. For example, the dramatic spike (to 81 per cent) in German support for increased education spending in 2006 followed a much-publicised OECD report on children's reading competence which placed Germany lower mid-table (OECD, 2004). And the 2006 downturn in support for "much more" health spending in Britain, from 43 per cent in 1996 to 27 per cent in 2006, followed a decade of Labour government involving very substantial public expenditure in this area. A similar picture is true in relation to education spending.

So far, we have focused on support for left-oriented policies. We turn now to examine whether the decline we have seen in support for the role of government in Britain and – to a lesser extent – in continental European countries is simply a reflection of a value shift to the right, rather than a more general weakening of ideological consistency. In line with our chapter in *The 24th Report* (Padgett and Johns, 2008), Table 3.8 indicates that there is little evidence of a shift to the right in attitudes across continental Europe between 1985 and 2006. We asked whether the respondent was in favour of or against "less government regulation of business". The Scandinavian countries and Spain mirror Britain, with consistently low levels of support for deregulation, and no significant increase in support over time. Under half (45 per cent), for example, were in favour of deregulation in Britain in 2006, down from 55 per cent in 1985. Only Germany shows increasing support over this period. It is difficult to tell, in the absence of more data and more time points, whether this reflects an underlying shift in German attitudes to the role of government, or a more short-term perception that the heavily regulated business environment has been a factor in the declining recent performance of the economy.

Table 3.8 Attitudes towards government regulation of business in six countries, 1985–2006[11]

% "in favour" or "strongly in favour" of less government regulation of business	1985	1990	1996	2006
Britain	55	43	42	45
France	n/a	n/a	66	60
Germany	41	39	52	73
Norway	n/a	53	46	44
Spain	n/a	n/a	43	35
Sweden	n/a	n/a	44	47

n/a = not asked
"Can't choose" and "Refusal" responses excluded

So far we have found some support for the view that party 'messages' and party system packaging helps to shape public opinion about the role of government and welfare. The bias of the Norwegian party system to the left is reflected in *increasing* support for government to play a role in income redistribution, a trend which was found in no other country. Moreover, Norway displayed solid support for a government role in employment and providing living standards for the unemployed. Conversely in Sweden, the offensive of the Moderate Party against the welfare state, and the ideological retreat of the Social Democratic Party in the 1990s may help to explain the erosion of support for government intervention in income distribution and employment. Spain also conforms to expectations. A less developed market economy means that citizen support for an activist government was high in comparison with the other countries we have looked at. The convergence of the main parties in the centre, however, is reflected in a decline between 1996 and 2006 of leftist standpoints towards the role of government.

France provides partial support for the linkage between the packaging of issues in the party system and public opinion. The resilience of support for a government role in income redistribution is consistent with the convergence of the main parties on the left. At the same time, however, we found a steep decline in support for the obligation on government to provide jobs for all, and for it to provide a living standard for the unemployed. This trend was also found in Germany, where it is consistent with the shift of its party system to the right. Here, though, if citizens' opinions are shaped by party messages, we would not have expected them to remain so supportive of the government's role in income distribution. Comparison between France and Germany shows striking similarities in public opinion towards the role of government that – in view of their different party system dynamics – we would not have expected.

Party systems and ideological consistency in public opinion

We have two main findings so far. First, trends in public opinion on the role of government are clearly far from uniform across western Europe. Second, when these cross-national variations are examined alongside data on parties' ideological positions, there is at least some evidence that public opinion is moving in line with the nature and dynamics of a country's party system. The link between party systems and public opinion is therefore worth closer scrutiny. In this section, we look in particular at levels of ideological consistency within public opinion and how this relates to the ideological structure within a party system.

It is worth beginning with a few remarks on why ideological consistency, often referred to as 'constraint', matters. Ideology is a crucial means of giving structure to political debate, and simplifies things both for voters and for parties (Feldman, 2003). The number and diversity of political issues is enormous, such that virtually no citizen can claim detailed knowledge of all of them. When called upon to make a judgement on an issue, citizens are helped considerably if they can apply an ideological principle or value. For instance, judgements on a range of public policy questions can be straightforwardly derived from a person's broad view of the role of government: would they generally like government to do more or to do less (Alvarez and Brehm, 2002)? If they do not have that general principle to apply, citizens will find it more difficult to reach a judgement and there is no guarantee – given relatively low overall levels of political interest and knowledge – that they will invest the effort to do so. Put bluntly, then, ideology helps public opinion to exist (Luskin, 1987). It also helps political parties by saving them from the need to convey information issue by issue to already over-burdened voters. Rather, they advertise their broad ideological stance – such as their general view of the role of government – and voters can choose more easily between them.

This last point highlights the potential role of the party system in affecting ideological consistency. If major parties converge on the centre ground, and cease to present ideologically coherent packages – couched in ideological terms – to the public, then that public is less likely to think about politics ideologically and less likely to have consistent attitudes. This process is likely to be gradual – citizens' more basic political attitudes change relatively slowly – and so we would not expect ideological consistency to fluctuate as sharply as the parties' positions. Nonetheless, these arguments give us reason to look for trends in ideological consistency within our six countries and, in particular, for signs that convergence weakens this consistency.

Measuring ideological consistency is not entirely straightforward. The first task is to find questions on which, in theory at least, we might reasonably expect consistent answers. For example, having speculated that citizens' priorities for the state might have shifted from labour market intervention to the provision of public services, we cannot expect their views on providing jobs and on education spending to be 'consistent' with one another – these are different dimensions of the role of government. We therefore focus on the four questions concerning whether it is the government's responsibility to reduce income differentials, provide jobs, maintain living standards of the unemployed and protect declining industries. Our anticipation is that these form a cohesive scale of attitudes to the role of government in the economy. The next step is to test whether this expectation is borne out in practice. The measure we use is Cronbach's alpha, the standard measure of the internal consistency of a scale of survey questions. Alpha is a summary of how closely responses to the different questions are correlated together, that is, of how similarly people answered them. It varies between 0 and 1 and, for a four-item scale like this one, an alpha of above around 0.6 would generally be considered respectable. Since the four-item scale meets that criterion in all six of our countries and in all time points, it is reasonable to use it to look at changes in ideological consistency.

Alongside these alpha statistics, Table 3.9 also includes our earlier measure of the ideological distance between the two main parties in each country (see Table 3.1). These figures are taken from the manifestos for the election *before* the survey year in question. Choosing the previous election – rather than simply the closest, which may have taken place after the survey – makes sense given our supposition that public opinion is shaped by the ideological content (or lack thereof) in parties' discourse. And the evidence points clearly in favour of that supposition. As predicted, the variations in attitude consistency over the years are a good deal smaller than those in distance between the parties, but the direction of this variation is often the same. This is confirmed by a simple correlation, based on pooling the data from all countries and waves of the survey, between party distance and public ideological consistency. Our previous analysis of British data suggests a positive relationship – the wider the ideological gap, the greater the attitude consistency – and so it proves, the correlation working out at r = 0.50, a moderate (bordering on strong) positive correlation.

This correlation summarises the overall relationship that exists between ideological distance in the party system and the extent of citizens' ideological consistency. We now turn to look in more detail at the patterns in each of the individual countries. The UK and France, the two clearest cases of party convergence during our period, also show pronounced declines in citizens' ideological consistency. Spain shows the narrowest distance between the major parties and also, in line with expectations, the lowest levels of ideological consistency among voters. Meanwhile, the greatest consistency is to be found in the more ideologically polarised Scandinavian countries.

One interesting contrast between the British experience and that elsewhere is the speed with which convergence seems to have weakened consistency. In Sweden, where in the 1990s the Social Democrats moved just as sharply to the right as did New Labour in Britain, there looks to have been no accompanying dip in consistency (which remained high, as if awaiting the system's return to polarisation). Equally, the spike in ideological distance in Germany's 1994 election – which was also a temporary phenomenon, in this case probably reflecting a post-unification adjustment of the party system – did not result in any upturn in consistency. Indeed, there is no instance in Table 3.9 of a marked *increase* in alpha: convergence tends to weaken consistency but divergence does not appear to strengthen it. There are relatively few cases of divergence in Europe's party systems over this period, so this asymmetry should not be overplayed. But it does raise questions about the likely impact on public opinion in Britain should Labour and the Conservatives once more move apart ideologically. On this evidence, an increase in ideological consistency among voters cannot be taken for granted.

Table 3.9 Ideological distance[+] between parties and citizens' ideological consistency (Cronbach's alpha) in six countries, 1985–2006

	1985	1990	1996	2006
UK				
Distance	68	44	58	18
Alpha	0.73	0.71	0.73	0.64
Base	*1530*	*1197*	*989*	*930*
France				
Distance	43	38	18	7
Alpha	n/a	n/a	0.73	0.65
Base			*1312*	*1824*
Germany				
Distance	37	24	45	28
Alpha	0.63	0.66	0.65	0.63
Base	*1048*	*3840*	*3470*	*1643*
Norway				
Distance	18	29	34	48
Alpha	n/a	0.70	0.68	0.67
Base		*1517*	*1344*	*1330*
Spain				
Distance	24	19	1	5
Alpha	n/a	n/a	0.63	0.61
Base			*2204*	*2257*
Sweden				
Distance	81	61	16	56
Alpha	n/a	n/a	0.75	0.74
Base			*1079*	*1032*

[+] Source: Manifestos data

n/a = not asked

Do parties and their supporters move together?

So far, we have been dealing with the entire electorate as a whole. This might be taken as implying that citizens react uniformly to changes in their country's party system. Yet plainly this is not the case, one obvious reason being that many people have an enduring attachment to one particular party. If a party shifts in a given ideological direction, this is likely to have most impact on its own supporters, rather less impact on those who do not support the party, and may even induce supporters of a rival party to move in the other direction (see the chapter by Curtice in this report). Hence, by comparing party movements with ideological shifts among their supporters, we obtain a cleaner measure of the impact of party-system change.

Unfortunately, the *International Social Survey Programme* data do not provide a consistent measure of partisanship across time and countries.[12] This obviously limits the scope for genuinely comparative analysis. However, we can go some way to addressing the question for this section. The key point is to use the same measure of party support in a given country so that any trends are genuine changes rather than simply the result of examining different groups. Spain is excluded from this analysis since, with just one time point, no trend can be measured.

Having identified supporters of each party, we then need to measure their attitudes to the role of government. For this we will rely on the same four-item 'role of government in the economy' scale as used in the previous section. Previously our interest was in the internal consistency of this scale; here, we are concerned with overall scores on the scale (that is, when responses to each question are summed together). Since the manifesto left–right measure is scored such that high scores represent right-wing party platforms, we do likewise. To assist further in comparing trends in the two variables, we rescale scores on the survey scale so they range between -40 (the most left-wing response on each question) to +40 (the most right-wing response each time) – these are roughly the boundaries of the manifesto scores.

We report the full results of this analysis in the appendix to this chapter. Here we look to pick out general patterns and trends. A first point to note is that, as in the ideological consistency analyses, public opinion fluctuates a good deal less than party positions. This is not to say that individuals are all fairly stable in their views about the role of government. However, once opinions are averaged across the electorate, striking shifts are unusual. One corollary of that is that the differences between partisan groups within a country tend to be relatively narrow. Supporters of the right-wing party are more right-wing than supporters of the left party, but seldom by very much, and usually by markedly less than separates the parties' ideological positions. To that extent, we can say that these voters have already converged ideologically. Nevertheless, we can still look at changes in the extent of this convergence over time. (It should be acknowledged, however, that in the absence of data from before the 1980s we cannot rule out the possibility that the average supporter of these parties was always in the moderate range of the left–right spectrum.)

The available data give us seven pairs of elections across the five countries and hence (with two parties in each country) 14 trends to compare. In four of these 14 cases, the party barely shifted ideologically between one election and the next, and so there is no case for us to analyse. The remaining 10 cases are classified in Table 3.10. (Details of the precise definition of convergence and divergence are also provided in the appendix.) While plainly there are too few cases here to make definitive statements about the relationship between the two variables, the results are highly suggestive of a connection. Where parties shifted towards the centre, in all but one case they were accompanied by their supporters. For example, New Labour in Britain moved from a score of -30 to -3 between the 1992 and 1997 elections according to their manifesto data, while their supporters moved from -11 to 1. This is a more striking case of something that also happened with the PS in France and the SPD in Germany. Where parties shifted away from the centre, in only one case – Labour in the UK between the 1987 and 1992 elections – did their supporters even edge in the same direction according to the subsequent surveys. This is the same asymmetry as was identified in the previous section: convergence appears to have an impact on public opinion but divergence does not. Once again, there is a danger of overstating the point given that these shifts away from the centre ground were seldom very substantial – certainly not on the scale of New Labour's move in the other direction. Nonetheless, these results cast further doubt on the likely public reactions were the British parties to diverge as in the past. On the basis of the results summarised in Table 3.10, the voters cannot simply be expected to follow.

Table 3.10 Summary of parties' and their supporters' ideological shifts across 10 elections,1985 –2006

		Did supporters move in the same direction as their party?	
		Yes	No
How did party move between elections?	Towards centre	4	1
	Away from centre	1	4

In the previous section, we suggested that public opinion may take longer to react to party system change than we can easily detect with the available data. It could be, then, that the 1996–2006 attitude change among Social Democrat supporters in Sweden – from -12 to -5 on the left–right scale – was a response to the party's own rightward shift in the previous decade, and that the next few years will see a similar (albeit delayed) reaction, with supporters once again moving back out to the left. However, this seems unlikely given that our results provide no instance of public opinion diverging significantly from the centre ground. And that, in turn, raises the question of whether the party system is relevant at all. If core ideological values are weakening, even among self-proclaimed supporters of left- and right-wing parties, and these voters are converging on the centre ground regardless of the fluctuations in their parties' positions, the obvious explanation is that other factors are driving public opinion. On that reading, converging parties do not bring their voters with them; the voters were moving in that direction anyway. In the concluding section, we discuss what role, if any, we can reasonably ascribe to party systems in these public opinion processes.

Conclusions

The main purpose of this chapter has been to clarify the relationship between the party system and the structure and dynamics of public opinion. Does the ideological distance between the main parties have an effect on citizens' values and attitudes? Do party movements drive public attitudes, or are those movements simply coincident with shifts in public opinion resulting from social change? Cross-national comparison has certainly served to confirm the link between party systems and public opinion. The countries we investigated can be seen as having different political 'centres of gravity', towards which both parties and citizens incline. In Norway, for instance, both the major parties and the average voter are some way to the left of their equivalents in Britain. Similarly, there is greater ideological distance between the parties, and likewise greater ideological consistency among the public, in Norway than in Spain. However, these points do not address the issue of causality. Can parties shift that centre of gravity, or is more fundamental social change required to do so? Is party convergence the cause of ideological inconsistency in the electorate or a rational response to it?

Answering these questions requires us to move beyond 'static' comparisons across countries and to explore trends over time. And here the evidence that party systems have a causal impact was mixed. In particular, there was some evidence of an asymmetry in the relationship between party ideology and public opinion. While party convergence appeared to weaken ideological consistency and to lead to ideological moderation among voters, divergence failed to generate the opposite effects. At the very least, there are clearly factors at play other than the party system. A stronger conclusion might be that the party system is irrelevant: a combination of class dealignment and cognitive mobilisation has caused the weakening of ideology in electoral politics, an inexorable trend to which the ideological to-ing and fro-ing of parties is incidental.

Although these social trends are clearly important, and set the context within which parties as well as voters make their choices, we would argue against that conclusion. First, as we saw in the series of tables charting opinions on the role of government over time, there are marked cross-national differences that cannot be explained by social trends that run broadly in parallel across countries. For example, Britain saw by far the sharpest declines in the proportions of its citizens who deemed that government should "definitely" reduce income differences, provide jobs, support declining industries, and so on. In Norway, by contrast, support for government involvement in these spheres held quite steady. An obvious difference between the two cases is that, while their respective Labour parties began this period in a similar ideological position, the British party has since moved a long way to the centre while the Norwegian party remained resolutely 'old' Labour.

Moreover, the shifts in public opinion that we have recorded were not slow and steady in the way that might be expected were they simply a result of glacial social change. The impression given by these data is that, while there may be persistent external pressures towards ideological moderation in the electorate, parties can either accelerate this change or act as a brake on it, depending on how they position themselves ideologically. Returning to the British example, there were particular periods of steep decline in support for an expansive role of government, and the timing of the steepest fall – between the 1996 and 2006 surveys – is such as to implicate New Labour quite clearly.

Ultimately, this kind of argument – based on the chronological coincidence of trends – is as close as we can get to establishing causality. Moreover, the data available here, with at most four time points and up to a decade between them, offer only a very unrefined means of observing trends. If party messages were to be tracked in between as well as during elections, and the trends compared with monthly opinion polls, there would be scope for more compelling evidence about whether parties lead or follow public opinion. There are, nevertheless, good reasons to suppose that parties can shift voters' attitudes and, and in particular, can accelerate the process of ideological convergence within the electorate. Parties' desire to gain office means that they are not simply interested in following the opinion of their existing supporters. They are also looking to win converts, and typically these potential converts, or 'floating' voters, will be clustered in the less ideological centre ground (Downs, 1957). Hence, for example, although Labour supporters may have been drifting slowly away from the left, the party nonetheless had an incentive – to which, under Tony Blair, it responded – to 'overshoot' them in its move to the centre. This, in turn, seems to have led many Labour identifiers to accelerate their move in the same direction.

On the other hand, the norm appears to be for parties to be less moderate than their voters. That further reinforces the point that parties do not simply follow public opinion. It also provides a useful reminder to observers of more recent British politics that the current period of ideological convergence is not an irreversible or inevitable feature of electoral competition. Similar patterns of competition can be observed elsewhere but are far from universal, and indeed some parties have clearly bucked the trend towards convergence. (In any case, the period of extreme polarisation in Britain in the 1980s occurred at a time when the social changes thought to induce convergence were already in full swing.) However, our analysis casts doubts on whether future ideological polarisation in Britain's party system would have the beneficial effects that are often claimed for it. Judging by the patterns in Table 3.10, it is unlikely that ideological divergence between the main parties would reverse the decline in ideological consistency among the electorate. And, if parties do not take their supporters with them when moving away from the middle ground, it is more difficult to envisage that such a shift would rebuild voters' attachments to those parties. On the one hand, a perception that there is no difference between the leading contenders for government is widely thought to have driven voters away from parties and, ultimately, away from the polling booth. On the other hand, for an electorate increasingly moderate and uninterested in ideology, a choice between two unwanted radical options may not be much choice at all.

Notes

1. Further information on the *International Social Survey Programme* can be found in Appendix I of this report. Further details about ISSP can be found at www.issp.org.
2. The two parties selected for each country are the leading parties of left and right (respectively) across the five most recent elections covered by the Manifestos Project.
3. Bases for Table 3.2 are as follows:

% saying government should reduce income differences	1985	1990	1996	2006
Britain	1419	1137	913	870
France	n/a	n/a	1264	1732
Germany	968	3582	3230	1532
Norway	n/a	1423	1263	1280
Spain	n/a	n/a	2378	2409
Sweden	n/a	n/a	1163	1125

n/a = not asked

4. The level of item non-response fluctuates both across countries and across survey years, probably as a result of methodological differences. These responses have therefore been excluded from the analysis presented throughout this chapter so as to avoid confusing methodological differences with substantive change.
5. Bases for Table 3.3 are as follows:

% saying government should provide a job for everyone	1985	1990	1996	2006
Britain	1441	1136	935	861
France	n/a	n/a	1261	1698
Germany	1020	3680	3318	1564
Norway	n/a	1458	1313	1289
Spain	n/a	n/a	2421	2455
Sweden	n/a	n/a	1163	1136

n/a = not asked

6. Bases for Table 3.4 are as follows:

% saying government should provide decent standard of living for unemployed	1985	1990	1996	2006
Britain	1448	1139	924	844
France	n/a	n/a	1245	1680
Germany	1006	3639	3270	1532
Norway	n/a	1459	1294	1295
Spain	n/a	n/a	2393	2428
Sweden	n/a	n/a	1175	1135

n/a = not asked

7. Bases for Table 3.5 are as follows:

% in favour of government providing support for declining industry	1985	1990	1996	2006
Britain	1495	1181	960	873
France	n/a	n/a	1277	1743
Germany	1035	3765	3440	1547
Norway	n/a	1456	1310	1261
Spain	n/a	n/a	2353	2419
Sweden	n/a	n/a	1196	1122

n/a = not asked

8. A factor analysis of all of the questions used in this chapter confirmed this point. This method, which looks for the structure underlying a set of survey responses, revealed that there are (at least) two dimensions to people's thinking about the role of government. Opinions on what might be termed the 'role of government in the economy', such as providing jobs and protecting industries, were only modestly correlated with answers on the 'role of government in providing public services', notably health and education.

9. Bases for Table 3.6 are as follows:

% who would like to see more spending on education	1985	1990	1996	2006
Britain	1479	1158	961	887
France	n/a	n/a	1273	1730
Germany	1013	2717	3342	1599
Norway	n/a	1430	1286	1308
Spain	n/a	n/a	2339	2440
Sweden	n/a	n/a	1192	1154

n/a = not asked

10. Bases for Table 3.7 are as follows:

% who would like to see more spending on health	1985	1990	1996	2006
Britain	1497	1172	967	895
France	n/a	n/a	1279	1757
Germany	1019	2756	3395	1596
Norway	n/a	1461	1315	1314
Spain	n/a	n/a	2370	2470
Sweden	n/a	n/a	1204	1169

n/a = not asked

11. Bases for Table 3.8 are as follows:

% in favour of less government regulation of business	1985	1990	1996	2006
Britain	1472	1164	948	820
France	n/a	n/a	1263	1691
Germany	1030	3750	3422	1527
Norway	n/a	1418	1293	1199
Spain	n/a	n/a	2042	2123
Sweden	n/a	n/a	1171	1023

n/a = not asked

12. In 1985, all respondents were asked about their likely vote were an election to be held the next day. Thereafter, practice varies across countries and, in some countries, across time. Some asked a genuine partisanship question, seeking to gauge long-standing commitments to a particular party. Others asked about hypothetical votes. In Spain, no such question was asked at all in 1996, and in 2006 respondents were asked about their vote in the 2004 election.

References

Alvarez, R.M. and Brehm, J. (2002), *Hard Choices, Easy Answers*, Princeton, NJ: Princeton University Press

Bartolini, S. and Mair, P. (1990), Identity, *Competition, and Electoral Availability: The Stability of European Electorates, 1885–1985*, Cambridge: Cambridge University Press

Bromley, C. and Curtice, J. (2002), 'Where have all the voters gone?', in Park, A., Curtice, J., Thomson, K., Jarvis, L. and Bromley, C. (eds.), *British Social Attitudes: the 19th Report*, London: Sage

Budge, I., Klingemann, H-D., Volkens, A., Bara, J. and Tanenbaum, E. (2001), *Mapping Policy Preferences, Estimates for Parties, Electors and Governments 1945–1998*, Oxford: Oxford University Press

Dalton, R. (1984), 'Cognitive Mobilization and Partisan Dealignment in Advanced Industrial Democracies', *Journal of Politics*, **46**: 264–284

De Graaf, N., Heath, A. and Need, A (2001), 'Declining cleavages and political choices: the interplay of social and political factors in the Netherlands', *Electoral Studies*, **20**: 1–15

Downs, A. (1957), *An Economic Theory of Democracy*, New York: Harper and Row

Feldman, S. (2003), 'Values, Ideology, and the Structure of Political Attitudes', in Sears, D., Huddy, L. and Jervis, R. (eds.), *Oxford Handbook of Political Psychology*, New York: Oxford University Press

Franklin, M., Mackie, T. and Valen, H. (eds.) (1992), *Electoral Change*, Cambridge: Cambridge University Press

Heath, A., Jowell, R. and Curtice, J. (1985), *How Britain Votes*, Oxford: Pergamon Press

Inglehart, R. (1990), 'Values, Ideology, and Cognitive Mobilization in New Social Movements', in Dalton, R. and Kuechler, M. (eds.), *Challenging the Political Order*, Cambridge: Polity Press

Jaeger, M.M. (2006), 'What Makes People Support Public Responsibility for Welfare Provisions: Self-Interest or Political Ideology?', *Acta Sociologica*, **49**: 321–338

Johns, R. and Padgett, S. (2008), 'The role of government: public values and party politics', in Park, A., Thomson, K., Phillips, M., Curtice, J., Johnson, M. and Clery, E. (eds.), *British Social Attitudes: the 24 Report*, London: Sage

Klingemann H-D., Volkens, A., Bara, J., Budge, I. and McDonald, M. (2006), *Mapping Policy Preferences II: Estimates for Parties, Electors and Governments in Central and Eastern Europe, European Union and OECD 1990–2003*, Oxford: Oxford University Press

Knutsen, O and Scarbrough, E. (1995), 'Cleavage Politics', in van Deth, J. and Scarbrough, E. (eds.), *The Impact of Values*, Oxford: Oxford University Press

Luskin, R. (1987), 'Measuring Political Sophistication', *American Journal of Political Science*, **31**: 856–899

McQuail, D. and Windahl, S. (1981), *Communication Models for the Study of Mass Communication*, London: Longman

OECD (2004), *Learning for Tomorrow's World: First Results from PISA 2003*, Paris: OECD

Przeworski, A. and Sprague, J. (1986), *Paper Stones: a History of Electoral Socialism*, Chicago: University of Chicago Press

Rahn, W. (1993), 'The Role of Partisan Stereotypes in Information Processing about Political Candidates', *American Journal of Political Science*, **37**: 472–496

Rose, R. and McAllister, I. (1986), *Voters Begin to Choose*, London: Sage

Sarlvik, B. and Crewe, I. (1983), *Decade of Dealignment*, Cambridge: Cambridge University Press

Scarbrough, E. (1984), *Political Ideology and Voting*, Oxford: Oxford University Press

Sefton, T. (2003), 'What we want from the welfare state', in Park, A., Curtice, J. Thomson, K., Jarvis, L. and Bromley, C. (eds.), *British Social Attitudes: the 20th Report*, London: Sage

Taylor-Gooby, P. (1999), 'Markets and Motives', *Journal of Social Policy*, **28**: 97–114

Zaller, J. (1992), *The Nature and Origins of Mass Opinion*, Princeton, NJ: Princeton University Press

Acknowledgements

The *National Centre for Social Research* is grateful to the Economic and Social Research Council (ESRC) (grant number RES-501–25–5001) for their financial support which enabled us to ask the *International Social Survey Programme* (ISSP) questions reported in this chapter in Britain. The views expressed are those of the authors alone.

Appendix

The table below is the basis for the simpler summary shown in Table 3.10. It reports the mean 'role of government scale' score for supporters of each of the major parties listed, along with that party's left–right position at the election prior to the survey. For each country an indication is provided (in brackets) as to whether the measure of party support is a question about party identification or likely vote.

For each party the row marked 'Pattern' shows the trends in public opinion and in party position between the two relevant elections. The first letter in each cell reflects party ideological shifts: 'D' for divergence (movement away from the centre) and 'C' for convergence. In cases where the party shifted only negligibly (defined as less than five points), and so there is no possibility of gauging whether its supporters followed suit, we simply report 'n/a' for not applicable. Where the party did shift, we add 'Y' or 'N' to indicate whether supporters moved in the same direction. Since, as noted above, mean voter positions moved much less sharply, in this case we do not impose a minimum requirement for a shift to count as 'non-negligible'. For example, between 1990 and 1996 the Labour Party in Britain moved from a score of -14 to -30, a divergence or movement away from the centre (D). During the same period, its supporters moved from a score of -10 to -11, which denotes a move from the centre consistent with the movement seen in the party's manifesto (Y).

Table A.1 Ideological positions of parties and their supporters (via mean left–right scale scores)

		1985	1990	1996	2006
UK (party ID)					
Labour	Party		-14	-30	-3
	Supporters		-10	-11	1
	Pattern			D-Y	C-Y
Conservative	Party		30	28	15
	Supporters		7	8	9
	Pattern			n/a	C-N
France (party ID)					
PS	Party			-23	-16
	Supporters			-12	-9
	Pattern				C-Y
RPR / UMP	Party			-5	-9
	Supporters			2	5
	Pattern				D-N
Germany (vote)					
SPD	Party	-7		-18	-5
	Supporters	-7		-6	-2
	Pattern			D-N	C-Y
CDU	Party	30		27	23
	Supporters	1		2	1
	Pattern			n/a	C-Y
Norway (vote)					
DNA (Labour)	Party		-36		-38
	Supporters		-15		-10
	Pattern				n/a
Conservative	Party		-7		10
	Supporters		3		-3
	Pattern				D-N
Sweden (party ID)					
Social Democratic	Party			24	-18
	Supporters			-12	-5
	Pattern				D-N
Moderate	Party			40	38
	Supporters			10	10
	Pattern				n/a

'C'/'D' = party convergence/divergence; 'Y'/'N' = did the supporters follow; n/a = party did not move by 5+ points

Cells left blank in Table A.1 denote either that the ISSP questions were not asked in that year, or that no appropriate measure of party support was asked

4 Religion in Britain and the United States

David Voas and Rodney Ling[*]

Religion is a cause of perplexity to the British. On the one hand it is associated with Christian virtue, traditional values, the Dalai Lama and all things bright and beautiful. On the other hand it brings to mind violent fanaticism, reactionary morality, Osama bin Laden, abuse and oppression. After a long history of religious turmoil and mistrust we no longer much mind whether our leaders are Protestant, Catholic, Jewish or agnostic, but strong commitment makes us worried. Tolerance is the great commandment of the modern age – and hence we find it hard to tolerate exacting belief.

God seems more at home in the United States. Although the Constitution keeps prayer out of state schools, it also guarantees that no religion is officially preferred to another and that all are free to exercise their chosen faith. There is a widespread expectation that public figures will be religious (and will be the better for it). Churches, synagogues and temples have for generations served as welcome centres for newcomers, thereby assisting in the transformation of immigrants into Americans and of strangers into locals.

Elites in both countries hold up the other nation as a cautionary example. Britons shudder at public piety and the conviction that God's will coincides with the preacher's (or the president's). Americans see moral relativism and reliance on the state as symptoms of a lack of religious fibre. Each, for the other, has deviated from the preferred path of human progress and these religious tensions occasionally impinge on the 'special relationship' between Britain and America.

It is hard to understand the causes of religious change or the nature of modernisation itself without engaging in such transatlantic comparisons. The secularisation thesis – the idea that modernisation causes problems for religion – remains a key point of reference in the social scientific study of religion (Bruce, 2002), and Britain and the US are respectively example and apparent counter-example to it.

[*]David Voas is Simon Professor of Population Studies in the Institute for Social Change at the University of Manchester. Rodney Ling is Research Assistant in the Institute.

Notwithstanding the obvious differences in the strength of religion in Britain and the US, we will show that attitudes on many topics in this area are surprisingly similar in the two countries. One difference is inescapable, however. In the space of a few decades Islam has established a significant presence in Britain. The Muslim population reached 2.5 million by 2009 and is currently growing (through high fertility and immigration) at six per cent a year (Kerbaj, 2009). This growth coincided with the militant form of identity politics that surfaced in 1989 in the form of book burnings and death threats against Salman Rushdie. Islamism, or political Islam, has re-emerged sporadically in violent form, notably in the London bombings of 7th July 2005. By contrast the United States, where the total population is five times as large, has an estimated 1.3 million Muslims (Kosmin and Keysar, 2009).

Just when religious divisions were fading into insignificance, these perceived threats to national identity and public order have propelled religion back to the forefront of communal concern. Social class, sex and race may be objectively more important, but religion – and particularly Islam – now appears to provoke more anxiety than these other traditional distinctions. Perhaps in reaction to these tensions, some young Muslims increasingly see religious commitment as a form of cultural assertion and self-defence. While it is plausible that ethno-religious friction could also help to revive Christian identity, another possible outcome is hostility to religion in general, as promoted by authors such as Richard Dawkins and Christopher Hitchens.

What follows is a comparative look at attitudes towards religion and religious issues in Britain and the United States. We explore two theses that seem contrary to accepted wisdom. The first is that many people in the two countries have similar views about religion. The second is that people in Britain are actually *more* concerned about religion than Americans – a result, we suggest, of disquiet about Muslim integration. Our starting point is an overview of religious identity, belief and practice in the two countries. We then look at the generally positive views people have about personal faith, and their more critical opinions about public religion. Evidence on the extent to which religion has come to be a source of social division follows, with particular attention paid to how negative views about particular ethnic groups are related to attitudes towards religion. In our final section we consider the rather limited tolerance that now exists for unpopular speech and displays of religious commitment.

Many of our findings derive from a series of questions about religion developed as part of the *International Social Survey Programme*. In Britain, these questions are asked as part of the *British Social Attitudes* survey; in the US they are included on the General Social Survey.[1]

Religious identity, belief and practice

Religious diversity has been a significant feature of British life since the Reformation. Catholicism never disappeared, nor were the established Churches of England and Scotland ever able to prevent dissent and competition. Jews have lived in Britain for centuries, though the rapid growth in the non-Christian population is largely the product of immigration since the Second World War. More and more people are ceasing to identify with a religion at all. Indeed, the key distinction in Britain now is between religious involvement and indifference. We are thus concerned about differences in religiosity (the degree of religious commitment) at least as much as diversity of religious identity.

Religious belief is a basic sign of commitment, and profession of faith is often taken as an essential element of what it is to be religious. Actual religious behaviour, especially attendance at services, may be an even stronger sign. Of course, some people attend for personal, family or social reasons, but in general, religious practice serves as a good indicator of religiosity. We start, however, with simple affiliation. Table 4.1 shows the religious distribution of the population as measured by the question routinely included in the *British Social Attitudes* survey:

Do you regard yourself as belonging to any particular religion?

The fraction of respondents identifying themselves as Christian has fallen from two-thirds to a half since the *British Social Attitudes* survey series began in 1983 (Table 4.1). Most of the shift has been to non-affiliation, with 43 per cent now willing to say that they do not regard themselves as belonging to a religion.[2] Muslims and other non-Christians make up the balance. Apart from a modest under-representation of Muslims (which official estimates put at four per cent rather than three per cent of the total population), the *British Social Attitudes* survey well reflects the current size of religious minorities.

Table 4.1 Religious identity in Britain and the United States

	Britain		United States[+]
	1983	2008	2008
	%	%	%
No religion	31	43	15
Christian	66	50	76
Church of England/Anglican	40	23	1
Roman Catholic	10	9	25
Presbyterian	5	3	2
Methodist	4	2	5
Baptist	1	1	16
Christian – no denomination	3	10	14
Other Christian	3	2	13
Non-Christian	2	7	4
Muslim	1	3	1
Jewish	1	1	1
Other non-Christian	1	3	2
Base	*1761*	*4486*	*54461*

[+] Source: American Religious Identification Survey 2008

The declining Christian share is largely attributable to a drift away from the Church of England (C of E). While most of the growth has occurred in the "no religion" group, it is also noticeable that the Christian label (with no denomination specified) has become more popular in recent years. One might speculate that people who in the past might have given their identity as C of E are now inclined to describe themselves simply as Christian, thereby distinguishing themselves from Muslims and Hindus rather than from Catholics and Methodists. 'Ethnic nominalism', where religion is linked to ethno-national identity, may be gaining ground at the same time as religious practice is declining (Day, 2009). Not all of these respondents are merely nominal Christians, however. Some will be active members of independent non-denominational churches, and indeed 25 per cent of them attend services at least monthly.

The United States is certainly much more religious than Britain, but the common view that it is also more religiously *diverse* is debatable. The final column in Table 4.1 shows findings from the American Religious Identification Survey 2008;[3] some three-quarters of the population align themselves with Christianity, and four per cent with a non-Christian group.[4] There is undoubtedly more variety *within* the broad Christian category in the United States, although denominations of every kind also exist in Britain. If, however, we consider our top level headings – no religion, Christianity, and other faiths – the British population is more evenly spread.

The differences between Britain and the United States are most apparent in the areas of belief and practice. To measure belief in God, respondents were asked to choose which of the statements in Table 4.2 comes "closest to expressing what you believe about God".

Table 4.2 Belief in God in Britain and the United States

	Britain	United States
Belief in God	%	%
I don't believe in God	18	3
I don't know whether there is a God and I don't believe there is any way to find out	19	5
I don't believe in a personal God, but I do believe in a higher power of some kind	14	10
I find myself believing in God some of the time, but not at others	13	3
While I have doubts, I feel that I do believe in God	18	17
I know God really exists and that I have no doubts about it	17	61
Base	*1986*	*2023*

The contrast between the distributions in the two countries is remarkable. People in Britain are very evenly divided across the options, with a very slight skew in favour of atheism or agnosticism (37 per cent) rather than definite or doubtful belief (35 per cent). By contrast, only eight per cent of Americans are sceptics, while more than three-quarters (78 per cent) believe in God – the large majority of whom are free from doubt.

A similar story emerges when we look at self-assessed religiosity. We asked respondents:

Would you describe yourself as ...
... extremely religious
... very religious
... somewhat religious
... neither religious or non-religious
... somewhat non-religious
... very non-religious, or
... extremely non-religious?

These judgements are likely to depend on the context; a degree of commitment that seems high in one place might be regarded as ordinary in another. But while self-ratings may not be useful for comparisons along an objective scale, the figures in Table 4.3 do illustrate two important points. The first is that most people in both countries see themselves as moderate; half of Americans say that they are (merely) somewhat religious, while half of those in Britain either say the same or position themselves as neither one thing nor the other. The second point is that a quarter of the population in each country is willing to be more emphatic, but at opposite ends of the spectrum. For Americans, it is acceptable to be very or extremely religious, a stance taken by only seven per cent in Britain. By contrast, many people in Britain are comfortable describing themselves as very or extremely non-religious, compared with just nine per cent of Americans.

Table 4.3 Self-assessed religiosity in Britain and the United States

	Britain	United States
Respondent describes themselves as ...	%	%
... very or extremely religious	7	26
... somewhat religious	30	51
... neither religious nor non-religious	22	7
... somewhat non-religious	11	6
... very or extremely non-religious	26	9
Base	*1986*	*1365*

As Table 4.4 shows, the contrast is just as marked for attendance at religious services. We asked:

> *Apart from such special occasions as weddings, funerals and baptisms, how often nowadays do you attend services or meetings connected with your religion?* [5]

On this issue it is Americans who show a relatively uniform distribution across the main options (attendance at least weekly, monthly, annually or never). A substantial majority of people in Britain never attend ordinary services.

Table 4.4 Attendance at religious services in Britain and the United States

	Britain	United States
How often attends religious services	%	%
Never	62	22
Less than annually	5	7
At least annually	15	24
At least monthly	8	21
At least weekly	10	25
Base	*4486*	*2023*

As one might expect, the British pattern is heavily influenced by the large proportion of people who currently do not identify with *any* religion even though in many cases they were brought up in one. Nine in ten of this group never attend services (Table 4.5). Non-Christians – and to some extent Catholics – follow the American pattern of observance. Among self-identified Anglicans, not even a fifth attend church as much as once a month, and half never go at all.

Table 4.5 Attendance at religious services in Great Britain, by religious group

	Religious group					
	C of E/ Anglican	Roman Catholic	Other Christian	Non-Christian	No religion	All
How often attends religious services	%	%	%	%	%	%
Never	49	31	41	25	90	62
Less than annually	7	4	7	3	2	5
At least annually	26	23	18	20	5	15
At least monthly	10	15	12	22	1	8
At least weekly	8	25	21	28	1	10
Base	*1114*	*420*	*791*	*236*	*1903*	*4486*

There are substantial differences between the young and the old in religious identity, belief and practice. Previous research has shown that religious decline in Britain is generational; the gap between age groups arises not because individuals become more religiously committed as they get older, but because children are less religious than their parents. The results suggest that institutional religion in Britain now has a half-life of one generation, to borrow the terminology of radioactive decay. Two non-religious parents successfully transmit their lack of religion. Two religious parents have roughly a 50/50 chance of passing on the faith. One religious parent does only half as well as two together (Voas and Crockett, 2005).

Clearly, secularisation changes the environment in which children are raised and the likelihood of effective religious socialisation. How children are brought up has an enormous impact on their subsequent propensity to identify with a religion; once people reach adulthood their religious adherence is less likely to be affected by new conditions. What remains to be seen is how an environment that is increasingly diverse – in terms of both religion and religiosity – will affect the next generation.

Movement is not all in one direction, of course. The survey shows that 10 per cent of people in Britain who had no religious upbringing now regard themselves as belonging to a religion. Nor is the choice simply to stay or to go: nine per cent of respondents raised in one religion now identify with another. Nevertheless, the main shift is out of religion, something that characterises 36 per cent of people with a religious upbringing.

So far we have considered the three main measures of religious involvement: identity (or affiliation), belief (in God) and practice (specifically attendance at religious services). We can use these variables to classify people into one of three groups. We define people as 'religious' if they identify with a religion, believe (however tentatively) in God, and attend services (even if less than once a year). While this definition is exceptionally inclusive, it still covers only a quarter of people in Britain (see Table 4.6). We will label people 'unreligious' if they do not regard themselves as belonging to a religion, do not believe and never attend. This fairly conservative definition captures not quite a third of the sample. In between we are left with a large group who could be called the 'fuzzy faithful' (Voas, 2009): they identify with a religion, believe in God or attend services, but not all three.

Table 4.6 Religious typology for Britain and the United States

	Britain	United States
	%	%
Religious	26	70
Fuzzy	36	24
Unreligious	31	4
Base	*4486*	*2023*

In what follows we will use these categories to look at the relationship between religiosity and attitudes. (The classification is far less useful for the United States, where more than two-thirds of people qualify as religious and the unreligious group is very small.)

Personal faith and religious authority

We turn now to perceptions of the role of religion in contemporary society. We begin with the personal advantages that religion is seen to offer to the faithful, and then consider attitudes towards the relationship between religion and public life, looking particularly at the extent to which people feel that religion should be influential in politics. We explore the sources of moral authority and conclude by examining attitudes towards faith schools.

There is a widespread view that religion is functional for both individuals and society. We asked respondents how much they agreed or disagreed with the following statements:

> *Practising a religion helps people to…*
> *… find inner peace and happiness*
> *… make friends*
> *… gain comfort in times of trouble or sorrow*

As shown in Table 4.7, two-thirds of people agree that practising a religion helps people to find "inner peace and happiness"; few disagree (seven per cent). Religious Britons, like Americans, overwhelmingly back the statement. The idea that practising a religion helps people to make friends produces similar levels of support. The notion that religion is a comfort in times of trouble or sorrow is even more widely endorsed (not surprisingly, as critics of religion often describe it as a crutch).

Table 4.7 Attitudes towards the personal benefits of religion in Britain and the United States, by religiosity

	Britain				United States
	Un-religious	Fuzzy	Religious	All	
% agreeing that religion helps people to …	%	%	%	%	%
… find inner peace/happiness	49	63	88	65	86
… make friends	58	66	81	67	82
… gain comfort	68	80	92	79	95
Base	*638*	*806*	*531*	*1975*	*1365*

There is less consensus on the potential benefits of religion for society as a whole, although the principle receives support. We asked:

At the present time, do you think religion as a whole is increasing its influence on British life or losing its influence?

And then:

All in all, do you think this is a good thing or a bad thing?

Half of the sample views the influence of religion on British life as positive (most saying that it is waning and that this is bad, the rest saying that it is increasing and that is good). Not quite a third regard religious influence as unfortunate – they approve its decline or regret its increase – and the remainder are uncertain about either the trend or how to evaluate it (Table 4.8).

Table 4.8 Attitudes towards the influence of religion on British life

	% saying
Religion is increasing its influence	
Which is a good thing	6
Which is a bad thing	18
Religion is decreasing its influence	
Which is a good thing	13
Which is a bad thing	44
Religion neither increasing nor decreasing influence	6
Base	*1875*

People in Britain are, however, reluctant to see matters of faith intrude into the public sphere. As the proportion of the population that is religious has declined, the idea that religion should be a private matter has become ever more widely held (Bruce and Voas, 2007). People appear happy to accept pronouncements from religious leaders on certain topics – notably excluding sexual behaviour – provided they are matters on which everyone tends to agree (Bruce and Glendinning, 2003). Political life is a different matter, however. We asked respondents whether they agreed or disagreed with the following statements:

Religious leaders should not try to influence how people vote in elections

Religious leaders should not try to influence government decisions

Three-quarters (75 per cent) maintain that religious leaders should *not* try to influence voting behaviour while two-thirds (67 per cent) think religious leaders should stay out of government decision making. It is tempting to suppose that the situation is very different in the US, but in fact the figures there are almost identical (72 and 66 per cent respectively). This consensus has not inhibited religious leaders in either country from speaking on issues of political concern.

The responses to the following question are therefore not too surprising:

> *If many more of our elected officials were deeply religious, do you think that the laws and policy decisions they make would probably be better or would probably be worse?*

Nearly a half (45 per cent) of people in Britain take the view that laws and policy decisions would probably be worse in these circumstances, and only a quarter (26 per cent) think that decisions would probably be better. The example of Tony Blair and the war in Iraq was possibly influential for some respondents.

We also find only limited evidence that people in Britain see religion as a source of moral authority. Respondents were asked to pick which of these two statements came closest to their views:

> *In matters of right and wrong, some people say it is important to faithfully follow the leaders and teachings of one's religion*
>
> *Others say it is more important to follow one's own conscience*

Only six per cent think that people should faithfully follow their religious leaders; 89 per cent take the alternative view. These attitudes do not merely reflect a reluctance to be told what to do; most people simply do not believe that there *are* absolute standards. Sixty per cent agree that "there can never be absolutely clear guidelines of what is good and evil"; the same proportion agrees that "morality is a personal matter and society should not force everyone to follow one standard".

Moral relativism is characteristic of modernity, but it is also thought to be an especially European phenomenon. Once again, however, the US is less different than one might expect. Three-quarters (74 per cent) of Americans take the view that morality is a "personal matter", and 80 per cent acknowledge that "right and wrong are not usually a simple matter of black and white; there are many shades of grey".

Perhaps because religion is seen by most in Britain as a private matter, people are unwilling to be challenged about their beliefs. We asked respondents to pick which of these statements came closest to their views:

> *Some say it is okay for religious people to try to convert other people to their faith, others say that everyone should leave everyone else alone*

Only a sixth (17 per cent) of respondents think it acceptable for religious people to try and convert others; 81 per cent take the opposite view. There is also disquiet about the extent to which religious faith can lead to intolerance. Three-quarters (73 per cent) of Britons maintain that "people with very strong religious beliefs are often too intolerant of others". Naturally, agreement was highest among the unreligious (at 82 per cent), but even 63 per cent of religious people concurred. Two-thirds (66 per cent) of Americans agree as well, so the statement represents a widely accepted view on both sides of the Atlantic.

Despite some scepticism about the extent to which religion can be a source of moral authority, state-supported church-linked schools continue to be a major feature of the educational landscape in Britain. To gauge people's attitudes towards faith schools we asked:

> *Some schools are for children of a particular religion. Which of the statements on this card comes closest to your views about these schools?*
> *No religious group should have its own schools*
> *Some religious groups but not others should have their own schools*
> *Any religious group should be able to have its own schools*

Just over four in ten maintain that *no* religious group should have its own schools, and the same proportion thinks that that *any* religious group should have its own schools; the remainder would allow some groups but not others to have schools. As Table 4.9 shows, around half of the unreligious oppose religious schooling, as do a little more than a quarter of religious respondents. Support for faith schools is strongest among Roman Catholics, who at secondary level are the major beneficiaries of the current system: 63 per cent would allow any religious group to run schools. Even so, 21 per cent of Catholics do not believe that there should be religious schools.

Table 4.9 Attitudes towards faith schools in Britain, by religiosity

	Religiosity			All
	Unreligious	**Fuzzy**	**Religious**	
Attitude to faith schools	%	%	%	%
No religious groups should have own schools	51	44	28	42
Some groups should have own schools, not others	11	14	14	13
Any religious group should be able to have own schools	36	39	56	43
Base	*638*	*810*	*531*	*1979*

Religion and social division

Social cohesion is influenced by attitudes towards diversity, of which religious diversity is an increasingly important component. The multicultural ideal is for difference to be seen as beneficial, and this ideological norm can indeed be found in countries like Australia and the US. If a degree of uniformity is seen as important for social cohesion, though, religious diversity may not be welcomed (Bouma and Ling, 2009).

Attitudes towards religious diversity

Religious diversity in the abstract receives a reasonable degree of support in Britain: 70 per cent of people – including 60 per cent of the unreligious – agree that "we must respect all religions". To press the matter further, we asked people how much they agreed or disagreed with the statement "religious diversity has been good for Britain". As Table 4.10 shows, responses were mixed. Half of the country supports the assertion, but a majority of the unreligious disagree, as do more than a third of the religious. We will explore the possible reasons for these views later in this section.

Table 4.10 Attitudes towards religious diversity in Britain, by religiosity

	Religiosity			All
	Unreligious	Fuzzy	Religious	
Religious diversity has been good for Britain	%	%	%	%
Strongly agree	8	7	13	9
Somewhat agree	35	45	48	43
Somewhat disagree	32	33	26	31
Strongly disagree	22	10	9	14
Base	*354*	*425*	*325*	*1104*

A similar level of ambivalence is apparent on the issue of whether *all* religious groups in Britain should have equal rights. As Table 4.11 shows, barely half concur with the principle, with the remainder split between uncertainty and disagreement. Americans are considerably more supportive, as one might expect from the constitutional guarantee that the state will impartially protect all religions.

The most telling results are produced when we ask people whether they agree or disagree that "Britain is deeply divided along religious lines". Just over half (52 per cent) agree with this view. Only 16 per cent disagree, with the remainder (28 per cent) neither agreeing nor disagreeing with the statement. Although some people agree that the country is divided even while supporting diversity (and *vice versa*), the perception that religion is a significant source of division is strong and probably fairly new.

Table 4.11 Attitudes towards rights of different religious groups in Britain and the United States

	Britain	United States
All religious groups should have equal rights	%	%
Strongly agree	11	28
Agree	39	51
Neither agree nor disagree	21	11
Disagree	18	7
Strongly disagree	6	1
Base	*1986*	*1365*

Diversity in practice?

When the issue is brought closer to home, most respondents claim to be comfortable with the prospect of receiving someone of another religion into their families. We asked:

> *People have different religions and different religious views. Would you accept a person from a different religion or with a very different religious view from yours ...*
>
> *... marrying a relative of yours?*
> *... being a candidate of the political party you prefer?*

Three-quarters of people in Britain would accept a person from a different religious background marrying a relative (Table 4.12). But the level of definite acceptance in Britain is well below what one finds in the United States, where nearly nine in ten would accept mixed marriage. There are also marked variations between different religious groups. Roman Catholics in Britain come closest to the American pattern, with 80 per cent of them accepting mixed marriage. By contrast, only 60 per cent of non-Christians would accept it, while 26 per cent would *definitely* not, the highest proportion found across the different religious groups we surveyed. Differences between the religious and unreligious are fairly small; 73 per cent of the religious say they would accept mixed marriage, compared with 77 per cent of the unreligious. Replacing "marriage to a relative" with "being a candidate for office" makes little difference to the results, except that more people have no opinion.

The transatlantic contrast – with religious difference seeming to be a larger obstacle in Britain, despite its lower religiosity – points to a problem. It is to this issue that we now turn.

Table 4.12 Willingness to accept people of different religion in Britain and the United States

	Britain	United States
If wanted to marry relative	%	%
Definitely accept	24	40
Probably accept	51	47
Probably not accept	10	8
Definitely not accept	8	3
As a political candidate	%	%
Definitely accept	22	35
Probably accept	49	47
Probably not accept	10	12
Definitely not accept	5	3
Base	*1986*	*1356*

Attitudes towards different religious groups

We need to consider how far discontent with religious diversity reflects concern about particular religious groups. We asked respondents to express how they feel about people in various groups on a scale from 0 to 100, where 50 is neutral and higher or lower values represent "warm" or "cool" feelings respectively:[6]

> *I'd like to get your feelings towards a number of different ethnic and religious groups. I'll read the name of a group and I'd like you to rate that group using something we call the feeling thermometer. Ratings between 50 degrees and 100 degrees mean that you feel favourable and warm toward the group. Ratings between 0 degrees and 50 degrees mean that you don't feel favourable and don't care too much for that group. You would rate the group at the 50-degree mark if you don't feel particularly warm or cold towards the group. Feel free to use the entire extent of the scale*

The results are shown in Table 4.13. Each column shows the percentage of people who give "cool", "neutral" or "warm" scores to each of seven different religious groups. Most groups attract more positive than negative feelings. Nearly half of respondents, for example, feel warmly towards Protestants, 44 per cent are neutral and only six per cent express cool feelings. Two groups stand out for attracting more negative than positive feelings: Muslims and (marginally) the deeply religious. A third of people give Muslims a cool rating, while under a quarter give them a warm one. Responses towards these two groups are related; two-thirds (66 per cent) of those who feel warmly towards

Muslims are also positive about the deeply religious, and over half (56 per cent) of those who are negative about the deeply religious feel similarly about Muslims.

Table 4.13 Feelings towards different religious groups in Britain

	Religious group						
	Prote-stants	No religion	Catholics	Jews	Budd-hists	Deeply religious	Muslims
Score	%	%	%	%	%	%	%
Cool (0–49)	6	8	9	13	15	29	34
Neutral (50)	44	49	43	47	45	41	40
Warm (51–100)	47	40	45	36	35	27	23
Base	*2236*	*2236*	*2236*	*2236*	*2236*	*2236*	*2236*

As an aside, there is considerable variation in how positively people feel about members of their own group. Nearly two-thirds of Muslims feel very warmly about other Muslims (rating them 76 or more out of 100), and likewise half (50 per cent) of Catholics are highly positive about their co-religionists. Only a quarter (25 per cent) of those with no religion feel so warmly about fellow non-affiliates.

The fact that people make distinctions between Muslims and the followers of other religions is also evident when we consider responses to two questions about the building of a local mosque or church. A random half of respondents were asked:

> *Suppose some Muslims wanted to build a large Muslim mosque in your community. Would this bother you a lot, bother you a little, not bother you, or be something you welcome?*

The other half of respondents were asked:[7]

> *Suppose some Christians wanted to build a large Christian church in your community. Would this bother you a lot, bother you a little, not bother you, or be something you welcome?*

A majority (55 per cent) say that they would be bothered by the construction of a large Muslim mosque in their community, but only 15 per cent by a large church.

These concerns may be linked to perceptions of the extent to which Muslims want to integrate socially. When asked to agree or disagree with the statement "nearly all Muslims living in Britain really want to fit in", similar proportions agreed and disagreed (38 and 39 per cent respectively).

There is a clear relationship between negative attitudes towards Muslims and unease about religious difference. Among respondents with neutral or positive feelings towards Muslims, 62 per cent think that diversity has been good for Britain. Among those who have negative feelings for Muslims, exactly the same percentage disagree. A third of people (33 per cent) who deny that Muslims want to fit in – but only eight per cent of others – disagree with the view that all religious groups should have equal rights.

Similar attitudes towards religious diversity can be found among people who have negative feelings about other groups – Buddhists, for example – and one might therefore suppose that the figures show general anxiety about 'imported' religion rather than hostility to Muslims specifically. This interpretation is hard to sustain. First, far more people respond unfavourably to Muslims than to others. Second – and this is the crucial point – very few people are negative about any other group on its own. Of the people who feel cool towards Buddhists, 83 per cent are likewise cool towards Muslims. Of people who are neutral or positive about Muslims, a mere four per cent are negative about Buddhists. The same pattern can be seen when comparing attitudes to Muslims and Jews. Three-quarters (77 per cent) of people who see Jews in a poor light are likewise unfavourable towards Muslims, and of people who are at least neutral towards Muslims, few (five per cent) are negative about Jews. (The base for these values excludes Jews and Muslims themselves.) It is worth noting that of respondents who have adverse views of black people (10 per cent of respondents), 84 per cent also feel negatively about Muslims and 58 per cent are uncomfortable with Buddhists.

Education has a clear impact on attitudes towards Muslims; 44 per cent of respondents with no qualifications have negative feelings, as against 23 per cent of those with degrees. Perhaps surprisingly, given the importance of education, there are no sharp age differences, although 18–24 year olds are less likely than people aged 65 and over to have negative feelings (34 and 41 per cent respectively). Religiosity makes little difference to the prevalence of negative feelings towards Muslims, but the religious are almost twice as likely as the unreligious (31 per cent *versus* 17 per cent) to express feelings that are positive rather than neutral.

Three key points emerge from this analysis. Firstly, some of the antipathy towards Muslims comes from people with a generalised dislike of anyone different. Secondly, a larger subset of the population – about a fifth – responds negatively *only* to Muslims. Finally, relatively few people feel unfavourable towards any other religious or ethnic group on its own.

Some degree of generalised xenophobia is always likely to exist. Conceivably there is a spill-over effect, so that people who are worried about Muslims come to feel negatively about 'others' in general. In any case, the adverse reaction to

Muslims deserves to be the focus of policy on social cohesion, because no other group elicits so much disquiet.

When the feeling thermometer was used in the US General Social Survey in 2004, the ratings of Muslims were similar to those shown in Table 4.13 (28 per cent cool, 36 per cent neutral, 26 per cent warm). In a relative sense the results were even less favourable, because more people than in Britain felt warmly about Protestants, Catholics and Jews (51, 52 and 45 per cent respectively). Americans are more accepting of religious difference, but not because they have less negative views about Muslims. We suggest that Americans appear to be more tolerant in part because religious diversity is central to their national identity and ideology, and also because Muslims are a much smaller and less visible minority in the US than in Britain.

Religion and freedom of expression

Support for the free expression of unpopular or potentially dangerous religious views is weak, particularly in Britain. The following question was asked on both sides of the Atlantic:

> *Consider religious extremists, people who believe that their religion is the only true faith and all other religions should be considered as enemies. Do you think such people should be allowed ...*
> *... to hold a public meeting to express their views?*
> *... to publish books expressing their views?*

As shown in Table 4.14, only a quarter to a third of people in Britain would allow the meeting or book, as compared with more than half to three-quarters of Americans.

Table 4.14 Attitudes towards religious extremists in Britain and the United States

	Britain	United States
Would allow to hold a public meeting	%	%
Definitely	6	26
Probably	18	33
Probably not	24	20
Definitely not	45	20
Would allow to publish a book	%	%
Definitely	7	38
Probably	27	40
Probably not	23	10
Definitely not	34	9
Base	*1986*	*1365*

It is difficult to be sure without further testing, but one wonders whether the term 'religious extremist' is interpreted in different ways in the two countries. In Britain it is almost certainly taken to refer to violent Islamists; in the US it might be thought by some to include sectarian Christian fundamentalists. This conjecture receives some support from the similarity in responses to questions that explicitly mention antagonistic Muslims. One can compare different but related questions in the two countries. In Britain, respondents were invited to agree or disagree with the view that:

> People have a perfect right to give a speech defending Osama bin Laden or al Qaeda

Two-thirds (66 per cent) disagreed with this statement. In the US, people were asked to consider whether "a Muslim clergyman who preaches hatred of the United States should be allowed to speak", to which a substantial majority (57 per cent) responded in the negative. While support for free expression still seems slightly higher in the US than in Britain, these scenarios suggest that the acceptable limits are not so different in the two countries and that attitudes towards Muslims are similar.

Further similarities can be found in relation to material that criticises or mocks religion. Take, for example, the following question:

> Some books or films offend people who have strong religious beliefs. Should books and films that attack religions be banned by law or should they be allowed?

More than a quarter (27 per cent) of people in Britain are willing to ban these works. One might expect things to be different in the United States, in view of the strong constitutional (and ideological) support for free speech. There the following question was posed:

> There are always some people whose ideas are considered bad or dangerous by other people. For instance, somebody who is against all churches and religion ... If such a person wanted to make a speech in your community against churches and religion, should he be allowed to speak, or not? ... If some people in your community suggested that a book he wrote against churches and religion should be taken out of your public library, would you favour removing this book, or not?

Here, too, more than a quarter (26 per cent) would remove an anti-religious book from libraries, and nearly as many (23 per cent) would not allow someone to speak in opposition to religion. The comparison may not be fair, of course, to the extent that Americans are more religious than the British and hence will tend to be more offended by anti-religious material. Religious people in Britain are much more likely to support a ban than the unreligious (38 per cent *versus* 17 per cent, with the religiously fuzzy in between).

Turning to religious expression, we asked half of our respondents:

> *Should people be allowed to dress in a way that shows their religious faith, by wearing veils, turbans or crucifixes?*

Just over half (53 per cent) think that these symbols should be allowed, but 42 per cent say "no". Religiosity makes a difference; people who are unreligious or religiously fuzzy split fairly evenly on the issue, while 62 per cent of the religious would allow dress of this kind.

We asked the other half of our sample a similar but more restricted question:

> *Should people* who work with the general public *be allowed to dress in a way that shows their religious faith, by wearing veils, turbans or crucifixes?*

One might expect more people to respond negatively to this question than the other one, but in fact fewer people do so; only 30 per cent state categorically that religious dress should not be allowed in this situation, while 50 per cent would permit it.[8]

Conclusions

Britain and the United States might seem to be two countries separated by a common religion. Both are predominantly Protestant (in a broad sense, encompassing Anglicans), with sizable Catholic minorities and a leavening of non-Christians, but faith is far more vibrant in the New World than in the Old. It would be natural to suppose that attitudes towards religion are very different in the two countries. And if secularisation means the declining social significance of religion (Wilson, 1966), we would expect religion not to matter much in Britain.

As it turns out, these assumptions are not wholly correct. Americans and Britons are surprisingly similar in many of their attitudes. Most people are pragmatic: religion has personal and social benefits, but faith should not be taken too far. From politics to private life, many domains are seen as off limits to clerical meddling. People are generally tolerant, but signs of inflexibility are most quickly encountered in Britain. The reason, we suggest, is the degree to which Islam is perceived as a threat to social cohesion.

American views about Muslims and particularly anti-Western clerics are just as hostile as those found across the Atlantic. What is different is that the proportion of Muslims in the population is seven times higher in Britain than in the United States and growing rapidly. In that respect the better parallel, as others have observed, is with American unease at the prevalence of Spanish speakers. Some of the reaction comes from people who feel negatively about 'others' in general, but a larger number of people in Britain are unfavourable only to Muslims. The size and visibility of this group, as well as suspicion of extremists, have made religion seem important again.

This apparent threat to national identity (or even, some fear, to security) reduces the willingness to accommodate free expression. Opinion is divided, and many people remain tolerant of unpopular speech as well as distinctive dress and religious behaviour, but a large segment of the British population is unhappy about these subcultures.

Of course, Muslims are still only a small fraction of the British population, and most people have relatively little contact with them. Ironically this separation may make the problem more acute, as what from close up would seem benign looks threatening at a distance. Religion is increasingly associated with unfamiliar people practising an unfamiliar faith. It is a faith that provokes anxiety on both sides of the Atlantic, and the fact that the vast majority of adherents are loyal and peace-loving is scant reassurance if a minority are not.

Suspicion of 'risky' religion may have an impact on rights to free expression. Likewise, the strong opinion that religion should be confined to the private sphere could be an obstacle to the integration of those who believe otherwise. In any event it is not clear whether religious dress, education, language, and so on count as private or public. How does one classify the use of officially recognised Sharia tribunals to settle family disputes? When identity is salient, the personal becomes political.

There is, to repeat, considerable toleration in Britain of religion as a private pursuit. Few people are hostile to religious practice *per se*. Indeed, we have an interest in anything that might make other people behave well, and some nostalgia for traditional religion lingers. Religion has come to be associated with unpopular things, however: Islamist extremism, immigrants, George Bush, preachy morality, child abuse. Despite their engagement in worthwhile activities, religious groups have shown little talent for public relations. God is back on the agenda, but the faithful may yet come to be wistful about the days of dull secularity.

Notes

1. The General Social Survey 2008 is funded by the National Science Foundation and run by the National Opinion Research Center. It is based on face-to-face interviews in English and Spanish; N = 2023. The series began in 1972. For further information on the *International Social Survey Programme* see Appendix I of this report. Unless otherwise stated, all US data reported in this chapter come from the General Social Survey.

2. Responses concerning religion are known to be highly influenced by the wording of the question, the options offered, the context in which it appears, social norms and other factors (Voas, 2007). The 2001 Census elicited much higher levels of Christian identification (at the expense of 'no religion') for reasons that have been analysed elsewhere (Voas and Bruce, 2004).

3. The American Religious Identification Survey (ARIS) 2008 is a telephone survey of adults conducted in English and Spanish in the continental United States; N = 54,461. It is the third in a series that began in 1990.

4. The only other study of comparable size, the US Religious Landscape Survey conducted by the Pew Forum on Religion and Public Life, puts the figure at 4.7 per cent (http://religions.pewforum.org/).
5. In Britain, this question was asked of all respondents who identified with a religion or who said they had been brought up in a particular religion. Respondents *not* asked this question (that is, those who do not identify with and were not brought up in a religion) are included here in the "never" category.
6. The order in which respondents were asked about the different groups was randomised to avoid the possibility that question ordering might influence ratings.
7. Further randomisation meant that those respondents who were asked about the mosque/church were further divided into two. One group was presented with the answer options in the order shown in the text, i.e. running negative to positive. The other group were presented with answer options running from positive to negative.
8. It is unclear why people are less negative when the question is designed to induce a more hostile response. It is relevant that the first question appeared on the self-completion questionnaire while the second was asked by an interviewer as part of the face-to-face interview. The interview situation allows for more nuanced responses (which were then coded), such as "it depends on the job" or "it depends on the religion/symbol". It is also possible that respondents are reluctant to give frank but intolerant responses when speaking face to face.

References

Bouma, G.D. and Ling, R. (2009), 'Religious Diversity', in Clarke, P. (ed.), *The Oxford Handbook of the Sociology of Religion*, Oxford: Oxford University Press

Bruce, S. (2002), *God is Dead: Secularization in the West*, Oxford: Blackwell

Bruce, S. and Glendinning, T. (2003), 'Religious beliefs and differences' in Bromley, C., Curtice, J., Hinds, K. and Park, A. (eds.), *Devolution – Scottish Answers to Scottish Questions*, Edinburgh: Edinburgh University Press

Bruce, S. and Voas, D. (2007), 'Religious toleration and organizational typologies', *Journal of Contemporary Religion*, **22(1):** 1–17

Day, A. (2009), 'Researching belief without asking religious questions', *Fieldwork in Religion*, **4(1)**

Kerbaj, R. (2009), 'Muslim population "rising 10 times faster than rest of society"', *The Times*, 30th January 2009, available at
http://www.timesonline.co.uk/tol/news/uk/article5621482.ece

Kosmin, B.A. and Keysar, A. (2009), *American Religious Identification Survey Summary Report*, available at
http://www.americanreligionsurvey-aris.org/reports/ARIS_Report_2008.pdf

Voas, D. (2007), 'Surveys of behaviour, beliefs and affiliation', in Beckford, J. and Demerath, N.J. (eds.), *Handbook of the Sociology of Religion*, London: Sage

Voas, D. (2009), 'The rise and fall of fuzzy fidelity in Europe', *European Sociological Review*, **25(2)**: 155–168

Voas, D. and Bruce, S. (2004), 'The 2001 census and Christian identification in Britain', *Journal of Contemporary Religion*, **19(1)**: 23–28

Voas, D. and Crockett, A. (2005), 'Religion in Britain: Neither believing nor belonging', *Sociology*, **39(1)**: 11–28

Wilson, B.R. (1966), *Religion in Secular Society*, London: C.A. Watts

Acknowledgements

The *National Centre for Social Research* is grateful to the Economic and Social Research Council for the financial support (grant number RES-501–25–001) which allowed us to ask the *International Social Survey Programme* (ISSP) questions reported in this chapter. We are also grateful to the John Templeton Foundation (grant number 13362) and NORFACE for funding the additional questions about religion reported here. Responsibility for the analysis of these data lies solely with the authors.

5 Religious faith and contemporary attitudes

Siobhan McAndrew[*]

British society has become more secular over recent decades. Between 1983 and 2008 there was a sharp fall in the proportion of people who feel they belong to a particular religion and in the numbers who attend religious services frequently: from 69 to 56 per cent (identifying with a particular religion) and from 13 to 10 per cent (weekly or more frequent attendance). Belief in God has also declined, from 64 per cent in 1991 to 48 per cent in 2008. There appears to be a generational decline in the proportion of respondents reporting that religious beliefs make a difference to their lives (Crockett and Voas, 2006).

At the same time, immigration and demographic change has led to a rise in affiliation to other world religions and pentecostal Christianity, and an apparent religious renewal among second and subsequent generations of arrivals.[1] Since this has occurred concomitantly with religious decline among the majority population, it appears that some polarisation of belief has occurred.

Over the last few decades, the issues which religious communities encounter have also changed markedly – the implications of technological change, for example, or the changing relationships and structures within British society. Religious authorities will often have unique moral messages about many of these developments and will attempt to impart these to their followers, albeit with varying degrees of success. In so doing, they will face increasing competition from other sources of moral authority. Given that immigrant communities in Britain are somewhat residentially concentrated, it is also conceivable that political parties might attempt to mobilise them on either religious or ethnic bases to maximise their share of the vote.

In this chapter we will explore these issues by examining the extent to which religious beliefs are linked to wider social attitudes more generally. We will focus on four areas of particular contemporary relevance:

- The first relates to bioethics, with long-standing questions about abortion rights and the acceptability of assisted dying having been debated

---

[*]Siobhan McAndrew is a Research Associate at the Institute for Social Change, University of Manchester.

throughout 2008. The culpability of those assisting suicide was tested at the High Court, while the Human Rights and Embryology Bill was debated in Parliament, with considerable lobbying against it by pro-life organisations.[2]

- The second area of relevance reflects the proliferation of new and complex family forms over the last few decades (Duncan and Phillips, 2008). Here we will examine people's attitudes towards personal relationships and family roles, focusing on issues such as sex outside marriage, homosexual rights, and gender roles within the family.

- We next examine the evidence for any relationship between religion and party political choices. It was traditionally thought that class loyalty formed the bedrock of politics in Britain, and that any political cleavage along religious lines at least within Great Britain, if not Northern Ireland, ended in 1922 when the 'Irish question' was finally answered with the creation of the Irish Free State. However, there has been some reassessment of this apparent lack of a relationship between religiosity and party support. The fact that some traditional loyalties are dissolving, and that immigration is changing the religious profile of certain areas, means that religion and social questions may be emerging as a site for mobilisation.

- Finally, we focus upon the possible links between 'social trust' and religion. Do the religious in Britain have the high levels of social trust often claimed for their US counterparts?

How might religion be linked to a person's attitudes and values? Some have argued that religiosity – like sex, education or class – *directly* helps shape political views and party choices (Andersen *et al.*, 2005). But religion could also have a more subtle effect on people's attitudes and values by influencing the choices they make about their peers, networks and organisations – in sum, the contexts which provide cues and information on socio-political issues. So religious peers or spouses, and religious environments such as churches and mosques, may well help shape attitudes towards a range of ethical issues and political preferences (Kotler-Berkowitz, 2001). Finally, relationships between religiosity and social attitudes could be confounded by personality differences: it is plausible that those seeking certainty in the religious domain do likewise in other areas of their lives.

Measures of religiosity

We begin by considering how best to measure a person's religiosity. In so doing, we ideally need to take account of the different dimensions that can make up religious faith and practise. For example, someone who is intensely personally religious – who prays every day and believes strongly in God and in the existence of an afterlife – might not attend religious services regularly. Another person might exhibit a high degree of practise – such as high involvement in organised religious activities – but not subscribe to the tenets of any religious faith. So relying on one measure, such as attendance at religious services, will only give a partial picture of someone's overall faith.

As far back as the 1960s, with the earliest large-scale surveys of religion, some writers have suggested that religiosity has different dimensions, each of which have different implications for social behaviour (Glock, 1962; Glock and Stark, 1968). For example, some US studies distinguish between belonging (affiliation), behaving (attendance and private practice) and believing (Leege and Kellstedt, 1993). This suggests that religiosity has at least three dimensions. A very recent study assumed that two dimensions exist and used a typology to distinguish Swiss survey respondents according to whether they were 'believers' or 'belongers' (Nicolet and Tresch, 2009). Here researchers tried to capture the form of religiosity characterised by a sense of institutional affiliation with long-standing churches, as well as post-traditional forms characterised by more individualised beliefs, where institutional affiliation may not be a given. They found that people exhibiting belief were more socially liberal than those who reported affiliation alone, while among the non-practising, significant differences existed between uncommitted Christians, 'believers without belonging', and the unreligious in selected political attitudes. It seems, therefore, that *how* you are religious matters as well as how far you are religious.

How might we capture this insight? A variety of methods can be used. For simple comparisons it is often enough to use a simple typology – such as the 'more religious', the 'unreligious' and those in between who may either believe in God without practising greatly or practise religion without believing strongly. Then, the characteristics of the more religious compared with the less religious can be illustrated in a straightforward and intuitive manner. Alternatively, we can use a more sophisticated scale which scores people according to their responses to a wider range of questions. We will now explore each of these options.

The religious, the unreligious and the 'fuzzy faithful'

Here we categorise respondents according to their responses to three questions: whether they identify with a particular religion, whether they believe in God and whether they attend religious services. We explored various ways of using these questions to divide up respondents. In particular, while it makes sense to distinguish between the highly religious (who believe in God, report an affiliation and attend services at least sometimes) and the unreligious (who do none of these things), it is less clear how to examine the intermediate group. It seems plausible that those who believe without reporting an affiliation (believers without belonging) might be distinct from those who report an affiliation but do not believe (belongers without believing). It also seems plausible that those who report belief and affiliation, but attend religious services less regularly than once a month, might still be distinctive compared with those who exhibit weaker beliefs or behaviours (the somewhat religious compared with the less religious). After some analysis, however, differences between these various intermediate groups were not readily apparent, and so, following the approach adopted by Voas and Ling elsewhere in this report (see in particular Table 4.6 p.71), we group this middle group together as the 'fuzzy faithful' (Voas, 2009). So we find little evidence for either a distinct group of socially traditional churchgoers who are secular in terms of belief or a group exhibiting intense post-traditional spirituality which is not linked to institutional forms.

In summary, our typology identifies three groups:

- **The religious:** Those who believe in God, belong to a religious group and attend religious services at least sometimes. Even on this broad definition of religiosity, this group comprises 28 per cent of respondents. We might expect this group to have attitudes which are distinct from the rest of the population.

- **The fuzzy faithful:** Those who exhibit some evidence of religious belief, affiliation or practice, either through belief in God, reporting a religious affiliation, or at least some attendance (but not all three). This category is likely to capture those with weak or no belief in a deity, or a weaker but residual loyalty to religious organisations and practices. This group covers 39 per cent of respondents.

- **The unreligious:** Those who neither believe in God nor belong to any religious group. We might consider this group to be the most clearly secularised. This group forms 33 per cent of respondents.

The religiosity scale

A second way of examining the impact of religiosity on socio-political attitudes and practices is to create a composite scale of religiosity. This method uses a larger number of items relating to personal religiosity and religious practise than the three used in the typology we have just discussed. Each individual is given a score depending on their responses to this wider set of questions, so that we can distinguish more clearly between the highly religious and the less religious. Fourteen items were used to create the scale, encompassing the following:

- being a member of a particular religious group
- being brought up in a particular religious group

- church attendance
- participation in church activities
- importance of religion in the respondent's daily life
- the respondent's self-perception as religious or not
- prayer
- belief in God
- belief in heaven
- belief in hell
- belief in the afterlife
- confidence in churches and religious organisations
- response to the proposition that we trust too much in science and not enough in religious faith
- response to the proposition that religion helps people find inner peace and happiness.

Some questions involve religious attitudes and behaviours which are so mild that even many agnostic or atheist respondents might indicate assent – such as the question regarding whether religion helps people find inner peace. Others are stronger: many highly religious people might yet report low levels of confidence in formal religious organisations or indicate that we do not trust 'too much' in science. Including such questions helps us distinguish between the unreligious who are yet favourably disposed in some way towards religion, and those who are not; and the religious who report pro-religious attitudes and behaviours across the board, and those who do not. In addition, we include three questions relating to belief in the afterlife, belief in heaven and belief in hell, because prior work has indicated that the less religious may reject belief in a traditional heaven but yet believe in an afterlife, and also that those who believe in heaven may yet reject the notion of a traditional hell (Branas-Garza *et al.*, forthcoming).[3]

To create the scale, the original answers to each of the fourteen questions were dichotomised to distinguish between those reporting at least a moderate level of belief or practice in the relevant question (scored as 1) and the rest (scored as 0). The scale was then created by simply adding the scores across the fourteen items for each individual. Further details are given in the appendix to this chapter. The maximum possible score was 14 and the minimum 0, with a mean score of 6.6.[4]

Figure 5.1 shows the distribution of responses along this religiosity scale in terms of the percentage of respondents given each score. The distribution of these scores is interesting: there appear to be two different peaks around which the scores are centring, with a religious peak, an unreligious peak and a group in between. This suggests that even with a larger array of measures of religiosity the threefold typology described earlier characterises respondents fairly. This is confirmed by Table 5.1, which gives the mean religiosity score for each of the three groups: the religious, the fuzzy faithful and the unreligious.

Figure 5.1 Distribution of scores on the religiosity scale

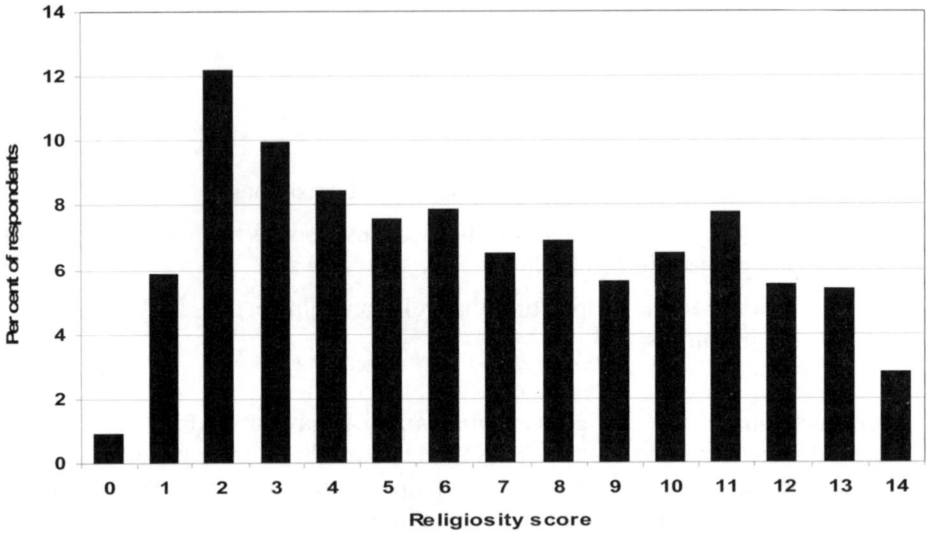

The data on which Figure 5.1 is based can be found in the appendix to this chapter

Table 5.1 Religiosity scores for the religious, fuzzy faithful and unreligious

Religiosity type	Mean score on religiosity scale	Base
Religious	11.0	528
Fuzzy faithful	6.7	791
Unreligious	2.8	623
All	6.6	1942

Dimensions of religiosity

We also carried out further analysis of these same fourteen questions to examine whether there are different *types* of religiosity. We did this by drawing on the extra information given in the responses as to the greater or lesser frequency of prayer, for example, or the intensity of self-assessed religiosity (the additive scale method simply captures whether the respondent engages in prayer or not, or identifies as religious or not).[5] Three dimensions of religiosity emerged as significant. The first accounts for the greatest variation, and relates to the following: whether the respondent is a religious adherent, whether they consider religion important in their everyday life, and whether they describe themselves as religious, believe in God, the afterlife and heaven, attend church regularly, and have confidence in churches. We can call this *generalised religiosity* – generalised in the sense that it is not specific to particular religious behaviours. The second dimension is associated most strongly with belief in an afterlife, heaven and hell. Belief in God is *not* associated with this dimension, which might seem surprising, given that belief in a personal God is a key aspect of most traditional religions in Britain. Neither is religious adherence associated with this dimension, while church attendance is negatively associated. So we might call this dimension one of diffuse *belief without belonging*.[6] Given the lack of association with adherence, belief in God and attendance, this dimension of religiosity seems to be one which our threefold typology fails to pick up. The third dimension encompasses people who were brought up in a particular religion, but indicators of religious activity such as church attendance are negatively associated. Adherence also correlates weakly with this dimension. We might consider this dimension to be one of *religious background*, where people have been brought up in a family with a religious identification but do not currently believe or practice; their religiosity may be of a more nominal type.

We will now use the religiosity typology to examine how religiosity appears linked to people's views about key contemporary issues.[7]

Bioethics and religion

We begin by examining public attitudes towards a range of bioethical issues. While the relationship between religiosity and attitudes towards abortion and euthanasia is well established, their high salience over the last few years makes it important to examine them afresh. The Human Rights and Embryology Bill was debated in Parliament during 2008, covering the creation of hybrid embryos for research, and the creation of 'saviour siblings'. An amendment by the 'pro-life' Conservative MP Nadine Dorries also proposed that the upper term limit for abortion be reduced. The legalisation of euthanasia was actively debated during the same period, reflecting Debbie Purdy's campaign to have the law on assisting suicide clarified, as well as ongoing discussions about the ethics of the Dignitas clinic in Switzerland.

We assessed public attitudes in this area through the following questions:

Do you think it is wrong to have an abortion if there is a strong chance of serious defect in the baby?

Do you think it is wrong to have an abortion if the family has a very low income and cannot afford any more children?

People have different views about the beginnings of human life. In your opinion, is an embryo a human being at the moment of conception?

Some people think that scientists should be allowed to use cells from human embryos for certain types of medical research. Others think this should never be allowed. ... what [do] you think?

Suppose a person has a painful incurable disease. Do you think that doctors should be allowed by law to end the patient's life, if the patient requests it?

Responses to each of these questions were coded on a four-point scale with responses to the two abortion questions running from "always wrong" to "not wrong at all", responses to the question on the beginnings of human life coded as "definitely true" (or untrue) or "probably true" (or untrue), and responses to the remaining two questions coded as "definitely should be allowed" (or should not) and "probably should be allowed" (or should not).

The proportions of people expressing the most 'liberal' responses to each of these questions are shown in Table 5.2. These findings suggest that, rather than the public exhibiting a dogmatic approach to bioethical questions, responses reflect the particular circumstances of each question. Over three-quarters believe that abortion is wrong only "sometimes" or "not at all" if there is a high risk that the baby will have a birth defect. By contrast, only around half believe the same when the issue is limited family finances. There appears to be a preference for reducing suffering: research on embryos (supported by 69 per cent) is justified because, presumably, respondents hope that it will lead to medical breakthroughs regarding conditions such as cystic fibrosis, muscular dystrophy, spinal injuries and diabetes, even though 53 per cent of respondents believe that human life begins at the moment of conception. Similarly, a very large majority (82 per cent) believes that a doctor should "probably" or "definitely" be allowed to end the life of a patient with a painful incurable disease at the patient's behest. Views on this issue have changed remarkably little over time (Clery *et al.*, 2007) ranging from 75 per cent support when we first asked the question in 1984 to 82 per cent now.

Not surprisingly, religiosity is strongly associated with people's views on these issues. As Table 5.2 shows, the unreligious are twice as likely as the religious to take the view that an embryo is *not* a human being at the moment of conception. And the religious are less supportive than the unreligious of abortion on medical grounds. In both cases, the views of the fuzzy faithful lie somewhere in between the two; in relation to abortion they are closer to the unreligious, but they are closer to the religious in their thinking on embryos.

To simplify our analysis we used these five questions to create a scale of attitudes to bioethical issues. Each response was given a score of 1 to 4, with 1

Table 5.2 Bioethical attitudes, by religiosity

	Religiosity			All
% saying …	Religious	Fuzzy faithful	Un-religious	
… abortion wrong only sometimes or not at all if strong chance of birth defect	67	81	86	78
… abortion wrong only sometimes or not at all if family cannot afford more children	35	50	60	49
Base	531	806	638	1986
… embryo probably or definitely not a human being at moment of conception	30	40	60	43
… medical research on embryos should probably or definitely be allowed	61	70	77	69
… a doctor should probably or definitely be allowed to end life of patient with painful incurable disease	71	85	92	82
Base	531	810	638	2250

being the most 'pro-life' and 4 being the most permissive. The maximum score was 20 and the minimum 5.[8] Table 5.3 shows the average scores for a selection of different religious and demographic groups, with higher scores indicating more liberal attitudes and lower scores indicating less liberal attitudes. That bioethical attitudes are strongly associated with religiosity is scarcely surprising, but it is interesting to note that attitudes vary much more strongly with religiosity than with age – which is often thought to be partly the cause of the less liberal attitudes of the more religious.

These results suggest that religious communities may be a fruitful site of mobilisation for 'pro-life' activists. At present, such mobilisation is relatively limited. During 2007 the Catholic Bishops' Conference of England and Wales lobbied against the requirement that adoption agencies treat same sex couples equally, and has also mobilised adherents against abortion and embryo research, and to support faith schools and reject quotas for the admission of children from other backgrounds. Besides that instance, pro-life and other religious activism does not appear to rely on support from large organisations, and has been primarily through the courts. For example, the rights of students to wear religious dress at school, contravening uniform policy, has been tested in the courts, notably by Lydia Playfoot in 2007. Her campaign to wear a 'purity ring' was funded by the pressure group Christian Concern for our Nation, an organisation founded in 2004, which also lobbied Parliament regarding bioethical issues and gay rights during 2007 and 2008.[9]

Table 5.3 Mean scores on bioethical attitudes scale, by respondent characteristics

	Mean score	Base
All	14.8	1499
Type of religious adherence		
Religious	13.0	392
Fuzzy faithful	14.9	585
Unreligious	16.2	515
Sex		
Male	15.2	682
Female	14.5	817
Age category		
18–24	15.1	103
65 plus	14.6	331
Education		
Degree	15.3	304
No qualification	14.3	300

Moral values, gender roles and changing family forms

Religious communities also claim to provide moral guidance on family life and relationships more broadly. The Church of England and Roman Catholic Church justify denominational education on the basis that students are taught according to a distinctive ethos, and a 2008 study of students and parents in faith schools in Bradford found that parents saw the transmission of religious values through faith-based education as a way of providing direction for their children (Howarth *et al.*, 2008). However, religious organisations face a great deal of competition in the provision of moral frameworks. People derive moral values from a variety of sources, including their family during formative years, the media, peers, the law as a frame of reference, and their own individual judgement. At the same time, society has become more complex, particularly with regard to family life, relationships and the place of women in society. Legislative and technological change has led to the role of marriage and family forms evolving considerably. From the 1960s, society has witnessed a fall in marriage rates while divorce has become common; many of those who divorce go on to remarry and their children accordingly enter 'blended families'. The entry of women into higher-paid occupations means that many women can find economic security outside marriage, removing an economic barrier to exiting low-quality relationships. Meanwhile, in 2003 the Employment Equality (Sexual Orientation) Regulations came into force, which rendered it unlawful to discriminate against workers because of their sexual orientation and, with the legalising of civil partnerships from 2005, the rights of gay couples have been formally recognised. Accordingly, norms towards family structure, gender roles and gay rights have changed markedly (for example, see Crompton and Lyonette, 2008; Duncan and Phillips, 2008).

How far do such norms vary with religiosity, or has a pragmatic secular norm supplanted traditional mores in order to accommodate these new relationship and household forms? Are those who are more religious more conservative with regard to issues of personal morality, and more supportive of traditional gender roles and family forms? To assess this we look at attitudes towards different forms of sexual relationships as measured by the following questions:

> *Do you think it is wrong or not wrong ...*
> *... if a man and a woman have sexual relations before marriage?*
> *... a married person having sexual relations with someone other than his or her husband or wife?*
> *... sexual relations between two adults of the same sex?*

Answers were coded on a four-point scale ranging from "always wrong" to "not wrong at all". We also look at answers to this question about traditional gender roles:

> *Do you agree or disagree: a man's job is to earn money; a woman's job is to look after the home and family?*

Table 5.4 shows how responses to these questions vary by religiosity. Unsurprisingly, the religious are the most likely to disagree with pre-marital sex, being ten times more likely than the unreligious to think it is wrong. Only 10 per cent of the fuzzy faithful feel this way. There is also a clear divergence between the religious and unreligious in relation to homosexuality; half of the religious think homosexual behaviour is wrong compared with one in five of the unreligious and just over a third of the fuzzy faithful. By contrast, there is little difference between the three groups in relation to the acceptability of cheating on a partner; a large majority of all groups think that this is wrong. The most religious group are also more likely to support traditional gender roles, with one in five doing so compared with one in ten of the unreligious.

This relationship between religiosity and values holds true even when we take account of other factors such as age. The results of multivariate analysis suggest that the religious are more likely to see homosexual sex as being wrong, even when we control for age and other socio-demographic characteristics such as education. This also holds true for the fuzzy faithful, indicating that even attenuated religiosity has an impact on social attitudes. With regard to gender roles in the home, the religious are more likely than the unreligious to support traditional gender roles, even after controlling for other relevant characteristics, although the fuzzy faithful are no longer significantly different from the unreligious on this issue.

Table 5.4 Attitudes towards personal and family relationships, by religiosity

% saying ...	Religiosity			All
	Religious	Fuzzy faithful	Un-religious	
... pre-marital sex is always or almost always wrong	29	10	3	13
... married person having sex outside marriage is always or almost always wrong	90	84	80	84
... homosexual sex is always or almost always wrong	50	35	19	34
... agree that man should earn money, woman should stay at home	21	18	10	16
Base	*531*	*806*	*638*	*1986*

We can also explore how religiosity relates to family formation and parenting responsibilities, by looking at responses to the following question about the role of non-resident parents:

> *Child maintenance law says that all parents should pay child maintenance even if they did not want to have a child or have not been in a committed relationship. Thinking about a non-resident parent in these circumstances, which of these comes closest to your view?*

> *They are just as responsible for supporting the child compared to other parents*

> *They are partially responsible for supporting the child but not to the same extent as other parents*

> *They are not responsible at all for supporting the child*

Here we find near unanimity between the religious, the fuzzy faithful and the unreligious when it comes to the extent to which non-resident parents are responsible for supporting a child born in these circumstances, with around eight in ten taking the view that non-resident parents are either just as responsible as other parents (79 per cent) or at least partially responsible (18 per cent). Only a small minority (2 per cent) think parents in these circumstances have no responsibilities at all. While religious organisations often promote the dignifying role of motherhood, and portray marriage and the family as the bedrock of society, there is perhaps little social teaching regarding responsibilities to families formed without religious sanction. Broader secular society has evolved norms regarding responsibilities to children – even if this might partly reflect a preference that the taxpayer should not step in where unwilling parents would rather not.

Party support

Confessional voting is not thought to characterise electoral behaviour in Britain. But in the European elections of 2009, the Christian Party, established in 2004, garnered 250,000 votes, or 1.6 per cent nationally. While this was not a significant result at the national level, it was nevertheless ahead of the Socialist Labour Party established by Arthur Scargill. The party also polled 2.9 per cent in London. Is this atypical, or does religion play a more general role in voting in Britain?

Traditionally, party support has been viewed as determined primarily by class and economic position. By comparison, many other European countries feature party systems which are two-dimensional, with party divisions based on religious lines as well as class lines. For example, both Germany and the Netherlands host Christian Democratic parties as well as large Social Democratic parties (Oskarsen, 2005). But in Britain, religious cleavages have been viewed as relevant only in Northern Ireland, or as having died with the old Liberal Party in the inter-war period. Before then, Irish Catholics tended to vote Liberal due to their policy on Home Rule. The Liberal Party was also associated with Nonconformism. According to the old adage, the early Labour Party 'owed more to Methodism than Marx'. In 1917, the social worker and preacher Maude Royden memorably called the Church of England 'the Conservative Party at prayer'.[10] With the collapse of the Liberal Party and the joint dominance of Labour and the Conservatives from the late 1920s, religion was not thought to be significantly associated with party support. Post-war immigrants with a distinct religious profile – such as Irish Catholics or new Commonwealth arrivals – were thought to vote in line with their class position, generally Labour.

However, recent work has suggested that religious faith does have a part to play in British party politics. For example, Kotler-Berkowitz has found that religion was significantly associated with voting behaviour in the 1992 General Election, with examples including a pro-Labour tendency among middle-class Catholics, and a secular middle-class tendency to vote against the Conservative Party (Kotler-Berkowitz, 2001). Middle-class 'Dissenting Protestants' (Methodists and other non-Anglican Protestants) were also found to be more likely to vote Liberal Democrat. Members of small religious communities – thought to be generally non-Christian, and likely to be of ethnic minority background – were more likely to vote Labour. Across all respondents, religious behaviour was associated with being less likely to vote Labour and more likely to vote Liberal Democrat. In a further study of the 1992–1997 and 1997–2001 electoral cycles, Andersen et al. (2005) report that religious identification was significant in predicting support for the Conservatives as opposed to Labour from 1997 to 2000, but was not a significant factor from 1992 to 1996 (Andersen et al., 2005).

We asked respondents to recall how they voted in the 2005 General Election. Table 5.5 shows how party choice differed between the religious, the fuzzy faithful and the unreligious. Although there wer some minor variations in party support between the different groups, the most obvious finding is that the unreligious were markedly less likely to vote for *any* party than either the fuzzy faithful or the religious.

Table 5.5 Party voted for in 2005 General Election, by religiosity

	Religiosity			All
	Religious	**Fuzzy faithful**	**Unreligious**	
Party voted for	%	%	%	%
Did not vote	28	28	36	31
Conservative	22	23	17	21
Labour	31	27	27	28
Liberal Democrat	10	7	9	9
Nationalist parties	1	3	2	2
Other	1	3	3	2
Not answered	6	8	5	7
Base	*302*	*388*	*318*	*302*

It is well known that party choice varies according to a wide range of other factors, such as age and education (Evans and Norris, 1999; Clarke et al., 2004). So to examine the independent effect of religiosity while taking account of these sorts of characteristics we used multivariate analysis to predict party support. As the vote choice question was only asked of a subset of respondents in 2008, we used party identification as a proxy for vote choice.[11] We used multinomial logistic regression to look separately at factors associated with identifying with each of the three main parties compared with not identifying with any party at all. Full details of this analysis can be found in the appendix to this chapter.

We found age to be significant in predicting party identification: older people are more likely to identify with all three of the main parties compared with identifying with none. Income and education are also significant in predicting party identification, with those in higher income quartiles and graduates being more likely to identify with each party (compared with none) than those in the lowest income bracket, or non-graduates. Having a professional or intermediate non-manual occupation as opposed to a routine manual one is also significantly associated with identifying with the Conservatives and Liberal Democrats, but not with Labour. (It is worth noting that education, income and occupation are so interrelated that it is difficult to be absolutely certain of the individual impact of each.) There is no relationship between being a member of an ethnic minority group and identifying with Labour, although ethnicity is significantly associated with *not* identifying with the Conservatives or the Liberal Democrats. Sex and marital status do not appear to make much of a difference to identifying with any of the three main parties.

Even when these factors are taken into account, the religious are more likely than the unreligious to identify with each of the three main parties, suggesting that religiosity is associated with an increased chance of identifying with *any* party rather than none. Multivariate analysis confirms this. It is not possible to say for sure what is behind this link between religiosity and party identification. However, if we repeat the analysis while distinguishing between the three dimensions of religiosity discussed earlier – generalised religiosity, 'believing without belonging', and the nominal religiosity associated with religious background – religious background emerges as the main component significantly associated with party identification. It may be that our measure of religious background is capturing the role of family socialisation in general rather than religious socialisation *per se*.

Social trust

Finally, we explore the question of social trust and whether this varies according to religiosity. In many studies of the decline of traditional community spirit and the emergence of new forms of belonging, 'generalised social trust' is used as an indicator of 'social capital', the bonds and social networks thought to be the basic pre-requisite for democracy to function fully (Putnam, 2000). Religious life provides one site for social capital and so might be expected to be associated with higher levels of civic engagement and social trust. The Saguaro Seminar on Civic Engagement's *Better Together* report, for example, found that in the US "houses of worship build and sustain more social capital – and social capital of more varied forms – than any other type of institution in America".[12]

Although the UK is more secular than the US, we might expect that here too those who are religious might have higher levels of social trust than the less religious. There are numerous possible explanations for this. Many religions encourage people to promote the interests of others or the common good ahead of their own narrow self-interest. In addition, the social aspects of religion bring people into contact with others more often, so that they learn through experience that others are willing to cooperate and are fundamentally trustworthy. Religious organisations can increase a sense of connectedness and community, and encourage people to act cooperatively. Religious practice in communal settings also reflects social capital investments already made. Perhaps religion provides a 'psychic insurance' effect in people's dealings with others, which makes them more willing to take a risk that others will act reciprocally (Kirkpatrick, 2005; Scheve and Stasavage, 2006).

Conversely, however, some argue that religious practice can promote only socialising with people from the same social or ethnic group, and that in fact divisions *between* such groups are entrenched. It has also been suggested that spending time on religious activities reduces productivity and the time available to engage in other, more trust-building, activities (Alexander, 2007). In this sense, religiosity might be associated with lower trust – as happens in sectarian societies. Some faith groups are hierarchical and authoritarian, and promote less civic engagement rather than more (Putnam, 1993). Furthermore, to the extent that religiosity is increasingly individualistic and personalised, the link between religion and social capital is weakened (Putnam, 2000). Finally, a third strand of the literature suggests that in Europe the link between religion and social capital is 'generally unsubstantial' (Halman and Petterson, 2001). This is because of the secularisation process in Europe: religion has increasingly less impact on public and social life, and has become increasingly privatised and personalised.

To measure social trust, we ask the following question:

> *Generally speaking, would you say that most people can be trusted or that you can't be too careful in dealing with people?*

Under half – 45 per cent – respond by saying that most people can "almost always" or "usually" be trusted.[13]

We found no significant relationship between religiosity (whether measured by our threefold typology or the fuller religiosity scale) and social trust. This may be because these measures of religiosity do not capture the social aspects of religion which might correlate more strongly with social capital. Alternatively, it may also reflect the fact that the measure of generalised social trust does not capture the variation in social capital which is associated with religious belief and practice: religious people may be strongly community minded and exhibit high levels of volunteering and reciprocity, without responding that people can generally be trusted. Finally, of course, there may simply be little or no relationship in Britain between generalised social trust and religiosity.

Multivariate analysis was carried out to examine the effect of religiosity, measured by the threefold typology, while controlling for various demographic and socio-economic factors. Full details can be found in the appendix to this chapter. Holding a degree, or being in the top income quartile are significantly positively associated with social trust, as is having a professional or intermediate job compared with a routine job. However, the most religious of our three categories are no more or less trusting than the unreligious, while the fuzzy faithful have slightly lower levels of social trust than the unreligious. Similar findings also applied when using the religiosity scale. There is little evidence, then, for the religious having higher levels of social trust than the unreligious, at least in Britain.

Conclusions

In this chapter we have examined whether religion still plays a role in shaping attitudes in British society. In certain aspects the highly religious are distinctive: they are more likely to be 'pro-life' and to exhibit less liberal attitudes towards abortion and voluntary euthanasia. They are more traditional in their views about gender roles and are much less liberal than the unreligious about homosexuality. These differences appear to hold even when controlling for confounding variables such as age.

In other regards, it is less clear that the religious are different. Religiosity does appear to be associated with political engagement, as measured via party identification. However, on the basis of the analysis included in this chapter it is not possible for us to be sure why this might be the case. Using more sophisticated measures of religiosity, it appears that religiousness in itself is not associated with the tendency to identify with any party compared with none. Instead, the relationship seemed to work through 'religious background', or a nominal type of religiosity which could be capturing family socialisation effects. Finally, we did not find any clear link between religiosity and generalised social trust. It may be that examining friendship or membership of voluntary associations would prove more fruitful in clarifying how religion might bring people together in modern Britain, but this awaits further study.

Perhaps these results are not surprising. British society has become increasingly secular over time. Despite the post 7/7 discourse regarding 'religious polarisation' and government engagement with religious groups, the vast majority of people do not attend church regularly or subscribe to strong religious beliefs. Even for those who practise, religion appears to be a private matter. Religious organisations do have a 'comparative advantage' with regard to bioethical questions, since most religions have a clear position on the parameters of life which scientists perhaps struggle to communicate in like manner. But on the evidence presented here, it is difficult to be certain that religion in Britain affects socio-political attitudes more widely.

Notes

1. Prior to the 2001 Census, evidence on growth of other world religions in Britain depended on opinion poll data, data on ethnicity and official data on number of religious buildings. Peach (1996) provides an overview of post-war British immigration, while Peach and Gale (2005) provide measures of the growth of Muslim, Sikh and Hindu places of worship. The growth in number of places of worship for 'other Christian' denominations from 1972 to 2004 has been documented in Weller (2007: 42). Meanwhile, Brierley (1998–2008) suggests that membership of pentecostalist churches has grown significantly. Survey evidence suggests that the transmission rate of religious identification between the first generation of immigrants and their children is high. Even if religiosity is on average lower for second-generation immigrants compared with their parents, their religiosity is higher than that of the white majority group, and this group is a growing proportion of the population. See, for example, Kaufmann (2007).
2. Human Fertilisation and Embryology Bill [HL] 2007–08. The Bill was first introduced to Parliament in November 2007; the eventual Human Fertilisation and Embryology Act 2008 (c.22) received Royal Assent in November 2008.

3. The data suggest that respondents are slightly more likely to accept that an afterlife exists than heaven, and in turn are more likely to accept that heaven exists than hell. Nine per cent of respondents consider that an afterlife exists but that heaven does not, while 11 per cent of respondents consider that heaven exists but that hell does not. This gives us confidence that the three items should be included separately. This is borne out by the fact that the mean score on the religiosity scale for those believing in the afterlife is lower than the score for the respondents who believe in heaven (which in turn is lower than the scores for those who believe in hell).

4. The usual method of testing whether such a scale is a reliable indicator of an underlying attitude is Cronbach's alpha. Cronbach's alpha for the fourteen items was 0.87, which indicates a very good level of reliability.

5. We used categorical principal components analysis, which reduces a large number of variables down to a smaller number of uncorrelated 'components' or dimensions. The categorical principal components analysis (CATPCA) method, in particular, suits data which are dichotomous or in ordered categories, rather than continuous measures. Full details of the results of the CATPCA analysis can be found in the appendix to this chapter.

6. This term was coined by Grace Davie, the leading exponent of the hypothesis that 'believing without belonging' characterises religiosity in Britain today (Davie, 1994).

7. There is a further practical distinction between our different measures of religiosity: sample size. While the typology is the simplest measure of religiosity, it does have the advantage of including the largest number of respondents (4,201). By contrast, the religiosity scale and the three component scores cover only 1,951 respondents. In order to maximise the number of respondents for whom we could calculate scale scores, we included cases where the respondent had responded to at least 11 of the 14 items, and in these cases replaced missing observations for the remaining items with the variable mean. The CATPCA procedure used the same set of cases, but instead treated missing values 'passively'; missing values were ignored in the analysis rather than imputations made. The inclusion of sets of responses where only three or fewer responses were missing ensured that valuable information was not lost, while imputation or non-inclusion was kept to a reasonable level.

8. In this instance, "don't know", "can't choose" and "refusal" responses were excluded. Cronbach's alpha for this scale was 0.67, indicating moderate internal consistency, which might be expected given that the scale is based on a small number of items. However, it suggests that analysis should be interpreted with some caution. (The score did not increase when individual items were dropped.)

9. As reported by BBC News in 2007 ("Chastity Ring' Girl Loses Case", available at http://news.bbc.co.uk/1/hi/uk/6900512.stm).

10. As reported in The Times in 1917 ('Church Reform. Restricted Spiritual Activity. The Demand For Freedom', 17th July).

11. Further details of the questions used to measure party identification can be found in Appendix I of this report.

12. Saguaro Seminar on Civic Engagement, Kennedy School of Government, Harvard University, Better Together (December 2000: 63). First edition of report available at http://www.bettertogether.org/pdfs/FullReportText.pdf

13. Two measures of social trust were included on the 2008 survey, one asked face to face and the other (described here) in a self-completion supplement. A slightly lower measure of social trust (40 per cent) was obtained on the face-to-face version of the question.

References

Alexander, M. (2007), 'Determinants of Social Capital: New Evidence on Religion, Diversity and Structural Change', *British Journal of Political Science*, **37**: 368–377

Andersen, A., Tilley, J. and Heath, A.F. (2005), 'Political Knowledge and Enlightened Preferences: Party Choice through the Electoral Cycle', *British Journal of Political Science*, **35**: 285–302

Branas-Garza, P., Garcia, T. and Neuman, S. (forthcoming), 'The Big Carrot: High-Stakes Incentives Revisited', *Journal of Behavioral Decision Making*

Brierley, P. (ed.) (1998–2008), *Religious Trends*, London: Christian Research

Clarke, H., Sanders, D., Stewart, M. and Whiteley, P. (2004), *Political Choice in Britain*, Oxford: Oxford University Press

Clery, E., McLean, S. and Phillips, M. (2007), 'Quickening death: the euthanasia debate', in Park, A., Curtice, J., Thomson, K., Phillips, M. and Johnson, M. (eds.), *British Social Attitudes: the 23rd Report – Perspectives on a Changing Society*, London: Sage

Crockett, A. and Voas, D. (2006), 'Generations of Decline: Religious Change in 20th Century Britain', *Journal for the Scientific Study of Religion*, **45(4)**: 567–584

Crompton, R. and Lyonette, C. (2008), 'Who does the housework? The division of Labour within the home', in Park, A., Curtice, J., Thomson, K., Phillips, M., Johnson, M. and Clery, E. (eds.), *British Social Attitudes: the 24th Report*, London: Sage

Davie, G. (1994), *Religion in Britain since 1945: Believing without Belonging*, Oxford: Blackwell

Duncan, S. and Phillips, M. (2008), 'New families? Tradition and change in modern relationships', in Park, A., Curtice, J., Thomson, K., Phillips, M., Johnson, M. and Clery, E. (eds.), *British Social Attitudes: the 24th Report*, London: Sage

Evans, G. and Norris, P. (eds.), (1999), *Critical Elections: British Parties and Voters in Long-Term Perspective*, London: Sage

Glock, C.Y. (1962), 'On the Study of Religious Commitment', *Review of Recent Research Bearing on Religious and Character Formation*, supplement to *Religious Education*, **57(4)**: 98–110

Glock, C.Y. and Stark, R. (1968), *American Piety: The Nature of Religious Commitment*, Berkley: University of California Press

Halman, L. and Petterson, T. (2001), 'Religion and Social Capital in Contemporary Europe: Results from the 1999/2000 European Values Study', *Research in the Social Scientific Study of Religion*, **12** :65–93

Howarth, J., Lees, J., Sidebotham, P., Higgins, J. and Imtiaz, A. (2008), *Religion, Beliefs and Parenting Practices*, York: Joseph Rowntree Foundation

Kaufmann, E. (2007), 'Shall the Religious Inherit the Earth?: Demography and Politics in the Twenty-First Century', Working Paper, Birkbeck College, London

Kirkpatrick, L.A. (2005), *Attachment, Evolution, and the Psychology of Religion,* New York: Guilford Publications

Kotler-Berkowitz, L.A. (2001), 'Religion and Voting Behaviour in Great Britain: A Reassessment', *British Journal of Political Science*, **31(3)**: 523–555

Leege, D.C. and Kellstedt L.A. (eds.) (1993), *Rediscovering the Religious Factor in American Politics*, Armonk, NY: M.E. Shape

Nicolet, S. and Tresch, A. (2009), 'Changing Religiosity, Changing Politics? The Influence of "Belonging" and "Believing" on Political Attitudes in Switzerland', *Politics and Religion*, **2**: 76–99

Oskarson, M. (2005), 'Social Structure and Party Choice', in Thomassen, J. (ed.), *The European Voter: A Comparative Study of Modern Democracies*, Oxford: Oxford University Press

Peach, C. (ed.) (1996), *Ethnicity in the 1991 Census: Volume Two: The ethnic minority populations of Great Britain*, London: The Stationery Office

Peach, C. and Gale, R. (2005), 'Muslims, Hindus and Sikhs in the New Religious Landscape of England', *The Geographical Review*, **93(4)**: 469–490

Putnam, R.D. (2000), *Bowling Alone: The Collapse and Revival of American Community*, New York: Simon and Schuster

Putnam, R.D. with Leonardi, R. and Nanetti, R.Y. (1993), *Making Democracy Work: Civic Traditions in Modern Italy*, Princeton: Princeton University Press

Scheve, K. and Stasavage, D. (2006), 'Religion and Preferences for Social Insurance', *Quarterly Journal of Political Science,* **1(3)**: 255–286

Voas, D. (2009), 'The Rise and Fall of Fuzzy Fidelity in Europe', *European Sociological Review*, **25(2)**: 155–168

Weller, P. (2007), *Religions in the UK Directory: 2007–2010*, Derby: Multi-Faith Centre

Acknowledgements

The *National Centre for Social Research* is grateful to the Economic and Social Research Council for the financial support (grant number RES-501–25–001) which allowed us to ask the *International Social Survey Programme* (ISSP) questions reported in this chapter. We are also grateful to the John Templeton Foundation (grant number 13362) and NORFACE for funding the additional questions about religion reported here. Responsibility for the analysis of these data lies solely with the author.

Appendix

The religiosity scale

When calculating the religiosity scale, indicators based on responses to the following questions were used:

Do you regard yourself as belonging to any particular religion; which?
Yes (any) = 1, No = 0

In what religion, if any, were you brought up: what was your family's religion?
Brought up in any religion = 1, No religion = 0

Apart from such special occasions as weddings, funerals and baptisms, how often nowadays do you attend services or meetings connected with your religion? [once a week or more, less often but at least once in two weeks, less often but at least once a month, less often but at least twice a year, less often but at least once a year, less often, never or practically never, varies too much to say]
At least once a month = 1, Less often = 0

How often do you take part in the activities or organisations of a church or place of worship other than attending services? [never, less than once a year, about once or twice a year, several times a year, about once a month, two to three times a month, nearly every week, every week, several times a week]
Any participation = 1, Never = 0

How important is religion in your daily life?[Version A/B: very important, somewhat important, not very important, not at all important; Version C/D: extremely important, very important, somewhat important, not at all important]
At least somewhat important = 1, Other response = 0

Would you describe yourself as religious? [extremely religious, very religious, somewhat religious, neither religious nor non-religious, somewhat non-religious, very non-religious, extremely non-religious]
At least somewhat religious = 1, Other response = 0

Now thinking about the present, about how often do you pray? [never, less than once a year, about once or twice a year, several times a year, about once a month, 2–3 times a month, nearly every week, every week, several times a week, once a day, several times a day]
Ever pray (even if less than once a year) = 1, Never = 0

Which statement comes closest to expressing what you believe about God? [I don't believe in God, I don't know whether there is a God and I don't believe there is any way to find out, I don't believe in a personal God but I do believe in a higher power of some kind, I find myself believing in God some of the time but not at others, while I have doubts I feel that I do believe in God, or I know God really exists and that I have no doubts about it?]
Believe in God at least some of the time = 1, Do not believe in a personal God = 0

Are you absolutely sure you believe in God, somewhat sure, not quite sure, not at all sure, or are you sure you do not believe in God?
Absolutely or somewhat sure = 1, Other response = 0.

Do you believe in heaven?[yes definitely, yes probably, no probably not, no definitely not]
Yes = 1, No = 0

Do you believe in hell? [yes definitely, yes probably, no probably not, no definitely not]
Yes = 1, No = 0

Do you believe in life after death? [yes definitely, yes probably, no probably not, no definitely not]
Yes = 1, No = 0

How much confidence do you have in churches and religious organisations? [complete confidence, a great deal of confidence, some confidence, very little confidence, no confidence at all]
At least some confidence = 1, Other response = 0

Please consider and tell me if you agree or disagree: we trust too much in science and not enough in religious faith? [strongly agree, agree, neither agree nor disagree, disagree, strongly disagree]
Agree/strongly agree = 1, Other response = 0

Do you agree or disagree that practising a religion helps people to find inner peace and happiness? [strongly agree, agree, neither agree nor disagree, disagree, strongly disagree]
Agree/strongly agree = 1, Other response = 0

Table A.1 gives the proportions scoring 1 for each item.

Table A.1 Responses to dichotomised items in the religiosity scale

	% respondents	*Base*
Religious adherent	56	*4464*
Was brought up in religion	87	*4470*
Attends church at least monthly	20	*3960*
Takes part in church activities at least occasionally	38	*1951*
Reports religion at least somewhat important in daily life	40	*4486*
Describes self as at least somewhat religious	38	*1891*
Prays at least occasionally	56	*1937*
Believes in God at least somewhat	48	*4222*
Believes heaven exists (probably or definitely)	48	*1703*
Believes hell exists (probably or definitely)	28	*1986*
Believes life exists after death (probably or definitely)	52	*1737*
Has at least some confidence in churches	50	*1986*
Agrees/strongly agree we trust too much in science	15	*1986*
Agrees/strongly agree religion helps people find peace	65	*1507*

Tables A.2 summarise the distribution of respondents along the religiosity scale, as shown in Figure 5.1.

Table A.2 Religiosity scale: Proportion of respondents given each score

Score on religiosity scale	% of respondents	Base
0	1	15
1	6	101
2	12	228
3	10	200
4	8	170
5	8	154
6	8	168
7	7	125
8	7	141
9	6	113
10	7	131
11	8	139
12	6	115
13	5	103
14	3	48
Total	100	1951

Categorical principal components analysis

Table A.3 Component loadings for each of the three dimensions of religiosity, by variable

	Generalised religiosity	Belief without belonging	Religious background
Whether respondent is religious adherent	0.71	-0.09	0.37
Importance of religion in respondent's daily life	0.77	-0.30	-0.01
Whether respondent brought up with religious affiliation	0.33	0.09	0.86
Respondent perception of how religious they are	0.90	-0.09	0.07
Whether respondent believes in God	0.78	0.01	0.11
Frequency of church attendance	0.70	-0.47	-0.41
Frequency of prayer	0.87	-0.16	0.02
Belief in afterlife	0.68	0.55	-0.20
Church activity outside regular services	0.69	-0.48	-0.23
Whether respondent thinks religion helps people find inner peace	0.33	-0.11	0.17
Whether respondent thinks we trust too much in science, not enough in religion	0.55	0.02	0.05
Whether respondent has confidence in churches	0.61	0.00	0.16
Belief in heaven	0.81	0.49	-0.18
Belief in hell	0.70	0.55	-0.23
Cronbach's alpha	0.9	0.3	0.3
Eigenvalue	6.7	1.4	1.3
Base	*1951*		

Regression analysis: Religion and party identification

Tables A.4 to A.6 show the results of a multinomial logistic regression analysis looking at whether the respondent has a particular party identification compared with no party identification. Table A.7 show the results of a binomial logistic regression analysis where the dependent variable is respondent has any party identification *vs.* none. In each case a positive coefficient indicates that the group is more likely than the reference group (shown in brackets) to identify with the party, while a negative coefficient indicates the group is less likely than the reference group to identify with the party. More details of logistic regression techniques can be found in Appendix I of the report.

Table A.4 Respondent identifies with Labour *vs.* no party identification multinomial logistic regression

	Coefficient	Standard error	p value
Intercept	1.318**	0.233	0.000
Age (increase by one year)	0.030**	0.004	0.000
Religiosity (unreligious)			
Religious	0.788**	0.161	0.000
Fuzzy faithful	0.369**	0.128	0.004
Sex (male)			
Female	-0.187	0.115	0.105
Married (no)			
Yes	-0.093	0.124	0.453
Ethnicity (white)			
Non-white	0.077	0.211	0.714
Income (lowest quartile)			
Second quartile	-0.016	0.158	0.918
Third quartile	0.140	0.168	0.403
Highest quartile	0.503**	0.198	0.011
Education (below degree)			
Degree	0.742**	0.180	0.000
Occupation (routine)			
Professional or managerial	0.158	0.148	0.283
Intermediate	0.015	0.152	0.921
Nagelkerke R2	0.15		

Base = 3283

* = significant at 95% level; ** = significant at 99% level

Table A.5 Respondent identifies with Conservatives *vs.* no party identification multinomial logistic regression

	Coefficient	Standard error	p value
Intercept	0.855**	0.236	0.000
Age (increase by one year)	0.043**	0.004	0.000
Religiosity (unreligious)			
Religious	0.872**	0.161	0.000
Fuzzy faithful	0.494**	0.128	0.000
Sex (male)			
Female	-0.218*	0.115	0.058
Married (no)			
Yes	0.017	0.125	0.893
Ethnicity (white)			
Non-white	-0.812**	0.243	0.001
Income (lowest quartile)			
Second quartile	0.375**	0.161	0.020
Third quartile	0.756**	0.169	0.000
Highest quartile	1.180	0.198	0.000
Education (below degree)			
Degree	0.352*	0.180	0.051
Occupation (routine)			
Professional or managerial	0.750**	0.146	0.000
Intermediate	0.764**	0.148	0.000
Nagelkerke R2	0.15		

Base = 3283

* = significant at 95% level; ** = significant at 99% level

Table A.6 Respondent identifies with Liberal Democrats *vs.* no party identification multinomial logistic regression

	Coefficient	Standard error	p value
Intercept	-0.904**	0.309	0.003
Age (increase by one year)	0.033**	0.005	0.000
Religiosity (unreligious)			
Religious	0.570**	0.199	0.004
Fuzzy faithful	0.130	0.167	0.438
Sex (male)			
Female	0.188	0.151	0.213
Married (no)			
Yes	-0.120	0.162	0.456
Ethnicity (white)			
Non-white	-0.788**	0.323	0.015
Income (lowest quartile)			
Second quartile	0.483**	0.211	0.022
Third quartile	0.757**	0.222	0.001
Highest quartile	0.778**	0.260	0.003
Education (below degree)			
Degree	1.054**	0.209	0.000
Occupation (routine)			
Professional or managerial	0.632**	0.189	0.001
Intermediate	0.497**	0.198	0.012
Nagelkerke R2	0.15		

Base = 3283

* = significant at 95% level; ** = significant at 99% level

Table A.7 Respondent identifies with any party *vs.* no party identification logistic regression

	Coefficient	Standard error	p value
Intercept	1.940**	0.215	0.000
Age (increase by one year)	0.033**	0.003	0.000
Religiosity (unreligious)			
Religious	0.666**	0.147	0.000
Fuzzy faithful	0.349**	0.115	0.002
Sex (male)			
Female	-0.167	0.102	0.103
Married (no)			
Yes	-0.084	0.112	0.456
Ethnicity (white)			
Non-white	-0.390**	0.190	0.040
Income (lowest quartile)			
Second quartile	0.133	0.145	0.358
Third quartile	0.383**	0.149	0.010
Highest quartile	0.700**	0.170	0.000
Education (below degree)			
Degree	0.670**	0.161	0.000
Occupation (routine)			
Professional or managerial	0.670**	0.161	0.000
Intermediate	0.434**	0.133	0.001
Nagelkerke R2	0.12		

Base = 3284

* = significant at 95% level; ** = significant at 99% level

Regression analysis: Religion and social trust

Table A.8 shows the results of a logistic regression analysis looking at social trust. The dependent variable is coded so that 1 = respondent thinks people can always or usually be trusted and 0 = respondent thinks "you can't be too careful". In each case a positive coefficient indicates that the group is more likely than the reference group (shown in brackets) to trust other people, while a negative coefficient indicates the group is less likely than the reference group to trust other people.

Table A.8 Respondent thinks most people can be trusted vs. "you can't be too careful" logistic regression

	Coefficient	Standard error	p value
Intercept	-0.799**	0.217	0.000
Age (increase by one year)	0.013**	0.003	0.000
Religiosity (unreligious)			
Religious	0.075	0.141	0.594
Fuzzy faithful	-0.210*	0.122	0.086
Sex (male)			
Female	-0.130	0.107	0.225
Married (no)			
Yes	0.123	0.116	0.287
Ethnicity (white)			
Non-white	0.146	0.219	0.505
Income (lowest quartile)			
Second quartile	0.190	0.148	0.200
Third quartile	0.056	0.161	0.729
Highest quartile	0.477**	0.184	0.009
Education (below degree)			
Degree	0.605**	0.149	0.000
Occupation (routine)			
Professional or managerial	0.467**	0.133	0.000
Intermediate	0.564**	0.139	0.000
Nagelkerke R2	0.09		

Base = 1633

* = significant at 95% level; ** = significant at 99% level

6 Understanding the dynamics of attitude change

Andy Ross and Amanda Sacker[*]

Since its inception in 1983, one of the main aims of the *British Social Attitudes* survey series has been to chart changes, or lack of change, in public attitudes, values and beliefs over time. Some examples from recent reports illustrate the point. For example, the trend towards more liberal views on pre-marital and homosexual sex contrasts with a lack of change in attitudes towards extra-marital sex (Duncan and Phillips, 2008). More liberal views on working women and working mothers seemingly conflict with a lack of increase in men's involvement in household work (Crompton and Lyonette, 2008). The trend towards declining racial prejudice, which had been in evidence since the mid-1980s, appears to have gone into reverse in recent years (Creegan and Robinson, 2008). Commitment to civil liberties has eroded over the last 25 years (Johnson and Gearty, 2007), but, contrary to common perceptions, social trust has not declined over the same period (Clery and Stockdale, 2009).

These changes in attitudes across time are considered to be the result of three general processes: generation (or cohort) replacement, lifecycle (or age), and period effects. *Generation replacement* represents changes in the attitudes at the level of the nation that occur not because individuals change, but because the attitudes of older, dying generations are being superseded by the attitudes of the young. It is a process of change that is relevant to attitudes that we develop as part of our early socialisation, and that remain fairly fixed across the rest of the life course. Differences in the attitudes between generations are a result of growing up in different times. A good example is religious affiliation. Most people develop a faith very early in life and while life events can mean that this faith feels stronger at some times than others, it generally remains constant throughout the life course. However, because new generations are being born into an increasingly secularised world, religious affiliation is in steady decline. This type of change is also known as inter-individual change, as it describes change that occurs as a result of differences *between* individuals. Alternatively, change in attitudes can be intra-individual, occurring because the attitudes of individuals change. This can be as a result of a specific event, for example as

[*] Andy Ross is a Senior Researcher at the *National Centre for Social Research*. Amanda Sacker is a Research Professor at the Institute for Social and Economic Research, University of Essex.

happened during the late 1980s when, as a nation, we became less tolerant of homosexual relationships following the AIDS epidemic. However, individual change in attitudes can also be a slow process as a response to a sequence of different events or general cultural change within society. Until the AIDS epidemic, our attitudes toward homosexual relationships were becoming increasingly tolerant or accepting and, after the panic in the 1980s, this trend resumed.

On the whole, evidence suggests that we are on average becoming more tolerant or accepting of different ways of living. As well as other people's sexual orientation, this also includes, for example, the choice to live in cohabiting relationships or to bring up a child as a single parent. This liberalisation of attitudes has been attributed to what some theorists term the 'individualisation of society'. Antony Giddens, a leading sociologist, argues that our lives have become dislocated from traditional and very structured ways of living, and that we have instead become more active in constructing our own individual biographies. As a result of this, our lives have become more varied and we have become and are becoming more accepting of different ways of living (Giddens, 1991).

Of course, tolerance is not forthcoming for all types of living or ways of being, and even for those which we now consider more acceptable, a sudden event or a culmination of other factors can counteract this trend. The AIDS scare is one example that has already been mentioned. Another is the increase in immigration and – in particular – the increase in media coverage of immigration which seems to be linked to an increase in anti-immigrant hostility and racism (McLaren and Johnson, 2004).

The type of intra-individual change described above is called a *period effect* because changes in attitude are a result of the context (or period) in which people are living. There is, however, another kind of intra-individual change that also relates to a person's age. This change is termed an age effect, or more appropriately a *lifecycle effect*, because it is a change that relates to reaching or passing through different stages in the life course. This could include entering the world of work, paying taxes, getting married (or not), buying a house, having children (or not), retiring, and so on. A good example of this type of change was described by Berrington *et al.* (2008) in a study of women's attitudes to gender roles. They found that women typically became more traditional in their views following the birth of their first child when accompanied by a reduction in working hours.

While these three general processes describe changing attitudes over time, in truth, changes that occur across society are often a combination of generational, period and lifecycle processes. Changes that are associated with new stages in the life course will always be situated in a particular context or period and will also be shaped by the period in which a person grew up. Quite often it has been the task of the researcher to try to identify which of these three processes is the dominant driver of change.

An example of a detailed discussion using *British Social Attitudes* data is the chapter 'The generation game' in *The 17th Report* (Park, 2000). Park uses a technique known as cohort analysis to compare the attitudes, values and beliefs of age groups ('cohorts') of respondents to the 1983 *British Social Attitudes* survey with a sample of equivalently aged people 15 years later in 1998. For example, she finds a large decrease in religious affiliation among the equivalent age groups in 1998. That is, the religious affiliation among individuals aged 18–25 in 1998 is lower than the religious affiliation among individuals aged 18–25 in 1983, and this pattern occurs across all the different age groups examined. This illustrates a clear generation replacement effect: new generations with more secular values are slowly replacing older, more religious, generations.

If, on the contrary, there had been change in attitudes *within* generations over time (that is, the samples from the same 'cohort' of individuals at two different points in time differ in their attitudes), and this pattern occurred across the age groups, that would suggest an age or lifecycle effect. If there had been both *within* and *between* generation change in attitudes, then this would have been evidence of a period effect.

The importance of establishing which of these processes dominates lies in the impact they have on what we can expect to happen in the future. Say we find that young people differ in their attitudes from old people. If the underlying mechanism is a generation effect, then we can expect it to lead to an average change in attitudes at the societal level, as young generations replace older ones, although in an ageing society the pace of change may slow down. If, on the other hand, the underlying mechanism is lifecycle based, average societal attitudes may not change at all over time, as each young generation grows up and become like their elders. Meanwhile, the evidence of period effects in the past should remind us that external events may cause ructions to either generational or lifecycle patterns that cannot be predicted.

Analyses of separate samples of respondents at different points in time on the *British Social Attitudes* surveys have enabled researchers to gain a rough understanding of whether generation, period or lifecycle effects are the dominant drivers of change on different issues. However, the approach is limited for several reasons. Since the comparisons are between different samples from the age groups at different times, not between the same individuals, the age groups have to be relatively broad in order to ensure big enough samples. If the age groups were too small, measurement error would increase, leading to a lot of variance – what is termed 'noise' – in the estimates, making 'true' comparisons very difficult if not impossible. Moreover, the approach uses only a limited number of points in time, usually just two, and assumes that any change in attitudes occur in one direction only. If there is a complex trend, such as a rise and subsequent fall in an attitude, this may be missed.

Moreover, this type of analysis is limited because of what is known as the *identification problem*. This arises because in standard linear models the three measures are perfectly confounding (Jacobs *et al.*, 1999): if you know someone's age and the period in which they are living, then you can predict perfectly the cohort to which they belong (age + period = cohort). As a result, you can only estimate two out of the three effects at any given time. To get around this problem, assumptions need to be made about the most likely processes at work. The researcher must draw the most appropriate conclusion given the evidence, which in most instances will be more than adequate, but not necessarily conclusive.

For the analysis which follows, we depart from using the *British Social Attitudes* surveys and instead use data from the British Household Panel Study which is a study following the *same* individuals over time.[1] As a result, we can examine changes over time at the individual level. Because of this, it is much easier to distinguish inter-individual change (change attributable to the differences in attitudes between generations) from intra-individual change (changes which occur because the attitudes of individuals change, whether because of lifecycle or period effects). Instead of comparing the values and beliefs of different aged cohorts we can simply examine changes among the same individuals as they age. This also means we can carry out more complex kinds of statistical analysis that can account for more nuanced and complex dynamics of change. Because of the identification problem outlined above, it is still sometimes difficult to distinguish between period and lifecycle effects. However, as we shall demonstrate, by using a particular statistical technique and an innovative means of presenting our findings, we get a little closer to achieving this goal.

The technical term for the analysis used in this chapter is latent growth curve modelling (Duncan *et al.*, 1999). Although it is a more complex approach to analysing trends over time than cohort analysis, the graphs that we are able to plot from the results are quite straightforward to comprehend as we shall demonstrate. The technique enables us to measure change within individuals over time and relate this change to a person's age. As a consequence of this we can illustrate differences in values or beliefs that are as a result of a person's age, and those which are a result of the generation in which they were born.

First, we fit a number of different models to the data that reflect different underlying trends. Once we have found the best model for describing the underlying trends in the data (which is identified both by measures of 'model fit' and by the statistical significance of the estimated trends), we then construct vector graphs (Mirowsky and Kim, 2007) from these results that illustrate the change in attitudes of differently aged individuals.[2]

Figure 6.1 shows a hypothetical graph. Each arrow represents the change in attitudes of one age cohort over time: the start of the arrow shows the average attitudes within the cohort at the time of the first reading and the arrow head at the time of the last reading (the length of the arrow indicating the readings between these start and end points). By estimating and plotting change in this way we are able to describe generation, period and lifecycle effects. In Figure 6.1, all the age cohorts have similar attitudes and they have all changed their attitudes at the same time, presumably in response to some external influence which affected all of them. This is an example of a pure period effect.

Figure 6.1 Vector graph: a pure period effect

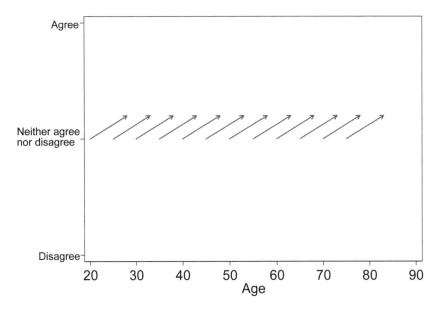

In figure 6.2, each age cohort holds a different attitude. Attitudes are not changing at the cohort level, but as younger cohorts replace older ones, average attitudes in society change. This is an example of a pure generational effect.

Figure 6.2 Vector graph: a pure generational effect

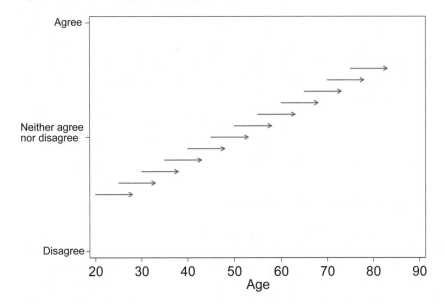

In Figure 6.3, each cohort changes its attitudes over time to become exactly like its predecessor. This is a pure age, or lifecycle, effect. A one-off survey of the population would show age-related differences in attitudes similar to those in Figure 6.2, but in this case there would be no change over time in attitudes at societal level.

Figure 6.3 Vector graph: a pure age effect

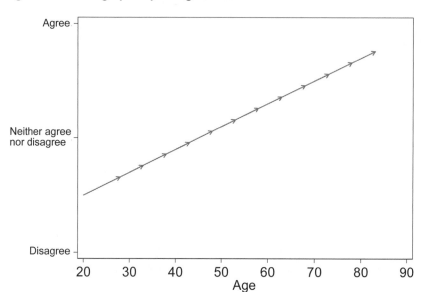

The British Household Panel Study is a multi-purpose study measuring a range of different attributes and is less focused than the *British Social Attitudes* on changing attitudes. Nevertheless, the study records a number of attitudinal measures and, more importantly, repeats them over (at least part) of the life course of the study. We have chosen a selection of attitudes to homosexuality, divorce, cohabiting parents and looking after the elderly to illustrate the different mechanisms of attitude change at work.

Attitudes are measured by presenting respondents with statements and asking them whether they "strongly agree", "agree", "neither agree nor disagree", "disagree" or "strongly disagree". In the statistical method used to estimate change, we work with the population mean or average score.[3]

Attitudes to homosexual relationships

As already mentioned, attitudes to homosexuality present an interesting case in attitude change. The *British Social Attitudes* data in Table 6.1 illustrate how the proportion saying "sexual relations between two adults of the same sex" are "always" or "mostly wrong" rose from 62 per cent in 1983 to 75 per cent in 1987 and has since declined steadily to reach 36 per cent at the most recent reading in 2007. As already mentioned, the rise in prejudice in the late 1980s has been linked to the AIDS scare. Previous analysis of *British Social Attitudes* data has indicated that the subsequent growth in tolerance has the characteristics of a generation replacement effect (Evans, 2002).

Table 6.1 Attitudes to homosexual sex, 1983–2007[4]

Sexual relations between two adults of the same sex are …	83	85	87	89	90	93	95	98	99	00	03	06	07
	%	%	%	%	%	%	%	%	%	%	%	%	%
Always/mostly wrong	62	70	75	69	69	64	57	52	49	47	40	32	36
Sometimes wrong	8	7	8	9	8	7	10	11	9	9	9	11	7
Rarely wrong	4	4	2	4	4	5	7	8	7	7	7	11	10
Not wrong at all	16	13	11	14	14	19	21	23	28	33	37	38	39
Base	*1719*	*1769*	*1390*	*1470*	*1353*	*1494*	*1182*	*1080*	*1055*	*3426*	*2148*	*1089*	*1041*

The British Household Panel Study asks a different question which, nevertheless, taps similar attitude change. Respondents were asked to agree or disagree with the statement:

Homosexual relations are always wrong

As seen in Table 6.2, the decline in prejudice is noticeable even over the shorter period of 1998–2006.[5] Moreover, since the question was asked of the same respondents on each occasion, we can analyse inter-individual and intra-individual change in a direct way.

Table 6.2 Attitudes to homosexuality, 1998–2006

Homosexual relationships are always wrong	1998	2000	2002	2004	2006
	%	%	%	%	%
Strongly agree	14	12	11	10	10
Agree	13	13	11	12	10
Neither agree nor disagree	37	36	36	35	35
Disagree	24	25	26	27	28
Disagree strongly	12	14	16	16	18
Mean score	2.94	2.86	2.75	2.72	2.66
Base	*9215*	*9006*	*8188*	*8619*	*8484*

Source: British Household Panel Study

In Figure 6.4 we examine this change in relation to a person's age or generation by using separate arrows for each age cohort. In 1998, the beginning points of the arrows are vertically quite far apart, suggesting that people's attitudes to homosexual relationships depended very much on their age or generation; that is, older people were much more likely to agree with the statement than younger people. In fact, individuals aged 55 and over in 1998 were more likely to agree with the statement that homosexual relationships are always wrong, whereas individuals aged 50 or younger were more likely to disagree with this statement.

The direction of the arrows shows the change over the period 1998–2006. If, as in Figure 6.2, the arrows joined up, that would suggest a lifecycle effect. But this is not the case: the arrows remain far apart, indicating that the differences observed represent generational differences in people's attitudes to homosexual relationships. Younger generations continue to be more accepting or tolerant. The predominant mechanism of change is a generation replacement effect.

Figure 6.4 Agreement with view "Homosexual relationships are always wrong", by age, 1998–2006

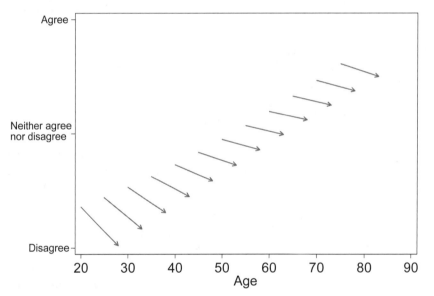

Source: British Household Panel Study

In addition, Figure 6.4 allows us to do much more than just distinguish between age and generation effects. All of the arrows are sloping downwards, suggesting there is also a period effect going on. On average, all age groups have become more liberal in their attitudes towards homosexual relationships between 1998 and 2006. This supports the theory of increasing individualisation outlined in the introduction.

Nor should we write off lifecycle effects entirely: another feature of the graph is that the arrows for younger generations have a steeper slope than the arrows for older generations. This means that younger generations became relatively more liberal than older generations within the same time period. One explanation for this might be that older generations are slower at changing their attitudes than younger generations (Heath, and Martin, 1996). Another possibility is that it is associated with the expansion of higher education, as other studies have indicated that tolerance increases with education (Evans, 2002). As more young people benefit from this expansion, their attitudes are more likely to change during the period.

What do these findings tell us about likely future changes in attitudes towards homosexual relationships? The generation, period and additional lifecycle effects are all acting to change attitudes in this same direction towards greater acceptance and tolerance, and we can expect this to continue. However, events of the 1980s should caution us: external events such as the AIDS epidemic can cause period effects which cannot be easily predicted.

Attitudes to divorce

As discussed in *The 24th Report,* marriage is much less important in family formation than was previously the case, and the heterosexual, co-residential couple is no longer considered the central social norm (Duncan and Phillips, 2008). In a similar vein, the chapter by Harrison and Fitzgerald in this report discusses British social norms in a European context. As with homosexuality, these changing norms in society have been attributed to a growing individualisation, in which these kinds of decisions are more about individual choice than adherence to long-standing tradition. If things do not work out as planned, then we are more willing to dissolve a marriage and start again. Table 6.3 shows responses on the British Household Panel Study to the statement:

It is better to divorce than to continue an unhappy marriage

With four-fifths of respondents agreeing with this statement in 2006, this certainly seems to be a viewpoint held by the majority of the British public.

Table 6.3 Views on divorce, 1992–2006

It's better to divorce than to continue an unhappy marriage	1992	1994	1996	1998	2000	2002	2004	2006
	%	%	%	%	%	%	%	%
Strongly agree	24	23	23	26	26	28	26	28
Agree	54	55	55	54	56	53	54	53
Neither agree nor disagree	16	16	17	16	15	15	16	16
Disagree	5	5	4	3	3	3	3	3
Disagree strongly	1	1	1	1	*	*	1	1
Mean score	3.96	3.94	3.96	4.03	4.03	4.05	4.02	4.04
Base	*9845*	*9481*	*9438*	*9215*	*9006*	*8818*	*8619*	*8484*

Source: British Household Panel Study

Over time there appears to have been little change. The cumulative change has been one of a slight increase in agreement with the statement. Although the change is very slight, it is statistically significant.[6]

What about change in attitudes at the individual level? Are the findings similar to attitudes regarding homosexual relationships? Do older generations hold much more traditional views, considering the institution of marriage important and worth saving at the cost of the actual quality of the relationship within?

Figure 6.5 shows the attitudes and change in attitudes to divorce of different generations within the British population. There does appear to be some difference between the attitudes of younger and older generations, with older generations showing a little less support for divorce. However, these differences are actually very small. Even those in their 60s, who were the least likely to favour divorce, were far more likely to agree than disagree with the statement, suggesting that we have come a long way from the times when divorce was considered a scandal.

Figure 6.5 Agreement with view "It's better to divorce than to continue an unhappy marriage", by age, 1992–2006

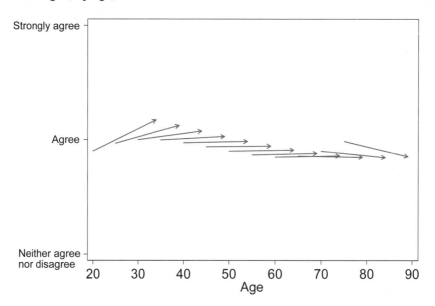

Source: British Household Panel Study

What is more significant is the interrelated relationship between a person's age, their generation and the period which they are living through. Looking at the beginning of the arrows which signify people's attitudes in 1992, the very young and people aged between 45 and 60 were slightly less likely to agree that divorce was preferable to an unhappy marriage, whereas individuals in their 30s and early 40s were more likely to favour divorce. In addition, the direction of the arrows for the youngest generations suggest that their attitudes towards divorce change quite significantly as they reach their 30s and early 40s. The most relevant interpretation of this change is one of a lifecycle effect. As they reach the age at which either they or perhaps members within their circle of friends are most likely to divorce (national statistics suggest average age for divorce is the early 40s for men and late 30s for women), their views on divorce change and they become more favourable towards divorce than other age groups.

In addition to this lifecycle effect, there is also evidence of an increase in the difference between generations in 2006, perhaps what we would consider a joint effect of period and generation. As these younger generations reach their 30s and early 40s they have more liberal views regarding divorce than the previous generations before them (signified by the fact that the end point of their arrows finishes higher than the beginning of the previous generations). Once this life-stage has been reached people's attitudes toward divorce then remain fairly stable over time.

Finally, there is a slight indication that the attitudes of the very old (that is, people in their mid 70s) were a little more liberal on average in 1992, and then became slightly more conservative on this issue as they aged. However, we have to retain a certain degree of caution when interpreting the trends of this older age group because the estimates become less reliable as some people in this group have died. One interpretation of the trend might be to do with survivor effects. Those who survive to older age may have more positive attitudes to life and may therefore also have different attitudes. Or they may on average be from different social backgrounds to those who die. Hence the (very slight) increase in conservatism is difficult to interpret.

Given this dynamic of changing attitudes toward divorce, what might we expect in the future? Assuming these trends continue, then we are likely to see further increases in the acceptance of divorce among younger generations, particularly as they reach an age when they or others they know are most likely to experience a divorce. However, in light of the changing demographics of Britain in which more and more people live beyond their eightieth birthday, the effect of this change on the population average is likely to be slight, offset by the stability of older generations.

Attitudes to cohabiting parents

As a nation we have become much more accepting of the fact that some couples choose to live together without ever planning to get married. Table 6.4 shows responses to a question asked on *British Social Attitudes*: the proportion who think that people who want to have children should get married has declined from almost three-quarters of the population in 1989 to about half in 2002. Again, this may be considered an indication of a more individualistic society in which alternative ways of living are becoming more and more acceptable.

Table 6.4 Attitudes to cohabiting parents, 1989–2002

	1989	1994	2000	2002
People who want to have children ought to get married	%	%	%	%
Agree strongly	25	18	21	14
Agree	46	39	33	37
Neither agree nor disagree	10	14	19	17
Disagree	14	21	20	22
Disagree strongly	3	6	6	8
Base	*1516*	*984*	*2980*	*1984*

The precise level of agreement is, however, rather dependent on the wording of the question. Since 1998, the British Household Panel Study has asked individuals how far they agree or disagree that:

> *It makes no difference to children whether their parents are married or just living together*

As shown in Table 6.5, this wording suggests that overall we are fairly undecided on this issue, with a population average that sits close to neither agreement nor disagreement. But, as with the *British Social Attitudes* question, there is evidence that we became increasingly tolerant of parents choosing not to marry in the period up to 2002.[7] After that, attitudes have remained very stable.

Table 6.5 Views on cohabiting parents, 1998–2006

	1998	2000	2002	2004	2006
It makes no difference to children whether their parents are married to each other or just living together	%	%	%	%	%
Strongly agree	8	9	11	10	11
Agree	30	34	34	34	34
Neither agree nor disagree	28	27	27	28	28
Disagree	27	25	23	23	23
Disagree strongly	6	5	5	5	4
Mean score	3.08	3.17	3.23	3.22	3.23
Base	*9215*	*9006*	*8188*	*8619*	*8484*

Source: British Household Panel Study

When we examine the change in attitudes among individuals in Figure 6.6 we get a far greater understanding of the different processes that are contributing to this population trend. Perhaps, unsurprisingly, younger generations are more likely to agree than older generations that the marital status of parents makes no difference to children, with older generations being more likely to disagree with this statement. What is also apparent is that differences between the generations are not evenly spread. There is greater difference between the attitudes of the 'middle generations', that is, those born between 1932 and 1963, compared with either younger or older generations (the arrows are much wider apart vertically).

This is probably because these 'middle generations' were growing up during the period when most demographic change was occurring in relation to this issue. In 1946, when those aged 65 in Figure 6.6 were aged just 20, it was still very stigmatising to be born to non-married parents; however, by 1986 when those aged 35 in Figure 6.6 were aged 20 it was becoming far more acceptable. Nowadays hardly anyone uses terms like 'illegitimate child' or 'out of wedlock'.

Figure 6.6 Agreement with the view "It makes no difference to children whether their parents are married to each other or just living together", by age, 1998– 2006

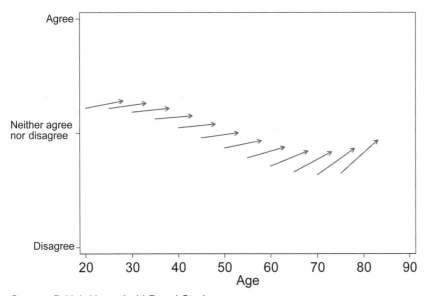

Source: British Household Panel Study

In addition to this generational change there is a clear period effect. Between 1998 and 2006, all generations became a little more liberal in their views on cohabiting parents. There is also a significant age or lifecycle effect. Those aged 60 or older in 1998 have become relatively more liberal over the intervening period than any other age group. Although we cannot be certain why this is the case we can offer a reasonable interpretation. As a result of more and more children being born to cohabiting couples, an increasing number of older people are also becoming grandparents to these children. Perhaps this personal experience, added to the fact older people are more likely to begin from quite a conservative viewpoint, explains why this generation is becoming liberal at a faster rate.

What of future attitudes? The certainty with which we might forecast any future change is complicated by the stability between 2002 and 2006. However, because of a continual rise in the number of children being born to cohabiting parents, and the demographic ageing of the British population, more people are going to become grandparents to children born to cohabiting parents and therefore we should expect attitudes to continue to become more liberal.

Looking after the elderly

Throughout this chapter we have made reference to the changing demographic of the British population. It is projected that by 2031 the UK population will include 3 million people aged over 85, and that the ratio of the number of people of working age for every person above the state pension age will reduce from 3.32 in 2006 to 2.91 by 2031 (ONS, 2008). This is leading us towards a care crises, where the taxation of the young working population will not be enough to pay for the pensions and the social and medical care of the elderly. Previous analysis of *British Social Attitudes* data has shown that public opinion is heavily divided on whether the state should meet the costs of personal care for all older people or only for some. Older people are more likely than younger ones to think that the government should foot the bill, but the difference between the generations is not very large (Ormston *et al.*, 2007).

The British Household Panel Study has since 1992 been asking respondents to agree or disagree with the following statement:

Adult children have an obligation to look after their elderly parents

Table 6.6 shows that as a nation we remain fairly undecided on this issue, with a population average that falls near to neither agreeing nor disagreeing with the statement. Over time there is some suggestion that we have become a little more caring toward the elderly, although overall the trend is fairly flat.[8]

What about the difference in attitudes across the generations? In particular, how do the attitudes of those who are expected to provide the care compare to those who hope to receive it? Figure 6.7 shows that, overall, differences between the generations in 1992 were very slight (the start of the arrows form an almost horizontal line). What is noticeable is the diverging change in attitudes over time. Far from feeling over-burdened by the dependency of an ageing population, younger generations appear to grow a little more generous regarding the care of their parents' generation as they get older. This could be a lifecycle effect, a sign of maturity, of becoming more socially aware and less egocentric. However, it could also be a period effect, an increase in the consideration of others as we move away from the hangover of the more self-obsessed decade of the 1980s to the more caring decade of the 1990s.

Table 6.6 Views on caring for the elderly, 1992–2006

	1992	1994	1996	1998	2000	2002	2004	2006
Adult children have an obligation to look after their elderly parents	%	%	%	%	%	%	%	%
Strongly agree	8	7	7	8	7	7	7	8
Agree	29	29	28	32	34	33	33	33
Neither agree nor disagree	32	33	33	30	30	31	30	31
Disagree	26	26	26	25	25	26	25	23
Disagree strongly	5	5	5	4	4	4	4	4
Mean score	3.08	3.05	3.06	3.14	3.14	3.13	3.14	3.17
Base	*9845*	*9481*	*9438*	*9215*	*9006*	*8818*	*8619*	*8484*

Source: British Household Panel Study

Figure 6.7 Agreement with view "Adult children have an obligation to look after their elderly parents", by age, 1992–2006

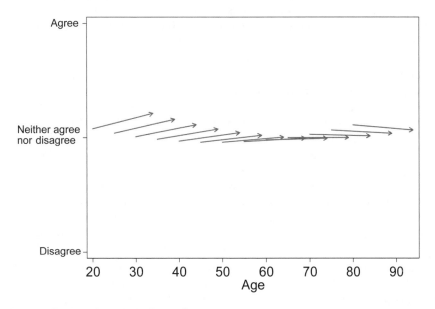

Source: British Household Panel Study

If we are witnessing a period effect, then it appears to be counteracted by the actual experience of the provision of care. The attitudes of people in their 50s and 60s, that is, those individuals who are most likely to be providing the care, remain fairly stable over time. It is fine to be altruistic in principle, but as is often the case with the relationship between attitudes and behaviour, it is behaviour that has the more important role in shaping attitudes rather than the other way around.

There is some indication that the very old, that is, those who are the most likely recipients of care, are more likely to agree with the statement than those most likely to provide it, although this difference is very small. However, as we noted earlier, we must remain a little cautious when interpreting the trends for older age groups because the estimates become less reliable as individuals die off.

What of the future? If the trends identified above continue, then we might expect to see a slow but increasing altruism towards our elderly parents. This is because the more generous attitudes of the very youngest generations are superseding the less generous attitudes of the preceding generations. However, because attitudes appear to stabilise during the period most associated with care-giving, this is likely to be a very slow pattern of change.

Conclusions

In this chapter, we have examined changing attitudes to four different social issues – homosexuality, divorce, cohabiting parents and care for the elderly. By using panel data from the British Household Panel Study we have been able to disentangle the mechanics of attitude change. On an issue like homosexuality, which most often is about the way 'other people' live their lives, the effect of a more secular and individualised world is that we have become more tolerant of other people's choices. This shows up in our data as a combination of a period and generational effect. Barring outside shocks, such as the AIDS crisis, we would expect attitudes to continue to change in a more liberal direction.

Attitudes to divorce and marriage may be closer to home – the majority of people have personal experience of intimate relationships. Perhaps this is why changes in attitudes in this area are more a case of lifecycle effects as individuals move into the age brackets where they are themselves forming and dissolving relationships.

The case of cohabiting parents is a complex combination of these. There are strong generational effects, as we would expect for an 'other people's lives' issue. But there are also complicated overlays of lifecycle effects; older individuals, who notably held the most conservative views on parenthood and marriage, were the most likely to change their views on this issue over time. As the number of children born to unmarried parents grows, the personal experience of becoming a grandparent of a child born outside marriage might be leading older people to take a more liberal view on this issue.

In the case of the care of the elderly, there seems to be a period effect of more realisation of the need to care for one's parents – perhaps an 'other people'-type attitude in the sense that it is the principle of caring for one's parents that has seen an improvement over time. This apparent increase in altruism, however, is counteracted by those in the age groups that are actually providing the care, suggesting again that lifecycle effects are more important when the experience is personal.

In summary, then, there are general processes at work – in general, we are becoming more liberal and tolerant. These period effects (which subsequently feed through into generational change), may relate to individualisation, secularisation, and so on. They dominate when the attitudes relate to distant values and 'other people'. However, our attitudes can be very much affected by what we are being faced with in our daily lives – these are more likely to be personal experience and hence lifecycle effects. In some cases, these effects enhance the generational replacement effect towards tolerance, but they can also counteract it.

Another interesting feature is the relationship between chronological age and attitude change – older people are less likely to change their views than young people, hence the tendency for generational change to be the underlying mechanism for 'distant' issues such as homosexuality. But this is not necessarily the case with issues that directly relate to older people. When it comes to situations that are relevant to them (for example, becoming grandparents to a child born to a cohabiting couple), then the elderly can also be seen to change their attitudes over time.

Notes

1. The British Household Panel Survey (BHPS) began in 1991. Its unique value lies in the fact that it follows the same representative sample of individuals over a period of years and is household-based, interviewing every adult member of sampled households. The main objective of the BHPS is to further our understanding of social and economic change at the individual and household level in Britain and the UK. The BHPS had an original sample size in 1991 of 5,500 households, covering England, Scotland and Wales. Additional samples in Scotland, Wales and Northern Ireland have been available in recent years. The total sample size is now around 9,000 households across the UK, providing annual interviews with some 15,000 individuals. A total of 18 years of panel data has been collected, making the BHPS one of the longest running panel surveys in the world.

2. The analysis was based on the sample of respondents who were still in the study at the end of follow-up. The models were estimated using the statistical package M*plus* 5.2 (Muthén and Muthén, 1998–2007) with the full information maximum likelihood estimator (FIML), which computes parameter estimates on the basis of all available data, including the incomplete cases due to item non-response, with sample weighting to take account of sample attrition and adjustment for gender.

3. We score the answer options from 5 = "strongly agree" to 1 = "strongly disagree". The statistical analysis treats the responses as ordinal, with the assumption that an unobserved or latent normally distributed continuum underlies the observed ordinal responses.
4. The decline in average score over time is statistically significant at the 0.1 per cent level.
5. The decline in average score over time is statistically significant at the 0.05 per cent level.
6. The increase in average score over time is statistically significant at the 0.05 per cent level.
7. The increase in average score over time is statistically significant at the 0.05 per cent level.
8. The increase in average score over time is statistically significant at the 0.05 per cent level.

References

Berrington, A., Hu, Y., Smith, P.W.F., and Sturgis, P. (2008), 'A graphical chain model for reciprocal relationships between women's gender role attitudes and labour force participation' *Journal of the Royal Statistical Society: Series A (Statistics in Society)*, **171(1)**: 89–108

Clery, E. and Stockdale, J. (2009), 'Is Britain a respectful society?', in Park, A., Curtice, J., Thomson, K., Phillips, M. and Clery, E. (eds.), *British Social Attitudes: the 25th Report*, London: Sage

Creegan, C. and Robinson, C. (2008), 'Prejudice and the workplace', in Park, A., Curtice, J., Thomson, K., Phillips, M., Johnson, M. and Clery, E. (eds.), *British Social Attitudes: the 24th Report*, London: Sage

Crompton, R. and Lyonette, C. (2008), 'Who does the housework? The division of labour within the home', in Park, A., Curtice, J., Thomson, K., Phillips, M., Johnson, M. and Clery, E. (eds.), *British Social Attitudes: the 24th Report*, London: Sage

Duncan, S. and Phillips, M. (2008), 'New families? Tradition and change in modern relationships', in Park, A., Curtice, J., Thomson, K., Phillips, M., Johnson, M. and Clery, E. (eds.), *British Social Attitudes: the 24th Report*, London: Sage

Duncan, T.E., Duncan, S.C., Stryker, L.A., Li, F. and Alpert, A. (1999), *An Introduction to Latent Variable Growth Curve Modeling: Concepts, Issues, and Applications*, Mahwah, NJ: Lawrence Erlbaum

Evans, G. (2002), 'In search of tolerance', in Park, A., Curtice, J., Thomson, K., Jarvis, L. and Bromley, C. (eds.), *British Social Attitudes: the 19th Report*, London: Sage

Giddens, A. (1991), *Modernity and Self-Identity: self and society in the late modern age*, Palo Alto Calif.: Stanford University Press

Heath, A. and Martin, J. (1996), 'Changing attitudes towards abortion: life-cycle, period and cohort effects', in Taylor, B. and Thomson, K. (eds.), *Understanding Change in Social Attitudes*, Aldershot: Dartmouth

Jacobs Jr, D.R., Hannan, P.J., Wallace D. (1999), 'Interpreting age, period and cohort effects in plasma lipids and serum insulin using repeated measures regression analysis: the CARDIA study', *Statistics in Medicine* **18**: 655–679

Johnson, M. and Gearty, C. (2007), 'Civil liberties and the challenge of terrorism', in Park, A., Curtice, J., Thomson, K., Phillips, M. and Johnson, M. (eds.), *British Social Attitudes: the 23rd Report – Perspectives on a changing society*, London: Sage

McLaren, L. and Johnson, M. (2004), in Park, A., Curtice, J., Thomson, K., Bromley, C. and Phillips, M. (eds.), *British Socila Attitudes: the 21st Report*, London: Sage

Mirowsky, J. and Kim, J. (2007), 'Graphing age trajectories: Vector graphs, synthetic and virtual cohort projections, and cross-sectional profiles of depression.' *Sociological Methods & Research*, **35(4)**: 497–541

ONS (2008), Population Trends, No. 131, London: The Stationery Office, available at www.statistics.gov.uk/downloads/theme_population/Population_Trends_131_web.pdf

Ormston, R., Curtice, J. and Fawcett, H. (2007), 'Who should pay for my care – when I'm 64?' in Park, A., Curtice, J., Thomson, K., Phillips, M. and Johnson, M. (eds.), *British Social Attitudes: the 23rd Report – Perspectives on a changing society*, London: Sage

Park, A. (2000), 'The generation game', in Jowell, R., Curtice, J., Park, A., Thomson, K., Jarvis, L., Bromley, C. and Stratford, N. (eds.), *British Social Attitudes: the 17th Report – Focusing on diversity*, London: Sage

Acknowledgements

The British Household Panel Survey (BHPS) is funded by the Economic and Social Research Council.

The authors would like to thank James Trinder for his preparation and descriptive analysis of the data.

7 A chorus of disapproval? European attitudes to non-traditional family patterns

*Eric Harrison and Rory Fitzgerald**

The concept of the social norm has been central to sociology since its emergence in the 19th century. Emile Durkheim (1893) famously traced the transition from simple societies bonded by 'mechanical' solidarity to the increasingly complex structures in the new industrial, urban societies that were reliant on what he called 'organic' solidarity. In both cases social cohesion was maintained through the existence of common sets of values and behaviours, which for the sake of simplicity we can describe as social norms. In order to be successful, such norms must either command universal (or at least widespread) support, or they must be supported by a system of sanctions imposed upon those who break them. In traditional societies the Church often took on the role as enforcer of social norms; in modern societies this role more commonly belongs to the State underpinned by the legal system.

In recent years there has been much concern and associated discussion about the perceived breakdown of shared norms and values in Britain. This has manifested itself in numerous forms, with the debate about the existence of an underclass, and the continuing controversy over multiculturalism being two of the most enduring. The argument in its simple form is thus: many of our traditional social norms originally derive from the Christian tradition in Europe. With industrialisation and urbanisation has come a creeping secularisation that has weakened the sanctions that formerly underpinned these norms. Moreover, the process of modernisation has weakened much of the economic rationale underlying these social norms; women are no longer reliant on marriage to provide them with financial security while children are no longer viewed as an economic resource for the family in the way they once were. Reactions to these developments are polarised. Social liberals see this as a progressive development, allowing individuals more freedom to shape their own lives and adopt a diversity of behaviours in relation to marriage, fertility and child-rearing. Social conservatives are scornful of such an easygoing attitude to this

* Eric Harrison (Senior Research Fellow) and Rory Fitzgerald (Deputy Director) are both based at the Centre for Comparative Social Surveys (CCSS) at City University London. CCSS houses the European Social Survey.

increased diversity of lifestyles, seeing instead the breakdown of such norms as highly dysfunctional (Wilson, 2008). Indeed, in recent years, the term 'broken society' has come into circulation to describe a whole range of social problems believed by those who use it to be related to shifting family and fertility patterns. Many of the things that were once thought of as frowned upon in Britain and many other European countries – such as cohabitation, having children outside of wedlock, divorce and mothers going out to work – are now far more common than they once were. For example, in the UK between 1970 and 1994, the number of unmarried couples living together rose from about 500,000 to almost 3.7 million while between 1980 and 1994 the number of children under 15 living in cohabiting households rose from 27 per cent to 35 per cent (Rodriguez, 1998). Change over time in Britain in attitudes to cohabiting couples and divorce is further discussed in the chapter by Ross and Sacker in this report.

Why should norms like these have weakened? It can be argued that when the Church was strong, those who broke social norms faced both the direct sanction of the clergy and the indirect disapproval of other members of the congregation. Even as the theological basis for behavioural norms waned, the risk of censure from one's friends and neighbours remained a strong incentive to conform. In contemporary society behavioural norms still vary between social groups and with the context of the social situation. To this extent we are using the term in the sense of what Schultz *et al.* (2007) call an 'injunctive norm', that is, one that refers to people's perceptions of what is commonly approved or disapproved of within a specific culture.

Given the differences in the religious traditions across different European countries, their varying degrees of secularisation, and their distinctive patterns of institutional development, it is logical that the prevalence of social norms varies across countries too. It is common to argue that such norms have been in sharp retreat right across the board in recent times, alongside the decline in the Christian tradition in countries such as Britain. However, talk of a decline of religion in Europe and its associated moral values needs, perhaps, to be treated with caution. As Greeley states:

> In fact, if one looks at Europe with a relatively open mind, prepared to be surprised by its complexity, one discovers a wide variety of religious phenomena. (2003: xi)

He notes that while religion has declined in some countries (most notably Britain, the Netherlands and France), in others it has increased (most notably the former communist countries and especially Russia) and in others it remains relatively unchanged (the traditional Catholic countries).

Equally, the decline in the prevalence of organised institutional religion may not automatically lead to changes in individual values. As Davie (1994) noted in the British case, religion for many remains important, albeit characterised by "believing without belonging". (See also the chapter by Voas and Ling in this report which looks at current attitudes towards religion in Britain.)

This chapter explores the extent to which 'injunctive norms' remain strong in a comparative European perspective. The specific focus is on data from the European Social Survey 2006/7,[1] more specifically a group of questions on attitudes to the timing and sequencing of particular behaviours across the life course (for further details, see Billari *et al.*, 2006).

The countries

The analysis in this chapter is restricted to a subset of countries that reflect the different geographical, political and religious contours of Europe. In selecting our set of countries, we wanted to investigate to what extent the attitudes of respondents matched the overall 'state of play' in that society with regard to the patterns of modernisation and secularisation discussed above. If one accepts that there is a single trajectory of what has been called "de-traditionalisation" (Heelas *et al.*, 1996) where the power of established norms and conventions is progressively eroded, then different countries are likely to be at different points on that journey. How far they have travelled should predict the degree to which respondents are tolerant of behaviour that breaks with established social norms.

However, while it is commonplace to note in cross-national comparisons that countries are *different* from one another, it is quite another task to identify the variables that act as indicators of the degree and manner in which they differ. We briefly sketch out our approach to this problem here.

In constructing our set of 11 countries we were guided by the following principles. First, they should be broadly representative of the diversity of Europe in terms of geography and culture. Secondly, they should exhibit as much variation as possible in terms of the degree to which they had embarked on the path of de-traditionalisation. To address the first principle we constructed a fourfold typology loosely based on the different types of 'welfare regime' that are common in the social policy literature, most notably in the work of Esping-Andersen (1990).[2] Our typology is:

- Western European: UK, France, Germany, Netherlands
- Nordic: Denmark and Sweden
- Mediterranean: Spain, Portugal, Cyprus
- Post-communist: Slovakia and Poland

Our initial exploratory analysis suggested that each of these groups differed significantly in their attitudes to social norms. Compared to the reference category of 'western European', the Nordic countries were less disapproving of norm breaking while the Mediterranean and post-communist countries were more disapproving. Between them, these countries provide a sample size of over 20,000 cases from the European Social Survey.

However, this sort of approach does not take us much further than re-describing the differences we know exist; it certainly does not further the explanation. Many proponents of the comparative approach (for example, Przeworski and Teune, 1970) have suggested that wherever possible one should replace country variables with more specific empirical variables. As we are interested in the relationship between the level of de-traditionalisation and socially liberal attitudes, we have attempted to operationalise a simple measure of this in our analyses. We took four indicators: gross domestic product (GDP) per capita by purchasing power, the proportion of females in employment, the divorce rate (number of divorces per 100 marriages) and the country's religiosity (the proportion of individuals claiming to belong to some religious denomination). GDP was not designed to indicate a country's wealth *per se*, but as a broad proxy for its degree of economic development – in Durkheim's terms, how far advanced was the transition from a rural and agricultural society to one dominated by cities and focusing on industry and services. Female labour force participation and the divorce rate were chosen as being indicative of the existence of a liberal institutional context. Where both are high it suggests that de-traditionalisation is already embedded in the prevailing climate. The inclusion of an aggregate measure of religious belonging is to recognise that, regardless of whether an individual is religious, living among others who are may exert a contextual effect on their views.

Table 7.1 shows, for each of the countries selected for analysis, the values of these background indicators.

Table 7.1 Country profiles

	'Welfare type'	GDP (EU27= 100)	% of pop. 65+	Divorce rate per 100 marriages	% females working	% religious	Main religious group
UK	W-European	119	20.1	53	65.8	48.6	Protestant
France	W-European	113	15.0	39	57.7	48.8	Catholic
Germany	W-European	114	22.2	52	62.2	57.2	Catholic Protestant
Netherlands	W-European	132	16.5	40	67.7	40.6	Catholic Protestant
Sweden	Nordic	120	18.8	54	70.7	31.7	Protestant
Denmark	Nordic	127	20.2	45	73.4	57.2	Protestant
Spain	Med	102	20.1	22	53.2	69.6	Catholic
Portugal	Med	74	22.8	41	62	86.6	Catholic
Cyprus	Med	93	13.6	13	60.3	98.5	Orthodox
Poland	P-communist	53	16.1	25	48.2	92.1	Catholic
Slovakia	P-communist	64	15.9	41	51.9	76.1	Catholic

Sources:
GDP 2006, females in employment 2005 (Eurostat, 2008), divorce rate 2001 (OECD, 2005)
Per cent population 65+, per cent belonging to religious denomination taken from European Social Survey 2006/7 (design weighted)
Main religious denomination taken from European Social Survey 2006/7. Where the second ranked denomination is less than 5 percentage points below the first, both are shown

In addition to the four measures described, we show the major Christian denomination in the country (based on the proportion of individuals claiming to belong to the denomination) and the proportion of the population older than 65 (an older population being hypothetically more traditional in outlook). What is already clear from the table is the great diversity that is represented by these 11 countries on the various different indicators that we believe to be closely related to levels of disapproval of norm breaking.

Our 'welfare type' classification tends to overlap with GDP, with the post-communist countries having the lowest levels, followed by the Mediterranean countries, then all (bar one) of the western European countries with the Nordic countries at the top. The Netherlands is the exception, with a GDP higher than the Nordic countries.

In terms of religiosity, the Mediterranean and post-communist countries clearly have the highest levels and are also predominantly Catholic, with lower levels found in the Nordic and western European groupings where Protestantism is generally, although by no means always, prevalent. In terms of the proportion of working females the differences between countries are perhaps a little less clear-cut but the pattern is still broadly the same, with the lowest levels in the post-communist countries and the highest levels in the Nordic countries.

The aim of this chapter is not to prove or disprove whether the presence of these various background factors *causes* the levels of disapproval we identify, since a causal analysis is not possible with this cross-sectional data. Rather, the aim is to examine the extent to which they co-vary empirically.

The social norms

A discussion of the weakening of traditional social norms could encompass a very wide range of values. In this chapter we limit ourselves to a set of items relating to family and fertility. These have been central to debates about 'the permissive society', 'the underclass' and the 'broken society' in the UK and elsewhere in Europe in recent years. Unlike in many surveys where questions focus on individual behaviour, or elicit abstract notions of good and bad, the emphasis here is on injunctive norms – the degree to which one disapproves when another member of the society transgresses the norm.

Five controversial forms of social behaviour are captured by the following questions:

> *How much do you approve or disapprove if a man/woman ...*
>
> *... chooses never to have children?*
> *... lives with a partner without being married to her/him?*
> *... has a child with a partner he/she lives with but is not married to?*
> *... has a full-time job while he/she has children aged under 3?*
> *... gets divorced while he/she has children aged under 12?*

Respondents answered using a five-point scale of "strongly disapprove", "disapprove", "neither approve nor disapprove", "approve", "strongly approve". In the administration of the survey, half the sample was randomly assigned to be asked the questions in relation to women, and the other half in relation to men. This enables us to examine whether these social norms are applied differently to men and women and whether men and women apply the norms disproportionately to their own or the other gender.

Do social norms still exist?

We start by questioning whether any social norms remain at all in Europe. Table 7.2 shows the proportion of respondents in 2006/7 who said they would "strongly disapprove" or "disapprove" if someone transgressed each of the five items listed above.

Table 7.2 Respondents disapproving if social norms are transgressed in 11 European countries, 2006/7[3]

	Number of items disapproved of			% who disapprove of:				
	% dis-approve of none	% dis-approve of all five	Mean[+]	Divorce with child <12	Choice not to have child	FT job and child <3	Child outside marriage	Coha-biting
All	44	2	1.11	33	25	21	18	15
Slovakia	24	8	1.99	47	53	26	39	34
Poland	29	6	1.82	49	52	17	30	34
Cyprus	27	2	1.65	26	58	9	44	29
France	40	1	1.11	36	31	20	14	10
Spain	50	3	1.11	36	25	16	18	16
Germany	43	2	1.08	32	23	27	16	10
Netherlands	50	2	0.94	25	13	29	15	11
UK	52	1	0.90	27	8	21	20	14
Portugal	56	2	0.86	25	23	13	13	12
Sweden	69	1	0.48	18	7	15	6	3
Denmark	74	0	0.41	14	6	8	9	5

[+] Mean is mean number of answers stating "strongly disapprove" or "disapprove" across all five social norms
Source: European Social Survey 2006/7

The first row of Table 7.2 ('All') refers to the pooled data that includes all 11 countries with the data from each country weighted according to the size of its population. This simply and conveniently represents the data from these 11 countries. While it might provide some approximation of a European perspective, it cannot be considered as a statistical representation of an overall European average. However, it is clear from this row that levels of disapproval differ considerably depending upon which social norm is being transgressed. Getting divorced when one has children under 12 was disapproved of by a third of respondents while a quarter said they would disapprove if someone chooses never to have children. Around a fifth would be less than happy if someone had a full-time job with children under three or had a child with a partner to whom they are not married. The lowest level of disapproval was for living with a partner without being married. In this instance just 15 per cent said they disapprove.

The rest of the rows in the table show the findings for each country. As was the case across Europe, it was getting divorced with a child younger than 12 that led to most disapproval in most countries, including the UK. However, there are some notable exceptions. In Slovakia, Poland and Cyprus, for instance, it was choosing never to have children that led to most disdain (over half of the sample in all three countries), while in the Netherlands it was having a full-time job and children under three (29 per cent disapproving).

The first three columns of Table 7.2 show how many respondents disapproved of either *none* or *all* of the items, and the mean number of items disapproved of. The mean number of items where there was disapproval varied between countries, with the highest disapproval in the former communist countries and the lowest levels in the Nordic countries. The pattern from the countries in the Mediterranean and western European areas is less clear-cut. The UK had relatively low average levels of disapproval.

Looking at the first column in Table 7.2, we see that, in Denmark, around three-quarters of respondents did not disapprove of *any* of these norms being transgressed, while the figure was just over two-thirds in Sweden. This suggests that in the Nordic countries these are barely norms at all. In Slovakia, on the other hand, only a quarter of respondents did not disapprove in response to any of the items, closely followed by Cyprus and Poland, suggesting that at least some of these social norms are still considered important here.

In the UK just over half of respondents did not disapprove of any of the norms In other words, for half of all Britons none of these social norms (still) exist. There was a similar *lack* of disapproval on any item in Spain, the Netherlands and Portugal. Surprisingly, perhaps, this group of countries includes both the Catholic Mediterranean countries as well as the Protestant mid-European countries. Around 40 per cent of respondents in France and Germany expressed no disapproval, suggesting a slightly higher prevalence of social norms here. As we will see later in this chapter these patterns were usually (but not always) found across the individual social norms, with the former communist countries and Cyprus being the countries where the social norms were most prevalent, followed by France, Germany and Spain, then the UK, Netherlands and Portugal, with the Nordic countries an area where these norms barely exist.

On the other hand, we should also consider the second column in Table 7.2 which shows the proportion of respondents who said they disapproved of *all five* items. Although disapproval levels differed in ways we might expect between different groups of countries in Europe, what is significant is that even in Slovakia – the most disapproving country – only eight per cent disapproved of *every* item. Taken together with the fact that, on average across these 11 countries, respondents disapproved of just 1.1 of the five social norms they were asked about, the most notable finding is, perhaps, the overall *lack* of disapproval. It is clear, therefore, that disapproval if these various norms are transgressed is largely a minority sport. Perhaps it is not a chorus of disapproval but, rather, only a section of the choir who are singing with a disapproving tone.

Let us now consider each of the norms in turn.

Getting divorced with young children

In most of the countries between a quarter and just over a third said they would disapprove if a man or woman got divorced while their children were under 12. So even on the item that tends to generate most disapproval the vast majority of residents in these countries said they would not disapprove. In the two Nordic countries disapproval was even lower. In Poland and Slovakia, on the other hand, this seemed to be more of a live social norm; around half of the population said they would disapprove.

Choosing never to have children

This issue of choosing not to have children showed even greater diversity than divorce. The UK stands alongside Sweden, Denmark and the Netherlands as countries where disapproval of choosing childlessness was very low. In Germany, France, Spain and Portugal levels of disapproval ranged from around a quarter to a third of respondents. In Cyprus and the two former communist countries, over half of all respondents said they would disapprove of this decision.

Having a full-time job and a very young child

Disapproval of having a child under three and working full-time goes against the usual cross-country pattern seen on the other items. While Slovakia was again one of the most disapproving countries, the Netherlands and Germany also had around 30 per cent expressing disapproval. Poland and Cyprus – which on other items expressed comparatively high disapproval – were closer to the relatively approving Sweden and Denmark on this issue. Around a fifth of those in the UK said they disapproved of this choice.

Exploratory factor analysis suggested that attitudes to this social norm were not so closely related to the other four items.[4] Perhaps attitudes on this issue specifically reflect differences in the employment structure in these countries. Or in the historical development of female labour market participation. Further analysis is required to address this issue in detail.

Cohabiting

Two items deal with the issue of cohabiting: in general, disapproval was higher if someone had a child outside of wedlock than if they were simply cohabiting. On both of these issues the usual cross-country pattern returns, with the former communist countries and Cyprus most likely to say they disapproved and the Nordic countries the least. Respondents in the UK were slightly more likely to disapprove on these issues than their counterparts in France, Germany and the Netherlands, although the differences were small.

Does gender matter for social norms?

So far we have looked at levels of disapproval in general. However, a key question is whether men and women have a different view of the transgression of social norms and whether it matters if the transgressor is a man or a woman.

Male and female respondents

On the first issue, Table 7.3 shows that overall, male and female respondents had rather similar views except on divorce where there is a child under 12, where men were more disapproving than women.

Table 7.3 Disapproval if social norms transgressed in 11 countries, by sex of respondent (but regardless of sex of the transgressor), 2006/7

% who disapprove if man/woman ...	Men	Women
... gets divorced while has children aged under 12	37	30
... chooses never to have children	25	24
... has a full-time job while has children aged under three	22	20
... has a child with a partner they live with but not married to	18	19
... lives with a partner without being married	14	15
Base	9898	11269

Source: European Social Survey 2006/7

Within individual countries there was also little evidence of differences in disapproval between men and women, except on the issue of divorce when a child aged under 12 is involved. On this matter, men were more disapproving than women in a number of countries. These include the UK (34 per cent of men disapprove, as do 21 per cent of women), Spain (40 and 32 per cent), France (42 and 31 per cent), the Netherlands (29 and 22 per cent) and Sweden (31 and 22 per cent).

Male and female norm breakers

What of the gender of the transgressor? Is it more frowned upon for women to break social norms than for men to do so? This does seem to have been the case when talking about working mothers. Figure 7.1 shows that disapproval of working full-time while having a young child was overwhelmingly directed at women and this pattern was found in all countries. In the UK, for instance, 38 per cent disapproved if a mother of a young child worked full-time compared to just three per cent if a man chose to do so. Perhaps, in time, attitudes towards this issue will change and fall in line with the gender-equal attitudes seen elsewhere. Or perhaps there will always be a view that young children need their mothers more than their fathers.

Figure 7.1 Disapproval if person has full-time job and children under three in 11 countries, by sex of transgressor, 2006/7

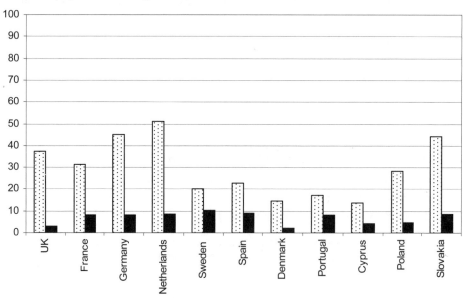

The data on which Figure 7.1 is based can be found in the appendix to this chapter
Source: European Social Survey 2006/7

In contrast, it was men who were the subject of greater disapproval for getting divorced while having children under 12. This difference was found in 9 of the 11 countries included in this study. But, as Figure 7.2 shows, these differences were less pronounced than for the full-time job issue. In the UK, for example, 23 per cent said they would disapprove if a woman got divorced compared with 32 per cent if a man did so.

Figure 7.2 Disapproval if person with child under 12 gets divorced in 11 countries, by sex of transgressor, 2006/7

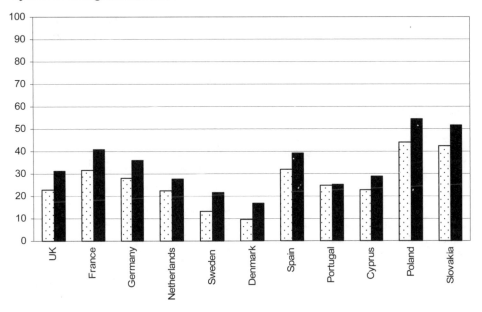

□ Asked about women ■ Asked about men

The data on which Figure 7.2 is based can be found in the appendix to this chapter
Source: European Social Survey 2006/7

On the other three norms (choosing not to have children and the two norms associated with cohabiting), there were no major differences in disapproval depending on whether the transgressor was a man or a woman.

Is there a gendered double standard at work?

We have seen that there was a mixed picture in terms of whether the gender of the person transgressing a social norm makes a difference to the levels of disapproval but that sometimes it made a large difference indeed. A related question, of course, is whether men were more disapproving of women than women are, and *vice versa*.

Table 7.4 summarises the disapproval toward different genders of transgressor by the gender of the respondent. Where a country appears in a cell it means that there was a difference of five percentage points or more between male and female respondents in the direction shown. No differences of five percentage points or more were found in Germany or Denmark.

Table 7.4 Gender differences (five points or more) in disapproval of transgression of social norms, by gender of respondent and transgressor[5]

	Men more disapproving than women...		Women more disapproving than men...	
	... when asked about men	... when asked about women	... when asked about men	... when asked about women
A person getting divorced while has children aged under 12	UK France Sweden Spain	UK France Sweden Spain Netherlands Cyprus Poland Slovakia	Slovakia	—
A person who has a full-time job while he/she has children aged under three	—	Spain Poland Slovakia UK	—	—
A person who has a child with a partner they live with but not married to	—	Cyprus	Cyprus	Netherlands Slovakia
A person who lives with a partner not married to	—	Cyprus Slovakia	Portugal Cyprus	—
A person who chooses never to have children	—	Netherland Cyprus	Cyprus Portugal Slovakia	—

Source: European Social Survey 2006/7

In terms of men and women getting divorced when their children are under 12, we see that in the UK, France, Sweden and Spain male respondents were always more disapproving than their female counterparts, regardless of whether it was a man or women going against the social norm. Male respondents in the Netherlands, Cyprus and Poland were more disapproving than female respondents of a *woman* getting divorced when her children were young. Slovakian men disapproved of a woman doing this, while Slovakian women disapproved of a man doing this. On other norms, however, the pattern is far less clear, although it appears that men were more disapproving overall than women. There is thus no clear picture to suggest respondents were more disapproving of the opposite gender, but the gender of the transgressor certainly mattered.

We can take this analysis further by combining the data across countries and using multivariate analysis to examine the influence of gender (of respondent and transgressor) on disapproval after controlling for other relevant factors such as country and age. The results of this analysis are shown in Table A.5 in the appendix to this chapter. In this analysis disapproval does emerge as a gendered process. Men were more likely than women to be disapproving in their attitudes to childlessness, cohabitation and parents divorcing. It was not just the sex of the respondent that affected the result. After controlling for country, age and a series of other demographic and attitudinal variables, respondents viewed issues differently depending on whether the transgressor was a man or a woman. The issue of working motherhood again stands out from the other measures of social disapproval. Among the whole set of countries, the odds of disapproval were more than three times higher for a woman working full-time with small children at home than for a man in the same situation. On other norms, women choosing to remain childless and divorce, respondents on average were less judgemental about women compared with men. However, there is evidence of a double standard at work; male respondents were more likely to disapprove when asked these questions about a woman than when asked about a man.

Are the old the conservatives?

It is often asserted that the young are more liberal in terms of social norms while older Europeans are more conservative. The process of attitude change in British society through generational replacement is discussed in the chapter by Ross and Sacker in this report. To examine this question in relation to social norms across Europe, we looked at the proportions disapproving of each of the social norms among men and women of different ages regardless of whether they were being asked about a man or a woman.

Given the relatively small number of respondents per age group in certain countries, these results should be treated with some caution. However, Figure 7.3 shows that it was men over 65 who were the most likely to disapprove if a woman decided never to have children. For Slovakia, Poland, Cyprus, Portugal and Spain there was broadly a linear pattern, with the youngest men in society being less likely to express disapproval than their older male counterparts. In the other countries, including the UK, the youngest men were not the least likely to express disapproval and here a more curvilinear pattern can be observed, with disapproval falling and then increasing again with age. Figure 7.4 shows that among women the relationship between age and disapproval was generally less strong, but in all countries the oldest age group were again more likely to disapprove. In the UK disapproval among women is lower than disapproval among men across all age groups.

Figure 7.3 Disapproval among men if man/woman decides never to have children in 11 countries, by age, 2006/7

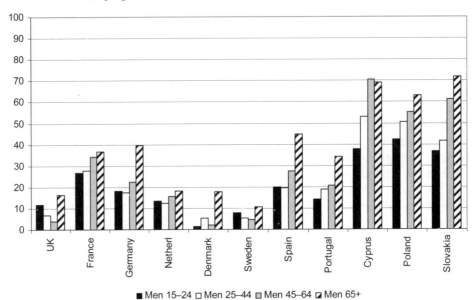

■ Men 15–24 □ Men 25–44 □ Men 45–64 ▨ Men 65+

Figure 7.4 Disapproval among women if man/woman decides never to have children in 11 countries, by age, 2006/7

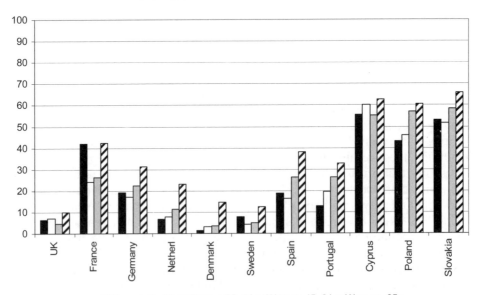

■ Women 15–24 □ Women 25–44 □ Women 45–64 ▨ Women 65+

The data on which Figures 7.3 and 7.4 are based can be found in the appendix to this chapter
Source: European Social Survey 2006/7

Modelling the predictors of disapproval across Europe

Three major findings have emerged so far. First, we have identified a reasonably consistent pattern of cross-national differences with regard to the proportions of respondents who personally disapproved of certain social behaviours. Secondly, we have established that levels of disapproval exhibited some variation according to the particular item under discussion. Thirdly, we have indicated that responses varied according to the age and gender of the respondent, as well as the gender respondents were asked to think of in answering the set of questions. However, these patterns were not identical for every country. In this section we present the results of multivariate analysis to further explore what might explain differences in attitudes towards social norms.

Differences in socio-economic context

We first conducted an analysis which combined data across all our countries and considered the extent to which differences in attitudes may be explained by the underlying socio-economic context in a particular country rather than or in addition to respondents' individual characteristics.[6] As discussed in the introduction, the countries in our analysis exhibit different degrees of modernisation as measured by four indicators: (GDP) per capita by purchasing power, the proportion of females in employment, the divorce rate (number of divorces per 100 marriages) and the country's religiosity (the proportion of individuals claiming to belong to some religious denomination). We combined these measures into an index which we call tradition–modernity and which was used in our analysis.[7]

This country-level indicator was included alongside a range of individual level characteristics (including age, gender, education and religion) in a logistic regression model exploring the factors associated with personal disapproval of each of the five social norms considered in this chapter. The results of this analysis are summarised in Table A.5 in the appendix to this chapter. Further information on regression can be found in Appendix I of this report.

We found that, even after controlling for a range of individual level characteristics, the country-level context mattered. Modernity produced a substantial and significant downward effect on personal disapproval for four of the five items. A one-point increase in the tradition–modernity score (towards being more modern) nearly halves the odds of disapproving of a person who chooses not to have children; it reduces the odds of disapproving of unmarried cohabitation by around a quarter. There were also significant reductions in disapproval of unmarried parenthood and divorce when children are younger than 12. The item that asks about those who work full-time while their child is under three behaved differently, as we noted earlier; here the evidence suggests that disapproval increases with modernity. For this item it would be preferable to have background data on the prevalence of working mothers rather than simply working women, and to have additional information on the availability of part-time work and childcare provision, both of which may additionally influence attitudes to working mothers.

Differences in respondent characteristics

In addition to the effect of these country-level factors, this multivariate analysis of all countries combined also confirmed the earlier findings with regard to the effect of respondent characteristics such as sex and age on attitudes. For example, the analysis confirmed that attitudes are age related, although the nature of this relationship differs according to the norm being considered. In the majority of cases social disapproval increased with age. However, looking at the data as a whole, it was not the youngest respondents that were the most 'permissive' but young adults aged 25 to 34. We can suggest that the attitudes of those under 25 are still influenced by their parents, and that they become less censorious as they move into adulthood and experience these events themselves. This finding is, in fact, a common one in the analysis of similar social attitudes in British data – see, for example, the chapter by Ross and Sacker in this report and Duncan and Phillips (2008).

As discussed above we also found significant differences in attitudes on the basis of sex (both of the respondent and of the transgressor). It is also notable that being married increased the chances of disapproving of cohabitation, and that those who are parents were also much more likely to disapprove of those who choose to remain childless.

Education appears to go hand in hand with social liberalism; higher education consistently lowered the odds of disapproval on all five items. The effect of an individual reporting personal happiness had the same effect, with an increase on an 11-point happiness scale leading to a reduction in the odds of disapproval. Another finding of interest is the persistence of the correlation between religious beliefs and social conservatism: a one-point increase in the strength of someone's religion increased the odds of them disapproving of cohabitation by 30 per cent and increased the odds of them disapproving of divorce by 12 per cent. Similarly, reporting that they felt part of a group that was discriminated against increased disapproval (over and above the effect of religiosity). The effects of perceived discrimination are quite large (for example, doubling the odds of disapproving of cohabitation) and it is not immediately apparent what is being picked up by this variable, but the size of the effect merits further investigation.

Respondent characteristics in individual countries

One of the pitfalls of comparative social analysis is that, in order to produce insights that travel across a number of countries, there is an inevitable loss in the subtlety of the message about individual countries. Consequently, we also conducted separate analyses for each individual country, using regression analysis to explore the relationship between respondent characteristics and their score on an index of personal disapproval (running from 0 to 5). This index combined attitudes to each of the five norms, with respondents awarded one point for each item of which they disapproved.

The results of this model (which can be found in Table A.6 in the appendix to this chapter) illustrate the different size of demographic, experiential and attitudinal effects across countries. For example, an effect for marriage was only present in four of the ten countries, and the link between parenthood and disapproval was only significant in two. The tendency for men to be more disapproving overall than women only appeared in five of the ten countries, while male disapproval, specifically in relation to women's social behaviour, was only significant in Germany and Poland. The effect of age on attitudes also varied across countries. In Portugal and in the Nordic countries, for example, age was seemingly important only in relation to the oldest cohort. In France young people had the strongest likelihood of disapproval. The most consistent effects across every country were from educational level and strength of personal religion; people with higher education were less likely to be disapproving, while the more religious people were, the more likely they were to be disapproving.

Focusing specifically on the analysis of attitudes in the UK we found that important factors influencing disapproval included age (those aged under 25 and over 65 were the most disapproving), sex (men were more disapproving than women), religiosity (with the more religious being more disapproving) and education (those with higher education were less disapproving). Taking all of the issues together, people in the UK were also more likely to disapprove when asked about a female transgressor compared with a male transgressor.

Conclusions

This chapter has attempted to describe and explain variations in the extent to which individuals express personal disapproval of lifestyle choices that run counter to established social norms such as marriage, family formation and the role of mothers in looking after children. The clearest message is that in most countries, including the UK, there will not be a 'chorus of disapproval' if these traditional social norms are transgressed. Rather, we are likely to hear only a minority of the choir singing with a disapproving tone. Certain sections are likely to sing more loudly than others, including men, older cohorts, the less educated and the more religious. However, the prevailing attitude towards individuals' lifestyle choices can perhaps best be described as indifference.

We have, however, demonstrated that respondents do not necessarily take a consistent approach to each and every norm and that the volume of disapproval may vary depending on the situation under discussion. Household formation and dissolution or fertility decisions were not viewed in the same way as the decision of women to combine work and childcare, with people generally being more critical of the latter. Furthermore, we uncovered some notable differences in attitudes depending on whether the transgressor of the social norm was a man or a woman. In particular, we found that people (especially men) were more critical of the idea of a woman with young children going out to work than a man in a comparable situation. The issue of maternal employment and child-rearing may be one domain where social attitudes will not get any more liberal; alternatively this may be the next stage of social liberalisation waiting to happen.

The volume of disapproval also varies across countries: disapproval of choices that run counter to social norms was far more likely to occur in Polish, Slovakian and Cypriot society, while it was barely audible in the Nordic nations. The UK, too, was found to be a generally tolerant nation with low levels of disapproval. As predicted, personal attitudes towards the transgression of social norms were found to be related to the underlying socio-economic context in particular countries, with disapproval felt more strongly in countries which remained objectively more traditional. So it is possible that disapproval of non-traditional choices will become increasingly muted across Europe, perhaps accompanied by the emergence of new social norms, as and when countries continue to undergo social change and development.

Notes

1. The European Social Survey (ESS) provides nationally representative probability samples of all residents aged 15 and over in more than 20 countries. Unlike the *British Social Attitudes* survey, ESS collects data for the whole of the United Kingdom including Northern Ireland. For further details see www.europeansocialsurvey.org. Individual country data are weighted by design weights. "All countries" data are weighted by design and population weights.
2. Readers familiar with Esping-Andersen's work will notice we have collapsed two of his categories, the corporatist and the neo-liberal, into a single western European type. In the context of this topic, and in comparison with the other selected countries, we felt that they were more similar than they were different from one another.
3. The bases for Table 7.2 are as follows:

All	21197
Slovakia	1766
Poland	1721
Cyprus	995
Spain	1875
France	1986
Germany	2916
Netherlands	1889
UK	2394
Portugal	2222
Sweden	1927
Denmark	1505

4. It has the weakest factor loading (0.488). A factor model run without this item explains 67 per cent of the variance, dropping to 57 per cent when it is included.
5. Further details of this analysis are available from the authors on request.
6. Analysis is based on data from 10 countries. Cyprus was dropped from this and subsequent analysis because of problems with the education variable.
7. In an exploratory factor analysis these four items formed a single factor that explained 83 per cent of the variance in our dataset. We then created a factor score for each country ranging from -2.116 for Poland ('most traditional') to 1.449 for Sweden ('most modern'). We used this as a single term in a regression model in place of dummy variables for individual countries.

References

Billari, F., Hagestad, G., Liefbroer, A. and Speder, Z. (2006), *Timing of Life: The organisation of the life course in Europe*, available at http://www.europeansocialsurvey.org/inde7.php?option=com_content&task=view&id=220&Itemid=309

Davie, G. (1994), *Religion in Britain since 1945: Believing without belonging*, Oxford: Blackwell

Duncan S, and Phillips M. (2008), 'New families? Tradition and change in modern relationships' in Park A., Curtice, J., Thomson, K., Phillips, M., Johnson, M. and Clery, E. (eds.), *British Social Attitudes: the 24th Report*, London: Sage

Durkheim E (1893), *The division of labour in society*

Esping-Andersen, G. (1990), *The three worlds of welfare capitalism*, Cambridge: Polity Press

Eurostat (2008), *Europe in Figures – Eurostat Yearbook 2008*, Eurostat

Greeley, A. (2003), *Religion in Europe at the End of the Second Millennium*, New Brunswick, NJ: Transaction Publishers

Heelas P, Lash, S. and Morris, P. (eds.) (1996), *De-traditionalization: critical reflections on authority and identity*, Oxford: Blackwell

OECD (2005), *Society at a glance 2005 – OECD social indicators*, available at http://www.oecd.arglels/social/indicators/SAG

Przeworski, A. and Teune, H. (1970), *The logic of comparative social inquiry*, New York: Wiley-Interscience

Rodriguez, H. (1998), *Cohabitation: a snapshot*, Center for Law and Social Policy, available at http://www.clasp.org/admin/site/publications_archive/files/0024.pdf

Schultz, P.W., Nolan, J.M., Cialdini, R.B., Goldstein, N.J., Griskevicius, V. (2007), 'The Constructive, Destructive, and Reconstructive Power of Social Norms', *Psychological Science*, **18**: 429–434

Wilson, A. N. (2008), *Our times: The age of Elizabeth II*, London: Hutchinson

Acknowledgements

The European Social Survey is funded jointly by the European Commission, the European Science Foundation and academic funding bodies in participating countries. Thank you to Sally Widdop for her assistance with this chapter.

Appendix

The data for Figures 7.1 to 7.4 are shown below.

Table A.1 Disapproval if person has full-time job and children under three in 11 countries, by sex of transgressor, 2006/7

	Asked about men		Asked about women	
	%	Base	%	Base
United Kingdom	3	1213	38	1181
France	8	1001	32	985
Germany	8	1469	45	1447
Netherlands	9	928	51	961
Denmark	11	771	20	734
Sweden	9	947	23	899
Spain	2	959	15	917
Portugal	8	1144	17	1078
Cyprus	4	507	14	488
Poland	5	863	28	858
Slovakia	9	867	44	899

Source: European Social Survey 2006/7

Table A.2 Disapproval if person with child under 12 gets divorced in 11 countries, by sex of transgressor, 2006/7

	Asked about men		Asked about women	
	%	Base	%	Base
United Kingdom	31	1213	23	1181
France	41	1001	32	985
Germany	36	1469	28	1447
Netherlands	28	928	23	961
Denmark	22	771	13	734
Sweden	17	947	10	899
Spain	39	959	32	917
Portugal	25	1144	25	1078
Cyprus	29	507	23	488
Poland	54	863	44	858
Slovakia	52	867	42	899

Source: European Social Survey 2006/7

Table A.3 Disapproval among men if man/woman decides never to have children in 11 countries, by age, 2006/7

	Men 15–24		Men 25–44		Men 45–64		Men 65+	
	%	Base	%	Base	%	Base	%	Base
United Kingdom	12	124	7	362	4	354	16	239
France	27	102	28	330	34	334	37	164
Germany	18	191	17	464	23	480	40	302
Netherlands	13	73	12	325	16	303	18	167
Denmark	1	73	6	237	2	283	18	145
Sweden	8	150	5	321	5	323	11	157
Spain	20	143	20	348	27	255	45	156
Portugal	14	109	19	272	21	246	34	236
Cyprus	38	68	53	162	70	137	69	107
Poland	42	185	50	258	55	265	63	107
Slovakia	37	156	42	327	61	237	72	121

Source: European Social Survey 2006/7

Table A.4 Disapproval among women if man/woman decides never to have children in 11 countries, by age, 2006/7

	Women 15–24		Women 25–44		Women 45–64		Women 65+	
	%	Base	%	Base	%	Base	%	Base
United Kingdom	6	140	7	429	5	398	10	348
France	42	92	24	396	26	352	42	216
Germany	19	164	17	476	22	486	31	353
Netherlands	7	90	8	365	11	345	23	221
Denmark	2	65	3	242	4	301	15	159
Sweden	8	138	4	305	5	328	12	204
Spain	19	124	16	367	26	267	38	216
Portugal	13	115	20	399	27	447	33	398
Cyprus	56	55	60	164	55	221	63	81
Poland	43	170	46	274	57	293	61	169
Slovakia	53	158	52	325	59	275	66	138

Source: European Social Survey 2006/7

Predictors of disapproval across Europe: regression analysis

Table A.5 shows the results of logistic regression analysis looking at the factors associated with a respondent saying they disapprove of each non-traditional behaviour (*vs.* approve or neither approve nor disapprove). The analysis combined data across all countries. Separate models were run for each behaviour. Results are presented in terms of odds ratios. An odds ratio greater than one indicates that the group was more likely to disapprove of a particular behaviour whilst an odds ratio of less than one indicates that the group was less likely to disapprove.

Table A.6 shows the results of linear (OLS) regression analysis looking at the factors associated with disapproval of non-traditional behaviour. The dependent variable was an index of personal disapproval (coded 0 to 5) combining attitudes to each of the five behaviours, where 0 indicates that the respondent disapproved of none of the behaviours and 5 indicates that the respondent disapproved of all five. Positive coefficients indicate greater disapproval while negative coefficients indicate less disapproval. Separate models were run for each country.

For categorical variables, the reference category is shown in brackets after the category heading. Figures are shown for significant relationships only.

Table A.5 Respondent disapproves of non-traditional behaviour (versus approves or neither) logistic regression across 10 countries

	Chooses never to have children	Living with partner unmarr.	Has child with partner unmarr.	Has FT job with child under 3	Gets divorced when child under 12
	Odds ratio	Odds ratio	Odds ratio	Odds ratio	Odds ratio
Tradition–modernity score	.544**	.763**	.931**	1.095**	.779**
Age (25–34)					
15–24	1.389**		1.342**	1.261*	1.393**
35–44	.740**				
45–54		1.512**	1.420**	1.192*	
55–64		1.741**	1.755**	1.410**	1.591**
65+	1.609**	3.501**	3.254**	1.729**	2.820**
Male	1.122*	1.198*			1.453**
Married	1.221**	1.337**	1.333**		1.219**
Respondent a parent	1.662**			1.170*	1.115*
Education (lower secondary or below)					
Upper secondary education					.815**
Tertiary education	.716**	.792**	.829**	.691**	.631**
R lives in rural area					
R feels discriminated against	1.232**	2.050**	1.884**	1.366**	1.267**
Female transgressor	.709**			3.562**	.680**
Men asked about women	1.249**			1.249*	1.174*
R believes most other people would disapprove	5.279**	5.692**	5.896**	7.768**	6.924**
Score on left–right scale (0–10)				.995*	.997*
Religiosity (0–10 scale)	1.099**	1.293**	1.237**	1.087**	1.122**
Happiness (0–10 scale)	.947**	.933**	.942**	.975*	.959**
-2 log likelihood	15898.50	11448.70	13878.90	13988.18	18065.87
Cox and Snell R2	.215	.191	.183	.221	.241
Base	19,933	20,026	20,032	19,946	19,789

* = significant at 95% level; ** = significant at 99% level
Source: European Social Survey 2006/7

Table A.6 Score on disapproval index (0–5) OLS regression, by country

	DE	DK	ES	FR	UK	NL	PL	PT	SE	SK
	Coeff.	Coeff.	Coeff.	Coeff.	Coeff.	Coeff.	Coeff.	Coeff.	Coeff.	Coeff.
Age (25–34)										
15–24				.595**	.183**				.249*	
35–44	-.118*		-.209**							
45–54							.324**			
55–64	.172**		.265**	.158*			.571**			.617*
65+	.603**	.490**	.892**	.550**	.846**	.384**	.904**	.389*	.258*	1.147**
Male	.081*		.332**	.216**	.266**		.159*			
Married	.124**			.260**		.254**			.179*	
Respondent a parent	.138**		.189**							
Education (lower secondary or below)										
Upper secondary education	-.430**	-.217*	-.257**	-.323**	-.089*	-.204**	-.317**			
Tertiary education	-.554**	-.334**	-.401**	-.373**		-.407**	-.484**		-.215*	
R lives in rural area					-.095**		.190**			
R feels discriminated against	.524**	.475*	.481**	.180**	.214**	.451**			.258*	
Female transgressor	.218**				.228**	.289**				
Men asked about women	.150**						.239*			
Score on left–right scale (0–10)			.006**	-.005**	.005**		.031**			
Religiosity (0–10 scale)	.072**	.058**	.152**	.078**	.104**	.106**	.179**	.092**	.069**	.138**
Happiness (0–10 scale)	-.032**		-.029*	-.045**	-.020*		-.033*			
R^2	.138	.115	.287	.135	.202	.184	.197	.073	.088	.148
Base	*2812*	*1460*	*1841*	*1974*	*2344*	*1829*	*1590*	*2148*	*1861*	*1656*

* = significant at 95% level; ** = significant at 99% level
Source: European Social Survey 2006/7

8 Never too old? Attitudes towards longer working lives

Stephen McKay[*]

Most people in Britain expect to spend a significant number of years in retirement. Yet the notion of a spell of retirement is actually relatively recent, as people would previously have expected to work all their lives. The introduction of state pensions in the early 20th century reflected the fact that people might outlive their ability to work and hence to support themselves. Even after the introduction of state pensions, it used to be common for those of state pension age to continue working (though until 1988 this often entailed a reduction in their pension). But in more recent decades people have come to expect a longer period of retirement when they could be active, though active in the sense of leisure rather than paid work. Between 1931 and 1971 the proportion of men aged over 65 who were 'retired' increased from under one half to more than three-quarters. And the trend in employment has been towards leaving the labour market at earlier rather than later ages despite increases in longevity; by the start of the 21st century, the proportion of men over 65 who were retired stood at 92 per cent (while 91 per cent of women over the age of 60 were retired) (Smeaton and McKay, 2003). So retirement from paid work was once unexpected, then brief, and is now seen as a time of choice and leisure.

However, demographic changes and the rising costs of pensions are now threatening this 'modern' view of retirement. We are witnessing an ageing of the population, resulting from a lower birth rate (meaning fewer young people to replace older ones) and from rising life expectancies at older ages. In the 1970s and 1980s, government policy at times gave incentives for older people to retire early and make way for younger people, particularly at times of high unemployment (Walker, 1986). More recently, however, various factors have placed a different emphasis on retirement. With fewer younger people, older people represent an important source of labour – indeed, increasing the number of older workers in the labour market is part of the government's strategy (Department for Work and Pensions, 2006: 142). A further change, perhaps linked, is the recognition that age discrimination in employment is unfair,

---

[*] Stephen McKay is Professor of Social Research in the School of Social Policy at the University of Birmingham.

inefficient – and now illegal in some circumstances. However, perhaps the most critical issue is the increasing costs of pensions (for both individuals and government), and the related question of whether early departure from the labour market is sustainable financially. Government policy to address these challenges includes encouraging extended working lives beyond the current state pension age (*ibid*).

These changes raise a number of questions. How far have these legal and demographic changes permeated the public consciousness? Does the public regard older workers as valuable or as replaceable? To what extent is there support for working longer and delaying retirement? Irrespective of general attitudes, how have people's individual expectations for their own retirement changed?

In this chapter we first outline changes in life expectancy over the last century, and give some background to one of the main implications of these demographic changes – the question of how to fund increasingly lengthy periods of retirement. Against this backdrop, we ask how people regard old age, and how much support there is for government spending on pensions, including the question of who should have responsibility for ensuring that retirement is adequately financed. With this vital context in place, we turn to the main focus of this chapter – attitudes towards older workers and extended working – and ask how the public views older workers, and whether it is supportive of extending working lives beyond age 65. We then explore individuals' own expectations of leaving work and retirement ages, and ask whether these tally with people's attitudes about these issues. Finally, we consider three of the main factors which can affect choices about extending working lives: finances, ill health and flexible working, and ask whether these elements can explain people's expectations about their own retirement age.

This chapter draws not only on *British Social Attitudes* data (which cover Britain), but also on the European Social Survey 2006/7, which covers the UK. This is a valuable source of data as it not only asked about attitudes to ageing, but also included a wide range of European countries against which the UK may be compared.

An ageing population

Longer lives

It is well known that the UK population will age rapidly over the next 30 years. This reflects three distinct factors. First, the long-term reduction in the birth rate, which means there are fewer younger people relative to those of older and middle age. Second, a factor to which we soon return, an increase in life expectancies, especially for those who are already old or approaching old age. Third, the effect of a large cohort of people born in the 'baby boom' who are all now approaching or reaching retirement age.

One of the main social changes over the 20th century has been the inexorable rise in life expectancy at birth (see Figure 8.1). In 1901 a newborn boy might expect to live to 45, and a newborn girl to 47. By 2011 it is expected that newborn boys will live to an average of 77 years, and girls an average of 82 years. This is clearly an impressive achievement, and has led some to question just how long human life expectancy might reach in the future. These figures show few or no signs of reaching a plateau and are already exceeded in some other countries.

Figure 8.1 Life expectancy at birth (actual: 1901–2006, projected: 2007–2021), by sex

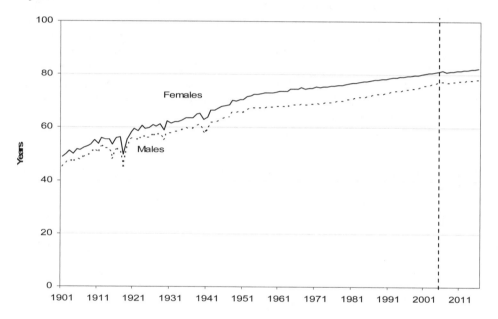

The data on which Figure 8.1 is based can be found in the appendix to this chapter
Source: Government Actuary's Department, 2001 projections

These overall increases in life expectancy mask two rather different trends: first, the decline in infant mortality, and second, higher life expectancy for those reaching later life. In the first half of the 20th century relatively few people used to die at these average life expectancies (i.e. in their 40s or 50s). Rather, these low averages reflected the much higher chances of death at an early age, particularly in childhood and through infectious diseases. Most of the progress in increasing life expectancy, at least in the first half of the 1900s, was the result of increasing people's chances of living through childhood and beyond and into middle age (Laslett, 1996). There was less progress in increasing the *additional* years of life expectancy for those reaching later life. A man reaching the age of 60 in 1911 could expect, on average, to live an additional 14 years. By 1971 this had only increased by about a year, to an additional 15 years of life. Similarly, a woman reaching the age of 80 in 1911 might live an extra 5.6 years, and by 1971 this had only risen by an extra 1.3 years – during a period when women's life expectancy at birth had risen by some 21 years. In fact these figures for additional life expectancy for those in their 60s and older were very similar in the middle of the 19th century (*ibid*).

This is an area where change has been most marked since the 1960s. There has been a sharp increase in the additional years of life that may be expected by older people. By 2011 it is expected that men who reach the age of 60 will live an additional 21 years, and women for an extra 24 years. It is unclear whether these figures have any in-built natural limits, but these projections for the future may well increase.

While these improvements in life expectancy are clearly a positive development in some ways, there are less positive outcomes for some. The improvements have not affected all groups equally, meaning sizeable differences in life expectancy among different social groups. Higher deprivation is associated with short lives. The ONS has calculated that the longest lives may be enjoyed by those in Kensington and Chelsea (men living to 84, women to 88), more than a decade longer than the much poorer residents of Glasgow City (men 71, women 77) (ONS, 2008).
Source: ONS, *Social Trends 30,* 2000

Figure 8.2 Actual and projected additional years of life expectancy at 60 and 80, by sex, 1911–2021

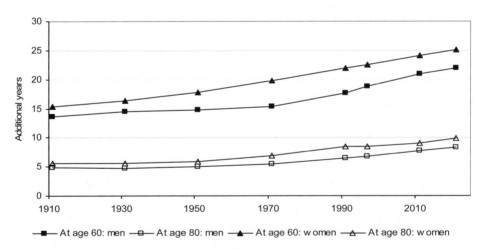

The data on which Figure 8.2 is based can be found in the appendix to this chapter
Source: ONS, *Social Trends 30,* 2000

Impacts on society and public policy

Both improved life expectancy and an ageing population have implications for society and for public policy. The fact that older people tend to have higher levels of disability or poor health impacts on individuals' quality of life and on public health services. In the 2001 Census, 37 per cent of those aged between 60 and 69 reported a limiting long-term illness, rising to 57 per cent of those aged 70 or older. A disability of this kind was also reported by 21 per cent of those aged between 45 and 59, but by only about one in ten of those aged between 30 and 44. Nevertheless, increased life expectancy is currently associated with more years of *healthy* life. People living longer may have more years with a disability (or ill health), but also more years without such conditions.

Perhaps most significantly, an ageing population has potentially far-reaching implications for pension provision and individuals' working lives. We have already noted that one factor contributing to an ageing population is the lower fertility level (Department for Work and Pensions, 2006: 177). This results in fewer young people in the workforce helping to fund the pensions of the growing number of retired people – a relationship known as the 'support ratio'. This only confounds the problems already mentioned which relate to improved life expectancy – i.e. longer periods spent being retired and economically inactive. Not surprisingly, then, the question of how to adequately fund retirement incomes has been high on the policy agenda for some time now, most notably in the work of the Pensions Commission and subsequent legislative reforms in two Pensions Acts in 2007 and 2008. In 2004, the Pensions Commission identified a trade-off between different policies needed to improve security in retirement. They rejected the view that society might allow pensioners' income to fall relative to those of workers, although that might happen if existing policies were unchanged. It was also seen as politically unacceptable to increase pensions through higher levels of general taxation (Pensions Commission, 2004). That left the two options of higher saving for retirement – which they were at pains to encourage – and later retirement. The latter was reflected in the key reforms proposed by the Pensions Commission – and directly taken forward by the government – through increases in state pension ages, and it is this measure that we focus on later in the chapter. As people live longer, it is possible to increase retirement ages while keeping the *proportion* of life spent in retirement roughly constant.

The 2006 White Paper, *Security in retirement: towards a new pensions system* shows its commitment to this approach in the chapter entitled 'Extending working life in an ageing society' (Department for Work and Pensions, 2006). In this, the government sets out one response to the challenges created by people living longer (139):

> ... we must enable and encourage people to work longer ... more needs to be done to change the culture and behaviour surrounding retirement. We will ... address the key barriers which prevent people staying in work for longer, and encourage more people to work up to and beyond State Pension Age.

When the first state pensions in the UK were introduced, few would have had an expectation of a long period of receipt of a pension, or indeed any receipt at all. The 1908 Old Age Pensions Act established pensions for some of those over the age of 70, at a time when life expectancy for men was around 49 years (for women, 53 years). This first pension was also means-tested, so that richer older people (with higher than average life expectancies) would not qualify. The current state pension ages of 65 for men and 60 for women were confirmed in the 1942 Beveridge Report, which provided the blueprint for the post-war system of social security. As we have seen, many people can now expect to live for a considerable number of additional years beyond these pension ages – and thus might expect to receive a state pension for a lengthy period. But from 2010, women's state pension age will begin to rise, and will reach 65 by the year 2020. As part of recent pensions reform, state pension ages will increase to 66 by 2026, to 67 by 2036 and then to 68 by 2046.

Changes in the state pension age do not necessarily mean delaying retirement and working longer – even if many companies have historically operated policies with a strong expectation of retirement at these ages, and expectations were shared with employees. Since 1989 there has been *no* requirement to stop work in order to receive a pension, or to see a pension reduced by other earnings. And yet increasing the age at which a person can draw a state pension is clearly linked to the idea of extended working lives – and as we have seen, it is a priority for government. If this policy is to succeed, it will be vital not only that the public supports such a change in principle, but also that individuals change their expectations and behaviour in relation to later working lives and retirement. We consider whether there is evidence of this public support later in the chapter.

Attitudes towards older people

Have the dramatic demographic and social changes witnessed in the 20th century impacted on public attitudes towards older people? Later in this chapter we explore changes in attitudes towards older workers and delaying the age of retirement. First, however, we consider two related, but broader questions –what do people think of as 'old age', and how much support is there for government spending on older people.

Who is 'old'?

We might anticipate that as people live longer, the notion of when someone is 'old' would change to reflect this different demographic profile. Unfortunately, we can't track attitude *change* on this issue, but we are able to look at a recent reading from the European Social Survey which indicates which groups people think of as 'old'. The survey included a series of questions about life-stages, including the following:

> At what age, approximately, would you say men/women reach old age?

Half of the respondents interviewed were asked about men, and half about women (selected randomly). As we show in Table 8.1, on average in the UK people were regarded as reaching old age in their late 60s (68 for women and 69 for men). There was only a slight difference in answers about men and women, with women more likely to be regarded as reaching old age at age 60 (18 per cent of respondents), coinciding with their current state pension age. In comparison, only 11 per cent believed that men were old at age 60. Close to one quarter of respondents (23 per cent) thought that people only reached old age after living for 75 years.

The question text does not pin down precisely what is meant by 'old age' – it is left to respondents to decide on this. But it is notable that the answers do not simply reflect current state pension ages or retirement ages. This suggests that 'old age' is seen as a life-stage that occurs *after* the end of economic activity, rather than coinciding with it. While we cannot know whether this amounts to a *change* in attitudes, we can speculate that this is a modern perception as we have already noted that the idea of an active retirement is a relatively recent one.

Table 8.1 Views of when women and men reach old age

	When women reach old age	When men reach old age	All responses
Timing of old age	%	%	%
It depends	4	4	4
Up to 59	6	4	5
60–64	20	12	16
65–69	17	20	19
70–74	31	35	33
75–79	9	11	10
80+	13	13	13
Base	*1213*	*1181*	*2394*
Mean (where specific age was given)	67.8	68.9	68.4
Base	*1128*	*1110*	*2238*

In practice most people gave answers that ended in either 0 or 5
Source: European Social Survey 2006/7

This table of results applies only to the UK, but it is possible to look at comparable figures for the other countries participating in the European Social Survey 2006/7. Out of 23 countries, the answers from the UK were the tenth 'oldest' for men, and the eleventh 'oldest' for women. Nordic countries (plus Ireland, the Netherlands and Switzerland) gave relatively 'older' answers. In both Denmark and the Netherlands the average overall response for reaching old age was around 70–71 years old. Perhaps most notably, the countries of eastern Europe tended to give 'younger' answers for when people became old (for example, in Hungary men were thought to become old at 63 and women at 61). Those living in the Russian Federation, Ukraine, Estonia, Hungary, Bulgaria, Slovakia, Poland and Slovenia on average suggested that men became old before the age of 66; all the other countries surveyed gave an answer of 66 or higher (often much higher).

These country-level attitude differences can be explained in part by differences in life expectancy. For example, the comparatively low ages given in countries of eastern Europe are mirrored by relatively low life expectancies in these countries compared to the other countries in the study. Indeed, there is a positive correlation between a higher life expectancy and a higher age at which people are regarded as being old in each of the 23 countries analysed (for men, r = 0.63, for women r = 0.65, p < 0.01).

However, differences in life expectancy cannot explain the different perceptions held about men and women. Women are regarded as becoming old at a younger age than men in most countries (if only by a year or two) despite the fact that in all of these countries women can expect to live at least four years longer than men, and often much longer. The only exceptions to this general pattern were in Sweden, Finland and (just) Ireland, where women were regarded as becoming old slightly later than men.

Funding retirement

In light of the wide-reaching implications of an ageing population on pension provision outlined earlier, we now ask how much public support there is for government spending in this area. We start by setting out people's priorities for welfare spending, to assess whether pensions are viewed as an important area for government funding, and whether that has changed over time. It is hard to anticipate which way opinion might have moved. Has the public become less supportive of state spending on older people (through the state pension) as it becomes increasingly costly and, perhaps, unsustainable – or is an increasingly old population recognised as problematic, justifying more spending on this area?

In previous years we have asked respondents about support for extra spending on benefits for different groups: retirement pensions, child benefits, and benefits for the unemployed, disabled people and single parents. Respondents are asked to choose a first and a second priority (see Chapter 9 for the full question text and data). As we show in Figure 8.3, support for higher spending on older people has been strong ever since our survey series started in 1983 – and it has increased markedly over the last 25 years. A majority of respondents have consistently identified retirement pensions as either the first or the second priority for higher spending on welfare benefits (Taylor-Gooby and Martin, 2007). Moreover, since 1996, a majority have said that retirement pensions are their *first* priority for additional spending on benefits, peaking at 60 per cent in 2005 and up from 40 per cent in the early 1990s.

In 2007, the last time these questions were asked, retirement pensions were a first priority for some 56 per cent of respondents. We should not place too much emphasis on one measure which might suggest a reversal of the longer-term trend of increasing support for pensions – this is something that we will need to examine in future years. However, even if this is the start of a downturn in support, it is notable that the next highest levels of support were much lower than this: 18 per cent prioritising benefits for disabled people, and 16 per cent identifying child benefits as the first priority. Only six per cent supported benefits for single parents as the first priority, and only two per cent benefits for unemployed people.

Figure 8.3 Proportion selecting retirement pensions as first or second priority for extra spending on social benefits, 1983–2007

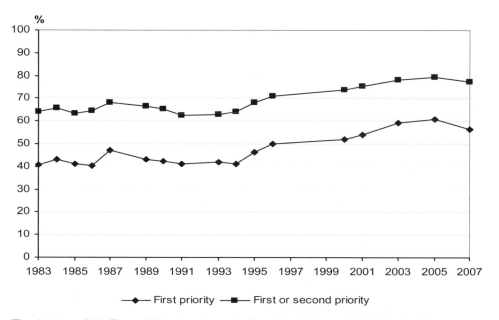

The data on which Figure 8.3 is based can be found in the appendix to this chapter

We should point out that we are unable to pin down the reason for the marked increase in support for spending on retirement pensions. It may, in part, reflect the fact that respondents answer this question with their own circumstances in mind; as the proportion of older people in the population increases, their choice of retirement pensions as a high priority would result in an increase at an overall level. Alternatively, it may be, in part, a recognition by the public as a whole of the increased funding required for an ageing population; however, it is likely that other factors were at the forefront of considerations when respondents were answering, including concerns about pensioner poverty. This might mean that people answered the question thinking of increasing the *level* of the state pension, rather than increasing the overall pot of money to fund a growing group of retired people experiencing longer periods of economic inactivity.

We also asked respondents who they think should be mainly responsible for ensuring people have enough money to live on in retirement, and, in particular, whether that responsibility falls on the state or the individual. Might regarding retirement income as a government responsibility seem outdated as this becomes increasingly expensive – or is this precisely the time that individuals are felt to need state support in funding increasingly long periods of retirement? As shown in Table 8.2, about six people in every ten believe that this is the responsibility of the government, three in ten that of the individual (and his or her family), and one in ten mainly that of the employer. These figures have fluctuated somewhat since 1998, but very much around these central figures. There is little evidence here of attitudes changing in response to the demographic trends we saw earlier.

Table 8.2 Views on responsibility for ensuring enough money to live on in retirement, 1998–2008

	1998	1999	2001	2003	2005	2008
Individual/group who should be mainly responsible	%	%	%	%	%	%
Government	56	58	62	58	56	58
Employer	9	9	7	11	10	10
Individual and their family	32	31	29	29	32	30
Base	3146	3143	3287	4432	3193	3358

A similar question was also asked in the European Social Survey, but one which allowed for a balancing of responsibilities between the government and the individual, rather than forcing a choice:

> *Choosing your answer from this card, please tell me who you think should be mainly responsible for providing people with an adequate standard of living in their old age? Please express your opinion on a scale of 0 to 10, where 0 means 'mainly the responsibility of the individual' and 10 means 'mainly the responsibility of the government'*

Results for the UK are illustrated in Figure 8.4 and give a broadly similar picture of views about responsibility. While the most popular single answer was in the middle of the two extremes, with over one quarter (27 per cent) of respondents giving an answer of five, the remaining responses were skewed towards the higher end of the scale, including a sizeable group (13 per cent) who opted for a response of 10, indicating that they believed that providing an adequate standard of living in retirement was mostly a matter for government.

Figure 8.4 Views on main responsibility for an adequate standard of living in retirement

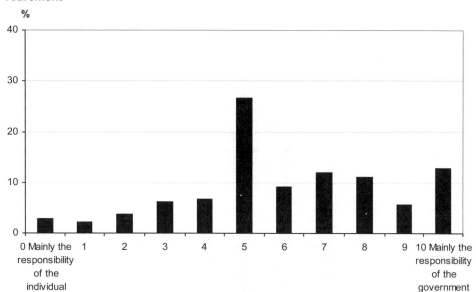

The data on which Figure 8.4 is based can be found in the appendix to this chapter
Source: European Social Survey 2006/7

While these results may suggest a high reliance on the government as being responsible for ensuring people have a decent standard of living in retirement, in most European countries there was an even *greater* emphasis on the role of the state. The average for each country varied from 4.9 for Switzerland, meaning that both the individual and the government were seen to have fairly equal responsibility, to a high of 7.7, indicating much greater emphasis on the role of the government, found in Bulgaria. The set of results by nation is shown in Figure 8.5.

It is perhaps unsurprising that the countries of eastern Europe tended to expect the government to take the main responsibility for retirement income. However, both Portugal and Finland also believed that the government should have the main responsibility. Some of those countries placing the greatest emphasis on individual responsibility – though still inclining towards retirement income remaining a government responsibility – in fact tended to have well-developed state pension systems (Germany, Austria). The Netherlands and the UK have perhaps the best developed system of occupational pensions. In addition, in Germany and Austria workers and employers contribute to state pensions, which might also explain the greater emphasis on individual responsibility in these countries.

Overall, on this evidence, there is little sign of attitudes changing over the last decade or so – pensions are still considered to be an important area of government spending, and a majority see living standards in retirement as mainly a government responsibility.

Figure 8.5 Views on main responsibility for an adequate standard of living in retirement, by country

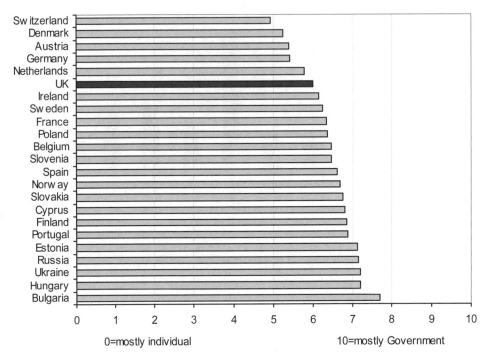

The data on which Figure 8.5 is based can be found in the appendix to this chapter
Source: European Social Survey 2006/7

Attitudes towards extended working lives

As we outlined earlier, the Pensions Commission argued for a combination of higher saving for retirement and later retirement as the solution to the pension provision problems. The policy of later retirement faces a number of hurdles (O'Connell, 2002). Over the 1970s and 1980s people tended to leave the labour market at a younger age. Many people continue to leave the labour market somewhat before the state pension age – and it is unclear whether changing pension ages will affect the age of labour market withdrawal ('retirement'). There is also the challenge of persistent class differences in life expectancy, and how far manual workers in particular are capable of either continuing to work or moving into alternative occupations in their 60s.

A number of recent reviews and studies have sought to identify the groups most likely to leave the labour market early, or to continue in paid work, and the policies that may be used to provide incentives for working longer (Humphrey *et al.*, 2003; Phillipson and Smith, 2005; Vickerstaff *et al.*, 2008). In this section we consider what people think about the role of older people and work. Our main focus is on society's attitudes towards people working later, before going on to examine individuals' own expectations at the ends of their working lives.

Views about older workers and early retirement

We start by considering attitudes towards the employment of older workers – whether employers treat older workers fairly, and whether older workers are seen as less important than younger ones (meaning that early retirement should be encouraged). Of course, there have been legislative changes in this area, with discrimination against older workers now illegal, so we are keen to see whether these changes are in line with, or have permeated, public opinion.

Many people leave the labour force before state pension age, and returning to work thereafter is particularly difficult, and rare. While the Pensions Commission proposed increases in state pension ages, they nonetheless recognised the challenge of keeping people in work until state pension age even now. The most recent survey included a question about opportunities for older people in the labour market that was also asked 25 years previously. We asked respondents to what extent they agreed or disagreed that:

Employers give too few opportunities to older people when recruiting

As shown in Table 8.3, the change in attitudes has been one of strength of feeling, rather than direction. In 1983 over six in ten agreed with the view that older people were given too few opportunities when recruiting. Now, a similar number are in agreement, although they tend to "agree" rather than "strongly agree". So, many continue to suspect that older people do not enjoy the same employment opportunities that firms offer to others (see also Macnicol, 2006).

Table 8.3 Views about older people's employment opportunities, 1983 and 2008

	Employers give too few opportunities to older people when recruiting	
	1983	2008
	%	%
Agree strongly[1]	27	10
Agree	35	56
Neither agree nor disagree	24	20
Disagree	10	6
Disagree strongly	3	1
Base	*1610*	*2998*

We also asked respondents two more direct questions concerning discrimination on the grounds of age, and especially above the age of 50:

How often do you think employers refuse a job to an applicant only because he/she is aged over 50? [A lot/Sometimes/Hardly ever]

Do you think it would be right or wrong to refuse a job to a person only because he/she is aged over 50?

As with the question above, people continue to believe that older workers face age discrimination. The vast majority (88 per cent) now think that job applicants over the age of 50 are rejected on grounds of age, either "sometimes" or "a lot". However, this does represent a small decrease compared to 2001, when 94 per cent thought this. In fact, most of the change can be put down to the fact that a higher proportion of people thought this happened "a lot" in 2001 than in 2008 (58 per cent compared to 47 per cent). Here, then, there is some evidence that perceptions of labour market practices relating to older workers have improved – possibly due to age discrimination legislation. Recent research in fact indicates that older workers face much less unfair treatment at work than is publicly perceived and than is experienced by those in the youngest age group (Fevre *et al.*, 2009); it may be that the media, which has tended to concentrate on older workers in its coverage of unfair treatment at work, has had a considerable impact on public views in this area.

While the public is now less likely to think that age discrimination happens frequently than in 2001, there is still a very strong view that this is an inappropriate way in which to behave (Table 8.4). In both 2001 and 2008, less than five per cent consider that such a move could be always or usually right. Over three-quarters, in each year, believe that this would be the wrong thing for employers to do.

Table 8.4 Views on acceptability of age discrimination in employment, 2001 and 2008

	2001	2008
View on refusing a job to 50+ on age grounds	%	%
Always right	1	1
Usually right	3	3
Neither right/wrong	13	15
Usually wrong	48	44
Always wrong	31	31
Base	*1883*	*2998*

These first three questions focused on adequate opportunities and fair treatment of older workers in the labour market. A further question raises the issue of whether older workers are seen as important as other workers, by asking whether "older people should be encouraged to retire earlier to reduce unemployment". Here we find a marked change in social attitudes (Table 8.5). In 1983 the public believed overwhelmingly that older people should be encouraged to retire earlier. Seven in ten agreed with this idea, with 36 per cent agreeing strongly, while only 15 per cent expressed disagreement. In 2008, however, only 13 per cent of people think that older people should be encouraged to leave work to 'make way' for younger unemployed people, while two-thirds (67 per cent) disagree.

Table 8.5 Views about encouraging early retirement, 1983 and 2008

	Older people should be encouraged to retire earlier to reduce unemployment	
	1983	**2008**
	%	%
Agree strongly[2]	36	2
Agree	34	11
Neither agree nor disagree	13	16
Disagree	10	51
Disagree strongly	5	16
Base	*1610*	*2998*

There are two important pieces of context that should be mentioned here, the economic situation and public policy, which distinguish the situation in 1983 from that of 2008 (and today). The first is the contrasting levels of unemployment. In July 1983 the number of people receiving unemployment benefit in the UK had reached three million. In July 2008 claimant unemployment was under 900,000, and (at the time) on a slowly rising trend that was only to accelerate towards the end of 2008. A second difference lies in public policy. It was part of government policy in the 1980s to encourage early retirement through the Job Release Scheme (1977–88). This scheme provided allowances to early retirees who were then replaced with unemployed younger people. So there was government support, and clearly a strong element of public support, for the idea of early retirement at a time of high unemployment. Indeed, as late as 1987, the *British Social Attitudes* series asked about the desirability of earlier retirement to tackle unemployment, and found that 82 per cent supported such a policy (with a similar result in 1985).

Today, however, it is considered important to retain older workers in employment, and age discrimination in employment has recently been outlawed. The New Deal for the 50 plus has aimed, with some success, at increasing the economic activity of older workers.

It seems that these steps are very much in line with people's views about the desirability of earlier retirement as a means of reducing unemployment. This turnaround in public support is remarkable, with few now supporting the view that older workers should somehow step aside for younger people.

Views about working beyond state pension age

It is clear, then, that the public feels that older workers should be fairly treated, and should not be seen as less important than others in the workforce. However, it is possible that attitudes may be different when it comes to people extending their working lives (rather than being encouraged to retire *early*). To explore this, we took the same issue – of older workers making way for younger ones – and asked about it in relation to working rather than retiring once they have reached "a certain age". We presented respondents with two options, as follows:

> *Some people say that it is wrong to make people retire just because they have reached a certain age. Others say that older employees must retire to make way for younger age groups. What about you? Which of the statements ... comes closest to your view?*

The responses confirm a trend away from assuming that older people should make way for younger people. In 2000, a majority (68 per cent) believed it would be wrong if simply reaching a certain age was sufficient grounds for making people retire. However, 30 per cent did think that older workers should step aside to make room for younger people. Now, there is even less sympathy for such a view. Respondents are split more than four to one against the view that the old should make way for the young, with 80 per cent thinking it is wrong to *make* people retire purely because they have reached a certain age, and just 17 per cent saying these workers should retire to make way for younger ones.

Despite this overwhelming rejection of older workers being forced to retire, there were rather different views about the right of employers to shed labour once people reached the age of 65 – the age from which a state pension is payable for men (and, from 2020, for women). We asked employees to what extent they agreed or disagreed with the following statement:

> *Employers should be allowed to decide whether or not to allow employees to work past age 65*

While employees tend to support rather than oppose this view, opinions diverge among the older age groups, as shown in Table 8.6. Well over half of employees agree with this proposition, while 28 per cent disagree. Those aged 55 or older are among the most likely to strongly support the view, but also the most likely to strongly oppose it – younger people are more likely to express an equivocal view, neither agreeing nor disagreeing.

Table 8.6 Views about employers' role in relation to working beyond 65, by age

	18–24	25–34	35–44	45–54	55+[3]	All
Employers should be allowed to decide if people work past 65	%	%	%	%	%	%
Agree strongly	10	9	14	16	16	13
Agree	42	47	47	46	36	44
Neither agree nor disagree	24	14	10	13	11	14
Disagree	20	22	25	20	24	22
Disagree strongly	3	6	4	5	12	6
Base	*113*	*353*	*420*	*388*	*275*	*1559*

Base: all employees

Lastly in this section, we consider a broader question about attitudes towards working well beyond state pension age. In the European Social Survey respondents were asked about general attitudes towards people working after the age of 70:

> *Apart from your own feelings, how do you think most people would react if a man/woman they knew well … carried on working after the age of 70?*

The answer options were that most people would "disapprove" (either "openly" or "secretly"), "not mind either way" or would "approve". In many countries, as shown in Table 8.7, a majority disapproved of women working after 70, and most countries tended to criticise women rather more than men for making such a choice. The UK emerges as one of the countries least likely to be critical of people working after 70 – though with Norway and Denmark even less likely to be critical. Even so, despite a relatively positive picture of support for working after state pension age, one third of UK respondents believed that most people would disapprove of women working after 70, and almost one quarter that there was public disapproval of men doing the same.[4] Those countries most opposed to women working past 70 were also those opposed to men doing the same.

Overall, attitudes towards older workers are largely positive. People are now more likely than in the past to think that older workers should be given job opportunities, and that this group should not be forced out of the labour market to make way for others – whether that is at age 65 or earlier. Discrimination against older workers is also clearly rejected by the public. However, there are some mixed messages. Minorities say they would disapprove of workers over the age of 70, and there is a view that decisions about extended working should be in the hands of employers, suggesting that this should not be seen as a right. In the next section we move on to look at individuals' expectations of retirement, and consider whether these correspond with the broadly positive public attitudes towards older workers that we have found.

Table 8.7 Attitudes to men and women working beyond age 70, by country

Country		Views about women working after 70				Views about men working after 70			
		Base	Openly dis-approve	Secretly dis-approve	Total dis-approve	Base	Openly dis-approve	Secretly dis-approve	Total dis-approve
Norway	%	869	3	14	17	871	3	12	16
Denmark	%	710	7	17	24	749	4	12	20
UK	%	*1193*	*13*	*20*	*33*	*1173*	*8*	*15*	*28*
Estonia	%	761	14	25	39	703	9	19	33
Ireland	%	851	16	23	40	881	10	18	34
Finland	%	957	16	29	46	908	13	26	42
Sweden	%	920	15	29	45	957	13	27	42
Portugal	%	1083	23	25	48	1018	17	26	45
Russia	%	1137	21	34	55	1133	14	26	48
Poland	%	835	25	30	55	829	17	28	50
Netherlands	%	901	27	30	57	938	18	27	51
Switzerland	%	909	18	37	56	839	13	35	52
Austria	%	1197	26	31	57	1040	19	27	52
Germany	%	1414	26	34	60	1403	19	32	56
Hungary	%	718	39	21	60	745	29	27	58
Ukraine	%	1001	32	32	64	847	23	29	58
Cyprus	%	486	27	43	70	464	20	33	62
Bulgaria	%	608	37	30	67	650	28	28	62
Belgium	%	860	38	33	71	931	27	29	64
Slovakia	%	847	33	35	69	875	22	36	64
Spain	%	929	38	31	68	896	28	31	64
Slovenia	%	694	36	35	70	737	24	40	67
France	%	991	42	30	72	985	35	31	69

Source: European Social Survey 2006/7

Individuals' expectations of working lives

Expected retirement age

We now turn to consider individuals' own motivations for working longer, and their plans for retirement. Are there signs in individuals' own behaviour and expectations that there is some acceptance of the necessity of extended working and delayed retirement? Table 8.8 confirms that there has been something of a shift in expectations of retirement age, even since 2004. In 2004 20 per cent of male employees and 23 per cent of female workers said they expected to retire from their main job in their 50s. By 2008 these figures had dropped to 14 per cent of men and 15 per cent of women. Conversely, now 10 per cent of men expect to retire in their 70s, roughly double the proportion in 2004 – with the proportion of women expecting to retire in their 70s also showing an increase.

Table 8.8 Retirement expectations, by sex, 2004, 2005 and 2008

	2004		2005		2008	
	Men	Women	Men	Women	Men	Women
Age at which plans to retire from main job	%	%	%	%	%	%
40s	2	2	2	3	2	2
50s	20	23	21	20	14	15
60s	68	65	62	65	67	71
70s	5	3	6	3	10	5
80s	*	*	*	1	1	*
At some other time	2	1	2	2	2	1
Not planning to retire	2	3	5	4	2	3
Base	*726*	*788*	*694*	*788*	*859*	*807*
Average (mean years)	n/a[5]	n/a	62.4	61.5	63.2	62.2
Average (median years)	n/a	n/a	65.0	60.0	65.0	63.0
Base	*n/a*	*n/a*	*537*	*594*	*564*	*687*

Base: all employees
n/a = not asked

We also asked employees for the precise age that they expected to retire from their main job. Men expect to retire, on average, at around 63.2 years and women at 62.2 years. The corresponding figures for 2005 envisaged retirement occurring around 0.8 years earlier than this. Overall, despite the slight upwards shift in the age at which people expect to retire in the last few years, the modal decade for expected retirement remains the 60s, and towards the earlier end of that range. This expected point at which people retire remains (at least on average) several years younger than the current state pension age.

It is worth adding that these figures relate only to those in employment. Those who have already retired early, or those out of the labour market at present for other reasons, are excluded. It is likely that many of this group would have indicated a younger age of retirement answer in to these questions.

The figures for precise retirement age include three per cent of men and eight per cent of women who said that they don't know when they will retire. For the remainder, most employees give an answer of 60 or 65. Over half (54 per cent) of all male employees give age 65 as their answer, and a further 21 per cent say 60, while only five per cent give any of the answers between 61 and 64. Among female employees, 42 per cent say they expect to retire at 65 and 34 per cent say age 60. Few other specific ages attract more than small numbers of respondents. Of course, it's likely that the reason these ages are popular is because 60 and 65 are the current state pension ages for women and men. If state pension ages drive retirement expectations, then we would expect that as these ages increase in future years, they may be less sharply associated with retirement expectations.

One way of testing this expectation is to examine whether younger people are more likely than their older counterparts to expect to work later in life, in line with changes in their state pension ages. Of course, it is harder for younger people to be aware of their likely incomes and resources, which might also affect the results. As we show in Table 8.9, younger people are more likely to state an expected retirement age of 65 or more than other age groups.

Table 8.9 Retirement expectations, by sex and age

	18–34	35–44	45–54	55+	All
Men					
Mean (years)	63.6	62.5	62.5	64.8	63.2
% saying 65+	69	56	56	76	64
Base	*109*	*183*	*167*	*109*	*564*
Women					
Mean (years)	62.7	61.6	61.8	63.2	62.3
% saying 65+	51	47	42	44	47
Base	*176*	*194*	*195*	*124*	*687*

Base: all employees

More specifically, those aged from 18 to 34 generally expect to retire about a year later than those aged 35 to 54 (the figures for the 55+ are biased because they are based on employees and hence exclude those who have already retired early). This may indicate that some kind of message about longer working lives is being received. Even so, an additional year across this age group is still insufficient compared with policy change that aims at raising state pension ages by one year for every decade.

Factors affecting retirement expectations

Many different things may affect a person's expectations about their retirement – including how much they enjoy their job, perceptions about 'normal' behaviour, caring responsibilities, poor health prospects, employer's policies and so on (Clery *et al.*, 2007). Here we report on a range of factors, but focus on two key elements: finances and health.

We directly asked employees about the reasons for their retirement expectations. Those who say that they expect to retire before the age of 65, effectively early, or at age 65 were asked to name the main reason why. As we show in Table 8.10 the main reason, given by 36 per cent of respondents, is simply because that is when they want to retire. However, responses that relate to retirement income seem lower because they are split across three separate codes: 17 per cent mention the availability of non-state pensions at their expected retirement age, 10 per cent the availability of state pensions and 15 per cent that this is when they can afford to – which may be reflecting the availability of pension income, either state or private. If these three categories are combined, then financial reasons become the most commonly mentioned explanation for expecting to retire early or at age 65, given by 43 per cent of respondents. This is clear for men, but for women the motivations of 'finance' and 'wanting to retire' were stated by similar proportions, 39 per cent the former and 38 per cent the latter.

Table 8.10 Main reason for expecting to retire early or at 65, by sex

	Men	Women	All
Main reason for retiring at, or before, 65	%	%	%
Financial reasons (any mention)	46	39	43
Of which ...			
... because you can receive occupational or personal pension	*20*	*14*	*17*
... because you can afford to	*16*	*15*	*15*
... because you can receive state benefits	*9*	*11*	*10*
Because you want to	34	38	36
Because you don't expect your employer will allow you to work beyond this age	11	9	10
To retire at same time as partner	3	8	5
Base	*557*	*712*	*1269*

Base: all employees who expect to retire at, or before, age 65

Two reasons given far less commonly are the expectation that their employer would not permit them to continue to work (10 per cent), and retiring at the same time as their partner – five per cent overall, but the figure is rather higher for women, at eight per cent. Until 2010, women have a state pension age five years before that of men, and this may suit couples where (as was the norm) the woman was younger than the man. When women's state pension age rises to 65, this would put such women in the position of having to choose between continuing to work, when their partner has retired, or retiring before a state pension would be available (to retire at the same time as their partner).

The self-reported emphasis on finances influencing retirement decisions observed in responses to the previous question is also supported by our analysis. There is something of a link between social class and expected date of retirement for men, but not for women (see Table 8.11). The expected retirement age of women is fairly constant across different classes. However, among men the higher the social class the earlier the expected retirement. In more middle-class occupations men are expecting to retire between 62 and 63, rising to 64 for those in supervisory occupations, and to 65 for those undertaking work in more routine occupations. Other research has also confirmed this link between finances and retirement decisions; for example, Clery *et al.*(2007) found that current income levels related to decisions to retire, with high earners more likely to expect to retire early (see also Phillips and Hancock, 2005).

Table 8.11 Average age at which men and women expect to retire from main job, by social class

	Managerial and professional	Intermediate occupations	Lower supervisory and technical	Semi-routine and routine	All
Men	62.6	62.2	63.7	64.5	63.2
Base	263	47	118	135	564
Women	61.9	62.7	62.1	62.4	62.2
Base	325	128	51	180	687
All	62.3	62.5	63.3	63.4	62.8
Base	588	175	169	315	1251

Base: all employees who provided precise age at which they expected to retire from main job

These differences to some extent belie variations in longevity. Higher social classes expect to retire earlier than average, but live longer on average. Of course, they are also likely to have acquired greater pension provision. If accurate, then these figures would mean a much longer time spent in retirement for those in higher social classes. In fact, the evidence tends to support the view that those from more manual backgrounds tend to leave the labour market rather earlier than average, typically as a result of health problems. Many of those in middle-class occupations with generous pension provision also leave the labour market relatively early – leaving the latest retirement ages to those who are not rich enough to retire, but still healthy enough to work and add to retirement provision, and includes a higher than average proportion of the self-employed (Smeaton and McKay, 2003).

Although our question didn't give people the option to say that the reason they expected to retire early or at age 65 was ill health, this is the reason that many people leave the labour market early. When people leave for ill health, their prospects of returning to work are much reduced. Ill health may also negatively affect incomes in retirement (Bardasi and Jenkins, 2002). We asked employees a hypothetical question that attempted to measure orientation concerning higher income in retirement, or better health for at least some of that time, specifically:

> *Imagine that you thought you would have poor health when you reached retirement. Which of these statements comes closest to your view?*
>
> *I would want to retire early to have a period of retirement in good health, even if this meant a smaller pension,*
> *OR*
> *I would want to continue working until state pension age to ensure I was better off, even if this meant I would have poor health for my retirement*

Employees are in little doubt that they want part of their retirement to be spent in reasonable health, even if this means a lower income in retirement. Some 85 per cent say they would stop early if facing poor health, to improve the quality of their retirement, if not their level of income. Only 13 per cent propose continuing to work in order to increase the value of their pension income.

In Table 8.12 we break down these results by the expected main source of income in retirement.

Table 8.12 Views about ill health and retirement, by expected main source of retirement income

Preference if had poor health approaching retirement	State pension	Company pension	Personal pension	Other savings	All
	%	%	%	%	%
Period of retirement in good health, even with smaller pension	79	89	88	89	85
Keep working, higher pension, poor health in retirement	21	11	12	11	13
Base	*399*	*664*	*173*	*205*	*1496*

Base: all female employees aged 60 or less and male employees aged 65 or less

The group most likely to suggest working longer, despite ill health, is those expecting to rely mostly on a state pension (and therefore the group with a relatively low retirement income), though, even then, only 21 per cent suggest this. Where the main source of income is a non-state pension, close to nine people in ten say they would want some of their retirement to be in good health, even at the expense of a lower pension. These responses seem to embody the idea of having a 'right' to some kind of active retirement, permitting people to continue non-work activities.

Working beyond 65

We have seen that most people *expect* to cease work at or before the age of 65. How many might actually want to work longer than this – or be encouraged to do so with different working arrangements? And what do employees know of their employers' policies on working beyond this age?

Relatively few employees (seven per cent) gave an expected retirement age that is later than 65 (representing 110 men and 86 women in the dataset). For those that did, we asked for their "main reason" for expecting to retire at this age, and the two most common reasons given are because they can't afford to stop earning money (41 per cent) and because they enjoy working (40 per cent).[6] Again, finances are a primary consideration when we attempt to explain retirement expectations. Interestingly, nine per cent said they didn't know what else to do – the third most common reason cited.

The government is focusing on flexible working arrangements to encourage extended working lives, as this has been shown as a key factor in helping older people stay in work (Department for Work and Pensions, 2006: 150). We didn't ask those respondents who *expected* to retire 'late' whether this was a factor for them. However, expectations may be different to what people want to do, so we asked employees whether they *wanted* to work past 65, and whether this decision might be different if they were able to work flexibly. Specifically we asked to what extent they agreed or disagreed that:

> I would want to work past age 65

> I would want to work past age 65 if I could work flexibly. This could involve working fewer hours, shorter weeks or just part of the year

The first column in Table 8.13 shows that many people do not want to continue working after the age of 65. A third (32 per cent) of employees want to work longer. About half do not want to work beyond age 65, with the remainder (15 per cent) uncertain.

The prospect of being able to work more flexibly increased interest in a longer working life beyond the age of 65 (which only a minority reach at present). With the promise of more flexibility, just over 60 per cent of employees say they would like to work past 65. This is a marked increase in comparison to the question that did not mention flexible working, and if it were translated into labour market behaviour, it would represent a remarkable change in working patterns. It should be borne in mind that the extent of flexible working depicted in this question might not tally with the arrangements that would be available to individual employees in practice; previous research has suggested that older workers desire a level of flexibility in working arrangements that employers, in practice, would not, realistically, be in a position to offer (Vickerstaff *et al.*, 2008). However, we should note that even with the promise of flexible working, three in ten are still sure they do not want to carry on working. There remains a strong attachment, among certain individuals, to ceasing work at age 65 – if not before.

Table 8.13 Views about working beyond age 65

	Would want to work past age 65	Would want to work past 65 if could work flexibly (e.g. shorter hours, part-year)
	%	%
Agree strongly	7	13
Agree	25	48
Neither agree nor disagree	15	11
Disagree	32	18
Disagree strongly	20	10
Base	*1559*	*1559*

Base: all employees

We now explore the groups who agree (or strongly agree) that they would want to work past age 65, and also those who said they would if they could work flexibly. In doing so, we are interested in discovering whether the expressed desire to work later in life is associated with particular characteristics. In Table 8.14 we illustrate the composition of each of these groups, compared to employees as a whole. The most notable difference between the composition of the different groups relates to age, with younger age groups forming a much smaller proportion of the group who would like to work beyond age 65, compared to employees as a whole. Specifically, 11 per cent of those who would like to work beyond 65 are aged under 35 years, compared to 31 per cent of employees in general. Conversely, older employees (those aged 55 or over) are over-represented in the group wanting to extend their working lives (35 per cent, compared to 16 per cent of all employees). However, we cannot necessarily take this to mean that younger employees are more opposed than their older counterparts to the notion of extended working. It may simply reflect the fact that, for this group, retirement is a long way off, and therefore they have not considered their plans in any detail (if at all). However, there are two reasons that this explanation is not particularly persuasive: first, the proportions of different age groups who "neither agree nor disagree" (or "don't know") do not vary significantly, undermining the notion that young people have simply thought less about this stage of their life; second, age differences are far less marked for the question about working flexibly after the age of 65, which is a similar issue. A more convincing argument could be made for the fact that the notion of extended working might not become an attractive one until an employee realises its potential effect on the quality of life that can be enjoyed in retirement, with this realisation occurring as individuals move closer towards retirement age.

Table 8.14 Characteristics of those who would want to work past age 65

	Would want to work past age 65	Would want to work past 65 if could work flexibly	All employees
Sex	%	%	%
Men	56	53	51
Women	44	47	49
Age	%	%	%
18–24	2	13	11
25–34	9	18	24
35–44	30	27	25
45–54	22	24	23
55+	35	17	16
Work status	%	%	%
Full-time	75	79	79
Part-time	25	21	21
Expected main source of retirement income	%	%	%
State pension	31	27	25
Occupational pension	31	38	41
Personal pension	12	13	12
Other savings	15	15	15
Social class	%	%	%
Professional occupations	5	7	6
Managerial and technical occupations	31	31	32
Skilled occupations (non-manual)	25	26	26
Skilled occupations (manual)	21	20	19
Partly skilled occupations	14	13	13
Unskilled occupations	4	3	4
Base	*499*	*927*	*1559*

Base: all employees

Erratum: Chapter 7 p.154

The correct data for Figure 7.1 are given in the table below.

Table A.1 Disapproval if person has full-time job and children under three in 11 countries, by sex of transgressor, 2006/7

	Asked about men		Asked about women	
	%	Base	%	Base
United Kingdom	3	1213	38	1181
France	8	1001	32	985
Germany	8	1469	45	1447
Netherlands	9	928	51	961
Denmark	2	771	15	734
Sweden	11	947	20	899
Spain	9	959	23	917
Portugal	8	1144	17	1078
Cyprus	4	507	14	488
Poland	5	863	28	858
Slovakia	9	867	44	899

Source: European Social Survey 2006/7

With the exception of age, there were only marginal differences, if any, between employees as a whole and those who might work longer, in general and if allowed to work flexibly. The group who wanted to work past 65, compared to all employees, were slightly more likely to be men (56 per cent, compared to 51 per cent of all employees) and less likely to be expecting an occupational pension to be their main income source in retirement (31 per cent, compared with 41 per cent of all employees). However, the overriding finding is that, apart from age, the composition of the groups who might work longer is virtually identical to that for employees as a whole.

Working past 65 depends on the willingness of employers to permit such arrangements. Workers may ask to work longer, but employers may still enforce retirement at 65. One in ten of those expecting to retire at 65 (or earlier) say the main reason is the perceived reluctance of their employer to permit working any later than this. In practice, however, many employees are unsure if their employer would allow this (25 per cent of men, 28 per cent of women). Perhaps unsurprisingly, younger workers were the least likely to know this information: as many as 48 per cent of employees aged 18–24 and 28 per cent of those aged 25–34 did not know whether their employer allowed working after the age of 65. Of course, employees in these age groups are a long way from retirement, and therefore are less likely to have sought out this information, or otherwise engaged with their employer's retirement policies. For those that do know, the proportion saying their employer permits work after 65 is twice that of those who say their employer does not (49 per cent and 24 per cent respectively). This is an area where information and knowledge for employees could be improved – and it might help the government achieve its targets of increasing the number of older workers.

We have already highlighted the additional likelihood that people would want to work after 65 if they had greater flexibility in their working arrangements. It is therefore logical to also ask whether employees believe that their employer would currently allow people to work flexibly beyond age 65 if they wanted to (this question was only asked of those who said their employer allowed working beyond age 65). Three-quarters (74 per cent) of those employees who say their employer allows working beyond age 65 also think that their employer would permit them to work flexibly at this age. The figure for employees as a whole is much lower: around half (48 per cent) think that their employers would allow both extended working beyond 65 and that this work could be undertaken with flexible working patterns. This finding is about perceptions of employer policies, rather than an objective measure of the availability of flexible working, but if the public is to change its own expectations about extended working, their perception of what is possible is a crucial factor. It may be that changing employer policies on flexible working after the age of 65 – or employee perceptions of them – could help to shift retirement expectations.

Earlier we found a broadly positive picture of attitudes towards older people remaining in the labour market, and being seen as important as younger workers. Yet individuals' expectations suggest that most do not want or expect to work until state pension age, let alone beyond it. One area which offers more promise for changes in future is flexible working; a majority of employees say they would want to work beyond age 65 if they could work flexibly.

Conclusions

The rise in life expectancy in the UK, an ageing population, and the related problems of funding increasingly long periods of retirement (through the state pension and/or private pension provision) have been partly addressed by government policy to increase state pension ages in future years. Tied to this is a government focus on encouraging extended working lives, both to increase the amount of time during which pension provision can be built up, and to reduce the length of retirement during which state or private pensions are paid out. This chapter has focused on whether these demographic and policy changes and developments are reflected in public attitudes, and in people's own expectations.

Certainly, it seems that attitudes towards older people and later working have shifted. People are now more accepting of the principle of later retirement, and believe that older workers are an important part of the workforce: they no longer support the idea of forcing people to retire early to make way for younger people. Going hand in hand with these changes we have also noted that the idea that age discrimination is in any way socially acceptable is much less prominent in Britain now than it was in the 1980s, and is also rather less common in the UK than in most European countries. People seem to believe that workers should be allowed to carry on if they want to and, crucially, if their employer also wants them to continue working. Respondents are, however, sceptical that older people are, in practice, offered equal opportunities compared to younger workers, though we have found that perceptions have improved in the last few years, no doubt due to the introduction of age discrimination legislation.

However, this general enthusiasm for older workers and the concept of longer working is not shared by many people when it comes to their own circumstances and expectations for retirement. The idea of retiring at or before 65 is strongly ingrained, and few want to work longer. Indeed, more than half of male employees expect to retire at age 65.

These findings on retirement expectations in part reflect different factors which may be seen as either incentives or barriers to extended working. A notable barrier is ill health – those facing a retirement in poor health suggest an early exit from the labour market as preferable to working longer, despite the negative consequences this would have for their lifetime income. Financial considerations are also important – either as barriers to extended working for some (it is those groups with higher incomes that expect to retire earlier), or as incentives for others (not being able to afford to retire is the most common reason given for expecting to work beyond age 65).

The incentive which, perhaps, offers most promise for retirement ages changing in future is the option of flexible working, which attracts considerably more people to the idea of later retirement, though a substantial minority will not be tempted, even with such an inducement. It is notable that many do not know their employer's policies on working beyond age 65, a majority feel it is up to employers to decide whether staff should be allowed to work beyond age 65, and only around half of employees think their employer would permit flexible working at this age. It seems that this is an area where increasing information and changing attitudes in the workplace could help to pave the way for an increase in some older workers' labour market participation.

Notes

1. In 1983 the categories 'agree' and 'disagree' were defined as 'just agree' and 'just disagree'. In addition, the answer categories were presented to respondents in the reverse order to that shown here. It is possible that the two different presentations of answer options may have impacted upon the responses obtained.
2. In 1983 the categories 'agree' and 'disagree' were defined as 'just agree' and 'just disagree'. In addition, the response options were also presented to respondents in the reverse order to that shown here. These differences are likely to have impacted upon the responses provided.
3. Separate analysis was not possible for employees aged 65 years and over, due to the small numbers in this group.
4. On a methodological note, these questions were asked in a 'split ballot' with half of respondents answering about men and half about women. So, while it is possible to compare within-country results in total, it is not possible to compare individuals' answers about men and women.
5. In 2004, unlike in 2005 and 2008, there was no follow-up question asking for the precise age of expected retirement, so we cannot calculate an average figure for this year.
6. These were the first two codes on the showcard (though they appeared in reverse order). The other answer options available were: "because your employer will allow you to work beyond 65"; "because you are not sure what else to do"; and "some other reason".

References

Bardasi, E. and Jenkins, S. (2002), *Income in later life: Work history matters,* Bristol: The Policy Press

Beveridge, W. (1942), *Social insurance and allied services,* White Paper Cmd 6404, London: The Stationery Office

Clery, E., McKay, S., Phillips, M. and Robinson, C. (2007), *Attitudes to pensions: the 2006 survey* DWP Research Report 434, Leeds: Corporate Document Services

Department for Work and Pensions (2005) *Security in retirement: towards a new pensions system,* White Paper Cm 6841, London: The Stationery Office, available at http://www.dwp.gov.uk/policy/pensions-reform/security-in-retirement/

Fevre, R., Nichols, T., Prior, G. and Rutherford, I. (2009), *Fair Treatment at Work Report: Findings from the 2008 survey,* Employment Relations Research Series No. 103, Department for Business, Innovation and Skills, available at http://www.berr.gov.uk/files/file52809.pdf

Humphrey, A., Costigan, P., Pickering, K., Stratford, N. and Barnes, M. (2003), *Factors affecting the labour market participation of older workers,* DWP Research Report 200, Leeds: Corporate Document Services

Laslett, P. (1996) *A fresh map of life: the emergence of the third age,* 2nd edition, Basingstoke: Macmillan

Macnicol, J. (2006), *Age Discrimination: An historical and contemporary analysis,* Cambridge: Cambridge University Press

O'Connell, A. (2002), *Raising State Pension Age: Are We Ready?,* London: Pensions Policy Institute

ONS (2008), 'Life expectancy at birth is longest in the South of England', *News Release,* 30 October

Pensions Commission (2004), *Pensions: Challenges and Choices. The First Report of the Pensions Commission,* London: The Stationery Office

Phillips, M. and Hancock, R. (2005), 'Planning for retirement: realism or denial?', in Park, A, Curtice, J., Thomson, K., Bromley, C., Phillips, M. and Johnson, M. (eds.) *British Social Attitudes: the 22nd Report – Two terms of New Labour: the public's reaction,* London: Sage

Phillipson, C. and Smith, A. (2005), *Extending working life: A review of the research literature, DWP Research Report 2009,* Leeds: Corporate Document Services

Smeaton, D. and McKay, S. (2003), *Working after State Pension Age: Quantitative Analysis,* DWP Research Report 182, Leeds: Corporate Document Services

Taylor-Gooby, P. and Martin, R. (2007), 'Trends in sympathy for the poor' in Park, A., Curtice, J., Thomson, K., Phillips, M., Johnson, M. and Clery, E. (eds.), *British Social Attitudes: the 24th Report,* London: Sage

Vickerstaff, S., Loretto, W., Billings, J., Brown, P., Mitton, L., Parkin, T. and White, P. (2008), *Encouraging labour market activity among 60–64 year-olds,* DWP Research Report, Leeds: Corporate Document Services

Walker, A. (1986), 'Pensions and the production of poverty in old age', in Philipson, C. and Walker, A. (ed.), *Ageing and Social Policy,* Aldershot: Gower

Acknowledgements

The *National Centre for Social Research* is grateful to the Department for Work and Pensions and the Department for Business, Enterprise and Regulatory Reform (now the Department for Business, Innovation and Skills) for their financial support which enabled us to ask some of the questions in this chapter. The views expressed are those of the author alone.

The European Social Survey is funded jointly by the European Commission, the European Science Foundation and academic funding bodies in each participating country.

Appendix

The data for Figures 8.1 to 8.5 are shown below.

Table A.1 Life expectancy at birth (actual: 1901–2006, projected: 2007–2021), by sex

	Male	Female
	Years	Years
2007	76.8	81.0
2008	76.9	81.2
2009	77.1	81.3
2010	77.3	81.4
2011	77.4	81.6
2012	77.6	81.7
2013	77.7	81.9
2014	77.8	82.0
2015	78.0	82.1
2016	78.1	82.3
2017	78.2	82.4
2018	78.3	82.5
2019	78.4	82.6
2021	78.5	82.7
2021	78.6	82.9

Source: Government Actuary's Department, 2001 projections

Table A.2 Actual and projected additional years of life expectancy at 60 and 80, by sex, 1911–1921

	Male		Female	
	At 60 years	**At 80 years**	**At 60 years**	**At 80 years**
	Years	Years	Years	Years
1911	13.7	4.9	15.3	5.6
1931	14.5	4.8	16.4	5.6
1951	14.8	5.0	17.8	5.9
1971	15.3	5.5	19.8	6.9
1991	17.7	6.4	21.9	8.4
1997	18.8	6.7	22.6	8.5
2011	21.0	7.7	24.1	9.1
2021	22.0	8.3	25.1	9.9

Source: ONS, Social Trends 30, 2000

Table A.3 Proportion selecting retirement pension as first or second priority for extra spending on social benefits, 1983–2007

% selecting pension …	… as first priority	… as first or second priority	Base
Year			
1983	41	64	1719
1984	43	66	1645
1985	41	64	1769
1986	40	65	3066
1987	47	68	2766
1989	43	67	2930
1990	42	65	2797
1991	41	63	2918
1993	42	63	2945
1994	41	64	1167
1995	46	68	1234
1996	50	71	3620
2000	52	74	3426
2001	54	76	3287
2003	59	78	3272
2005	61	80	3193
2007	56	78	3094

Table A.4 Views on main responsibility for an adequate standard of living in retirement

Responsibility for providing an adequate standard of living	% respondents
0 mainly the responsibility of the individual	3
1	2
2	4
3	6
4	7
5	27
6	9
7	12
8	11
9	6
10 mainly the responsibility of the government	13
Base	2373

Source: European Social Survey 2006/7

Table A.5 Views on main responsibility for an adequate standard of living in retirement, by country

Country	Responsibility for providing an adequate standard of living (0 = mainly the individual; 10 = mainly the government)	Base
	Mean	
Bulgaria	7.70	*1367*
Hungary	7.21	*1488*
Ukraine	7.20	*1971*
Russia	7.16	*2392*
Estonia	7.12	*1478*
Portugal	6.88	*2145*
Finland	6.86	*1885*
Cyprus	6.82	*952*
Slovakia	6.76	*1735*
Norway	6.68	*1745*
Spain	6.62	*1843*
Slovenia	6.47	*1448*
Belgium	6.46	*1793*
Poland	6.38	*1697*
France	6.36	*1979*
Sweden	6.26	*1904*
Ireland	6.15	*1717*
UK	6.01	*2373*
Netherlands	5.78	*1874*
Germany	5.42	*2886*
Austria	5.40	*2349*
Denmark	5.24	*1474*
Switzerland	4.94	*1787*
All	6.47	

Source: European Social Survey 2006/7

9 Lone parents and benefits: an obligation to look for work?

*Matt Barnes and Wojtek Tomaszewski**

Until recently lone parents have been able to claim Income Support solely on the basis of being a lone parent. In November 2008 the government introduced a new policy that requires lone parents to look for work if their youngest child is aged 12 or over. The age threshold for the youngest child drops to 10 years or over from October 2009, and seven years or over from October 2010. This new obligation for lone parents means that they will be required to take up support to look for work as a condition of their benefit receipt, an approach known as 'conditionality'.

This obligation for lone parents to look for work raises complex issues. For those with a traditional outlook on life, there is likely to be tension between, on the one hand, support for 'family values' which may suggest that women should stay at home and look after children and, on the other, a desire to cut benefits and hence public expenditure. When the former argument wins out, we would expect outright opposition to conditionality and support for maintained or higher benefits. Where the latter argument wins out, we would expect support for serious consequences for those who refuse to look for work, such as the withdrawal of benefits.

For those with a more left-wing outlook there may be a different tension: on the one hand, they would tend to support the welfare state; on the other hand, they may believe that work is the only realistic pathway out of poverty. The former argument would lead to support for higher, or at least maintained, benefits for lone parents and opposition to all forms of conditionality. The latter would lead to support for 'carrots' to encourage lone parents to take up work, but may also translate into support for 'sticks' that *force* lone parents to do so, at least if these are limited in nature and combined with 'carrots', that is, support for a limited amount of conditionality.

In this chapter we use *British Social Attitudes* survey data to try to tease out some of these complex patterns and to discuss to what extent current opinion is in line with public policy on lone parents. We supplement this discussion of the

---

* Matt Barnes is a Research Director (Analyst) and Wojtek Tomaszewski is a Senior Researcher (Analyst), both at the *National Centre for Social Research*.

public's views on lone parents by looking at how lone parents themselves view their own work prospects, using data from the Families and Children Study.

Lone parents, the labour market and the welfare system

Since 1997 the government has pursued an active programme of reform of the welfare system and labour market policy, much of which has been aimed at families with children. Many of these reforms have affected lone parents, partly because high numbers claim welfare benefits. This may arise either because they do not to work or because they need extra subsidy to top up low wages when in work – lone parents tend to be relatively under-skilled and work part-time hours. In addition, key government policy goals have been to raise employment rates, particularly for disadvantaged groups, and to eliminate child poverty. These two policy goals are closely linked with the aim to increase lone parent employment to 70 per cent by 2010, seen as a key tactic in attempts to 'end child poverty' (Harker, 2006).

Lone parents have also been directly affected by attempts to increase the financial incentive to work by 'making work pay'. This has seen the introduction of a national minimum wage, reductions in tax and national insurance contributions for lower-paid workers, and the introduction of a new system of income transfers to working people, in the form of tax credits, including a childcare element. Lone parents, along with other workers, have also benefited from policies related to flexible working, improved maternity and paternity rights, and greater rights for part-time workers. The National Childcare Strategy seeks to ensure the provision of good-quality affordable childcare (Daycare Trust, 2007).

In addition, there have been various policy interventions aimed specifically at increasing lone parents' participation in the labour market by helping them make the transition into work. The New Deal for Lone Parents was one of the New Deal programmes aimed at helping benefit claimants into work. Jobcentre Plus, which now integrates benefit claims and employment services, continues to offer a range of help to prepare lone parents for employment and ease their transition into work. The Employment Retention and Advancement Demonstration project specifically focuses on issues of employment retention and sustainability, offering two years of work-related services (one-to-one support from a dedicated adviser) combined with financial incentives for participants who work full-time (retention bonus) and for those who complete training while in work (training bonus).

The impact of these policy changes on lone parent employment has been well documented (Millar and Ridge, 2001). The positive effect has no doubt been enhanced by them coinciding with a period of low unemployment generally. The labour market participation of lone parents increased from 45 to 57 per cent between 1997 and 2008 – an increase of 12 percentage points. This should be seen in the context of an increase from 68 to 71 per cent for married and cohabiting mothers over the same period (Kent, 2009). Lone parents have thus been making progress in the labour market, although they are still some way behind the 2010 target employment rate of 70 per cent.

Despite the improvement in the lone parent employment rate, it remains low in relation to other OECD countries. Consequently many lone parents rely on Income Support as their main source of income. This, along with the fact that many lone parents in work suffer from low wages, helps to explain why over one third (36 per cent) of children in lone parent families are still living below the official child poverty line (60 per cent of median income, before housing costs) (Department for Work and Pensions, 2009).

The government decided that, with the right support package, it would be appropriate to increase the responsibility for lone parents with older children to look for work – a move intended to tackle both worklessness and child poverty. Given the substantial increase in childcare availability since 1997, the government proposed that, from November 2008, lone parents with older children would no longer be entitled to Income Support solely on the grounds of being a lone parent. Instead, these lone parents, as long as they are able to work, should apply for Jobseeker's Allowance, be supported to look for work and, as a condition of benefit receipt, should be obliged to take up that support (Department for Work and Pensions, 2008). Lone parents thus have to be actively seeking work in order to claim benefits.

To help lone parents make the transition from Income Support to Jobseeker's Allowance, a stepped approach is being introduced. From November 2008, lone parents have to be actively seeking work to claim benefits once their youngest child is 12 and over, falling to 10 and over from October 2009, and seven and over from October 2010. The threshold is being placed at the youngest child aged seven or over because by this age, it is believed that a family will have established a routine with the child going to school and therefore a parent returning to work will cause minimal disruption. Furthermore, by the time the final change is implemented in October 2010, schools in England should all be able to offer childcare to all children between 8 a.m. and 6 p.m. throughout the year.

The new obligations exempt lone parents who cannot work because of caring obligations (for example, for their disabled children), health conditions or disability. These lone parents will continue to be able to claim Income Support or another appropriate benefit. Lone parents with younger children will also continue to be able to claim Income Support and have access to the New Deal for Lone Parents.

Much has been made of the UK aligning benefit sanctions for lone parents with what happens in other European countries, which have much higher employment rates for lone parents than the UK. However, it is important not to forget the other factors that come into play here, such as lone parents in the UK tending to be younger and less qualified than their EU counterparts – as well as the different, arguably more focused, labour market policies of these other countries.

The success of the government's policies will depend in part on developments in the labour market – whether there are any jobs for lone parents. But it will also depend on the attitudes of the general public to the approach and the views and behaviour of lone parents themselves. It is these attitudes that we shall examine in this chapter.[1]

Public attitudes to welfare spending on lone parents

Levels of expenditure

Given that lone parents are one of the groups for which the government has particularly been trying to reduce the incidence of welfare expenditure, we start by comparing attitudes towards welfare spending on single parents with attitudes towards spending on other groups. The *British Social Attitudes* survey has from time to time asked:

> *Thinking now only of the government's spending on social benefits. Which, if any, of these would be your highest priority for extra spending?*

Table 9.1 shows that benefit spending on lone parents has consistently been seen by the public as a low priority. In 2007, only about one in twenty people thought that spending for lone parents should be given priority over spending on other groups, and this had not changed over the last decade. Even less of a priority was spending on benefits for unemployed people – a group many lone parents will now also find themselves classified as.

Table 9.1 Public priorities for government spending, 2000–2007

	2000	2001	2003	2005	2007
Highest priority for extra government spending	%	%	%	%	%
Retirement pensions	52	54	59	62	58
Benefits for disabled people	21	19	16	14	18
Child benefits	14	15	15	15	15
Benefits for single parents	7	7	5	6	6
Benefits for the unemployed	4	4	3	2	2
Base	3426	3287	4432	3193	3094

However, a low priority level for extra spending does not necessarily mean that the public wants cuts in spending on lone parents. Respondents were also asked this more specific question:

Some people think that there should be more government spending on social security, while other people disagree. Please say whether you would like to see more or less government spending on single parents than now. Bear in mind that if you want more spending, this would probably mean that you would have to pay more taxes. If you want less spending, this would probably mean paying less taxes

Table 9.2 shows that over a third of respondents think that more should be spent on lone parents, while a further two in five think the levels are about right. Moreover, these figures have remained fairly stable over the last decade.

Table 9.2 Attitudes to government spending on single parents, 1998–2008

	1998	1999	2002	2004	2006	2008
What should happen to government spending on single parents	%	%	%	%	%	%
Spend much more	5	4	6	4	5	5
Spend more	29	29	33	30	32	31
Stay the same	41	41	39	43	40	43
Spend less	18	19	14	15	16	15
Spend much less	4	4	3	3	3	2
Base	*3146*	*3143*	*3435*	*3199*	*3240*	*3358*

The popular press may malign lone parents as benefit scroungers, but this is not, in fact, reflected in the public's view, as demonstrated when we ask the following question[2]:

Think of an unemployed single mother with a young child. Their only income comes from state benefits. Would you say that they ...
   ... have more than enough to live on,
   have enough to live on,
   are hard up,
   or, are really poor?

This was supplemented by the following question with the same answer options[3]:

Now thinking again about that unemployed single mother with a young child. After rent, their income is £130 a week

As Table 9.3 shows, very few respondents think that single mums on benefits have "more than enough to live on", on either wording of the question.

ble 9.3 Standard of living of single mum on state benefits, 2000, 2004 and 2008

	2000	2004	2008
"State benefits"	%	%	%
Really poor	17	7	6
Hard up	51	44	45
Enough to live on	23	36	34
More than enough to live on	2	3	5
Amount in £s	%	%	%
Really poor	10	5	7
Hard up	43	38	44
Enough to live on	41	48	40
More than enough to live on	4	8	7
Base	*3426*	*3199*	*3358*

What is at issue is whether they have "enough to live on", are "hard up" or "really poor". When asked about "state benefits", without quoting the amount, around half of respondents think single mums have less than enough to live on. Although the proportion who think they are hard up or poor has declined since 2000, this may be mainly because of more knowledge about actual benefit levels – the gap between the answers to the "state benefit" question and the question quoting actual amounts has declined substantially between 2000 and 2008.

Lone parents may not be a priority for extra spending in the public's mind, but that does not mean the public wants to see benefits cut. At least half the population think that single mothers living on benefits are hard up or poor and four out of five want to maintain or increase spending. However, support for adequate benefits for those who have no alternative is not necessarily the same as opposition to 'conditionality' – the public may well think that it is in many lone parents' own best interests to be encouraged or forced to find work. That is the issue to which we now turn.

Conditions for benefit receipt

As already discussed, before November 2008, lone parents were not required to look for work in order to receive welfare benefits. The change in policy to make benefit receipt conditional on looking for work had been under discussion for some time before that. This shift in policy needs to be seen against change in the general background of attitudes to working women (see Crompton *et al.*, 2003 for a discussion of this in a previous *British Social Attitudes* report).

As can be seen in Table 9.4, there is a long-running trend towards greater acceptance of working women in general, and working mothers in particular. It has long been the view of the great majority that women need not stay at home once the youngest child is at school, and this is now near universal. Fifteen years ago, a majority used to believe that a woman should stay at home when the youngest child was under school age, but this has changed rapidly and is now a minority view (see also the chapter by Harrison and Fitzgerald in this report).

Table 9.4 Attitudes to working women, 1989–2006

% who agree that …	1989	1994	2002	2006
… a man's job is to earn money; a woman's job is to look after the home and family	28	24	17	16
% who think that women should stay at home …				
… when there is a child under school age	64	55	48	40
… after the youngest child starts school	11	8	5	3
Base	*1307*	*984*	*1960*	*1845*

However, there is a difference between thinking that mothers with young children may work if they choose and supporting conditionality, which involves an element of compulsion. Moreover, lone parents are a group for whom juggling work and childcare is particularly difficult and this may also affect people's views. We need to examine survey questions that have tapped this directly. The new conditionality conditions have been alluded to in the following question asked on a number of occasions on *British Social Attitudes* since 2000:

> *Suppose a lone parent on benefits was asked to visit the job centre every year or so to talk about ways in which they might find work. Which of the statements on this card comes closest to what you think should happen to their benefits if they did not go?*[4]
>> *Their benefits should not be affected*
>> *Their benefits should be reduced a little*
>> *Their benefits should be reduced a lot*
>> *Their benefits should be stopped*

As shown in Table 9.5, there is considerable support for conditionality, at least in a limited form. In 2007 only around one in six people thought there should be no cut in benefits for those who refuse the interview at the job centre. On the other hand, there is hardly unanimous support for hard line conditionality either. True, around a quarter thought benefits should be stopped, rising to two out five if we include those who thought benefits should be cut "a lot", and there is some sign that these views are gaining ground. Nevertheless, the largest group were

still those who thought benefits should be cut "a little", a position which seems
to indicate support for a limited 'stick' to encourage lone parents to find work.

**Table 9.5 What should happen to the benefits of lone parents who fail to attend an
interview at the job centre, 2000–2007**

	2000	2001	2002	2003[5]	2007
What should happen to lone parents' benefits	%	%	%	%	%
Not affected	22	17	16	15	17
Reduced a little	45	43	44	45	40
Reduced a lot	12	12	15	13	14
Stopped	18	23	21	24	25
Base	*3426*	*3287*	*2271*	*3272*	*3094*

How old should their youngest child be when lone parents are required to look for work?

As we have seen, conditionality has first been introduced for lone parents with
children aged 12 or over, but the intention is that this should be extended to
younger children over the next few years. Even if the public supports some
conditionality, there could be a mismatch between government policies and
public opinion on the age at which this is enforced.

A pair of questions that have been asked repeatedly on the *British Social
Attitudes* survey over the last decade deal with both the general issue of duty to
work *versus* duty to look after one's child and the age at which working
becomes appropriate. The first question asks:

> *Thinking about a single mother with a child under school age. Which
> one of these statements comes closest to your view?*
>
> > *She has a special duty to go out to work to support her child*
> > *She has a special duty to stay at home to look after her child*
> > *She should do as she chooses, like everyone else*

The question is then repeated for "a single mother with a child of school age".

As seen in Table 9.6, public views on the duty of lone mothers depend heavily
on the age of the children. Whereas, in 2007, only around one in six thought that
a lone mother with a pre-school child had a duty to go out to work, this rose to
over half for those with a school-age child. Conversely, whereas over a third
thought that a lone mother with a pre-school child has a duty to stay at home
and look after the child, this fell to less than one in ten for school-age children.
Recently there has been a decline in the proportion who think that lone mothers
should simply "do as she chooses, just like everyone else". But in the case of

pre-school children, the corresponding increase has gone into thinking she should stay at home, whereas with school-age children, it has gone into thinking she should go out to work. This suggests two things: firstly, that there has been a polarisation of attitudes on the duties of lone parents, and secondly, that a key factor in view of what they should do relates to whether the child is at school or not.

Table 9.6 Duties of lone mothers with children of different ages, 1998–2007

	1998	2002	2004	2005	2007
A single mother with a child **under school age** …					
… has a special duty to go out to work to support her child	16	14	17	14	16
… has a special duty to stay at home to look after her child	24	23	25	31	36
… should do as she chooses, just like everyone else	51	52	51	49	42
A single mother with a child **of school age** …					
… has a special duty to go out to work to support her child	44	45	47	42	52
… has a special duty to stay at home to look after her child	5	4	5	7	9
… should do as she chooses, just like everyone else	45	44	45	47	37
Base	*2531*	*2900*	*2609*	*914*	*913*

In 2008, just before the government's new lone parent obligation policy came into effect, we asked a question specifically designed to tap this latter issue:

> *Imagine a lone parent with a 1 year old child. The parent is living on benefits while they stay at home to look after the child. As the child gets older, do you think the parent should be required to look for work at any stage?*

If the respondent said yes, they were then asked:

> *How old do you think the child should be before the parent is required to look for work?*

As seen from Table 9.7, only one in ten respondents think the lone parent should not be required to look for work at any stage. Some element of conditionality is clearly desirable in the public's mind. On the other hand, an equally small proportion thinks that lone parents with pre-school children should be required to look for work. Again, starting school seems to be the key factor. A third of respondents pick this as the point at which lone parents should be required to look for work, and just over half pick either this or the early primary school years.[6] The government, therefore, seems to have caught the public's mood in its intention to push 'conditionality' down to the youngest child being age seven.

Table 9.7 At what age of child should lone parents be required to look for work?

Age of child	% respondents
Pre-school/nursery age (2–3 years)	9
Starting primary school age (4–5 years)	33
Early primary school age (6–7 years)	18
Late primary age (8–10 years)	10
Starting secondary school age (11–12 years)	11
During secondary school age (13–15 years)	4
Adult/working age (16–18 years)	2
Should not be required to look for work	10
Base	*3358*

Conditionality and lower public expenditure

One interesting question is why the public supports conditionality: is it because it thinks it will benefit lone parents or because it wants to cut public expenditure? We can get some insight into this by combining answers to the question about whether a single mother with a school-age child has a duty to work with answers to the question about benefits for single parents. Table 9.8 shows the results for 2004 when these questions were last asked together.

Table 9.8 Attitudes to government spending on single parents, by duty to work/stay at home of single mums, 2004

A single mother with a child of school age should ...	... go out to work to support her child	... stay at home to look after her child	... do as she chooses, just like everyone else
Government spending on single parents:	%	%	%
Spend much more	3	6	5
Spend more	26	31	33
Spend the same as now	43	35	46
Spend less	20	18	10
Spend a lot less	5	2	2
Base	*1197*	*138*	*1171*

It is true that people who think that single mothers have a special duty to work are more likely than others to want to spend less on benefits for single mums. But, even among this group, almost three-quarters want to spend the same or more. Hence it does not appear that a wish to cut public expenditure is the key factor. Rather, we can surmise that most respondents thought lone parent families would fare better if the parent made efforts to find work.

Varying views across the public

As we have seen, there is widespread support for some form of conditionality of benefits for lone parents with school-age children. However, if certain groups within the population have very different views to other groups, that could have important implications. For example, if the young have very different views to older age groups this may indicate that attitudes in the population as a whole will change as younger cohorts replace older ones.

We start by considering whether people think that lone parents should ever be required to go out to work. As we saw in Table 9.7, only one in ten think that lone parents should never be required to work whatever the age of their child. Table 9.9 shows that variation in this attitude across different parts of the population is only very limited

Table 9.9 Whether lone parents should be required to look for work as children get older, by demographic characteristics and political allegiance

	% saying lone parents should not be required to look for work at any stage	Base
Household type and employment status		
Respondent without children, working	8	1089
Respondent without children, not working	12	1252
Couple[+] with children, working	9	555
Couple with children, not working	14	198
Lone parent, working	8	126
Lone parent, not working	20	116
Party political allegiance		
Conservative partisan	7	502
Labour partisan	13	450
Lib Dem partisan	12	83
None	12	540
All	10	3308

[+] The category "couple" refers to all multi-adult households, not just those containing two married or cohabiting partners

The group most against requiring lone parents to work is – unsurprisingly – unemployed lone parents themselves. But even among them, only one in five think they should not be required to look for work at any stage. Conservatives are slightly more hard line than supporters of other parties, but the differences are hardly startling.

To confirm our results, we used multivariate analysis to take account of the effect of each of a number of factors, while holding the effect of others constant.[7] This analysis showed that the variables reported in Table 9.9 were the only ones that had a statistically significant effect. The sex, age, educational attainment, income and social class of the respondent did not have an independent effect.

We turn now to the second part of the question reported in Table 9.7: for those who thought that lone parents should be required to look for work at some point, what point should that be? We divide people's views into two groups that best reflected the age threshold used in the new government policy: those that thought the lone parent's child should be between two and five years of age (i.e. 'younger'), and those who thought the lone parent's child should be six years of age and older (i.e. 'older').

Table 9.10 shows slightly larger differences between different groups in the population. Younger people are more likely to think lone parents should be required to look for work when their child is younger, which supports findings from previous *British Social Attitudes* reports that there is a generation gap within modern Britain, with younger people placing more value on work than older age groups (Dench, 2008). It may also reflect a greater acceptance of working mothers in general among young people.

Women are also more likely to support this view, whereas unemployed lone parents think they should wait until the child is older. Interestingly, employed lone parents are more likely to favour enforcing the obligation when children are younger. Again, regression analysis was used to confirm the independent influence of these factors, while other factors such as educational achievement, income, political allegiance and social class did not have an independent effect.

The overall picture is one of relatively small differences in attitudes to conditionality across the population. To the extent that there are differences, these seem in part to be related to the more favourable attitudes to working mothers held by women and the young. This suggests that conditionality may become more acceptable over time as younger cohorts replace older ones.

There is, however, some doubt about the policy among unemployed lone parents themselves. Although most do not reject it outright, they are more hesitant, for example wanting the child to be older before requirements to work are introduced. And their views matter, of course. If lone parents were to resist the introduction of conditionality, the policy will be more controversial. We therefore need to look at their views in more detail and to do this we turn to a different survey which focuses directly on them.

Table 9.10 How old should their youngest child be before a lone parent is required to look for work, by demographic characteristics

		% saying lone mother should go to work when child is 2–5 years old	% saying mother should go to work when child is 6 years old and over	Base
Sex				
Male	%	42	58	1238
Female	%	55	45	1674
Age				
17–24	%	57	43	199
25–44	%	55	45	1004
45–64	%	43	57	994
65–74	%	44	56	384
75+	%	36	64	317
Household type and employment status				
Respondent without children, working	%	50	50	967
Respondent without children, not working	%	41	59	1057
Couple[+] with children, working	%	53	47	502
Couple with children, not working	%	56	44	166
Lone parent, working	%	57	43	115
Lone parent, not working	%	40	60	87
All	%	48	52	2912

Base: Those who say lone parents should be required to work at some point
[+] The category "couple" refers to all multi-adult households, not just those containing two married or cohabiting partners

The view of the lone parents

Our interest in this section is to gain an insight into the background, attitudes and plans of the type of lone parents who may well be required to look for work. To understand these issues we use data from the Families and Children Study. This is a large-scale survey of families with children and includes interviews with mothers about various aspects of their home and working life, as well as a host of background information on family circumstances and living standards.[8]

In the following analysis, we focus on lone mothers with a youngest child aged seven in 2007.[9] Approximately two-thirds (66 per cent) of these mothers were working for 16 or more hours per week and five per cent were working in 'mini-jobs' of between one and 15 hours per week. However, we are more interested in the lone mothers who were not in work at all (29 per cent). Four in five non-working lone mothers were claiming Income Support according to the Families and Children Study. Income Support is likely to be non-working lone mothers' major source of income – these lone mothers would most likely also receive Housing Benefit (often paid directly to the landlord), Child Benefit and Child Tax Credit.[10] We focus here on lone mothers who claim Income Support, as it will be these who get transferred on to Jobseeker's Allowance when their youngest child reaches seven years of age,[11] and compare their characteristics with those of lone mothers who work.

The demographic and economic characteristics and human capital of lone mothers

Detailed data on the demographic and economic characteristics of the lone mothers who participated in the Families and Children Study are presented in the appendix to this chapter. As this shows, non-working lone mothers are more likely than working mothers to be younger. This brings with it a number of other family characteristics, such as having younger children, and being more likely never to have married, rather than be separated, divorced or widowed. Non-working lone mothers are also more likely to be non-white compared with their working counterparts.

Turning to the economic characteristics of non-working lone parent families, previous research has shown that most live in low income households, and they are particularly likely to experience persistent poverty and deprivation (Barnes et al., 2008a). Hence it is not surprising to find that non-working lone mothers tend to be at the lower end of the income distribution scale. Two-thirds of non-working lone mothers are among the poorest 20 per cent of families with children. However, we also know from other research that finding work does not necessarily mean lone mothers escape low income (Barnes et al., 2008b): indeed, almost a third of *working* lone mothers still find themselves in the lowest income quartile.[12]

Non-working lone mothers are more likely not to receive any child support, live in rented accommodation, particularly social-rented accommodation, and in overcrowded conditions.

Over and above demographic and economic characteristics, levels of human capital may help determine the ease with which non-working lone mothers are able to find work and the types of job they move into. We see that non-working lone mothers are more likely to face a number of potential work-related barriers, including ill health and disability – both their own and that of their children. They also have lower levels of both academic and vocational qualifications, and are less likely to have a driving licence or access to a car. Lone mothers with health problems or with children with health problems are not required to look for work and will continue to be eligible to claim Income Support or another appropriate benefit. However, it is clear that there are some marked differences in the levels of human capital between lone mothers that do and do not work.

Non-working lone mothers' attitudes to work

Although we have seen differences in the socio-demographic backgrounds and levels of human capital of lone mothers that do and do not work, another influence on lone mothers' propensity to work is their own attitudes to work and family. We have already seen in our analysis of *British Social Attitudes* survey data that non-working lone mothers are more likely to think that lone parents should not have to look for work, and among those that do, only when their children are older. We now use Families and Children Study data to explore in more detail the attitudes of non-working lone mothers to work, being a parent and how the government views the role in the labour market.

In Table 9.11 we see that only one in five (19 per cent) of non-working lone mothers thought that children benefit from being looked after by other people. They were more likely to think that children do better when their mother stays at home and that people look down on you if you live on benefits.

Table 9.11 Opinions of work among non-working lone mothers with school-age children, 2007 (i)

Opinions of work		Strongly agree	Agree	Neither	Disagree	Strongly disagree	Base
Children benefit from being looked after by other people	%	2	17	39	31	9	237
If you live on social security benefits, everyone looks down on you	%	23	32	25	16	1	237

Base: Non-working lone mothers claiming Income Support with youngest child aged 7+
Source: Families and Children Study

On the other hand, Table 9.12 shows that, for several key issues, non-working lone mothers held more work-orientated views, including the positive role models working mums provide for their children and that having any job is better than being unemployed. The view that many non-working lone mothers are willing workers is supported by Ridge and Millar (2008).

These findings suggest that non-working lone mothers are not a homogenous group: they vary quite considerably among themselves on all the issues presented in Table 9.11 and Table 9.12. For example, whereas around a third of non-working lone mothers disagreed that having almost any job is better than being unemployed, over two-fifths agreed.

Table 9.12 Opinions of work among working and non-working lone mothers with school-age children, 2007 (ii)

Opinions of work		Strongly agree	Agree	Neither	Disagree	Strongly disagree	Base
Working mums provide positive role models for their children	%	8	30	44	12	2	237
Having almost any job is better than being unemployed	%	10	32	22	27	6	237

Base: Non-working lone mothers claiming Income Support with youngest child aged 7+
Source: Families and Children Study

This finding confirms other recent research which has identified distinct groups among the non-working lone mothers. Again using Families and Children Study data, D'Souza *et al.* (2008) found that non-working lone mothers were over-represented among mothers who reported a number of 'big factors' for not wanting or being able to work, such as a lack of qualifications or experience, low confidence, personal or family problems and health conditions. This group were particularly likely to think that society expects mothers to work. However, they found another group of lone mothers who also reported having difficulties due to a health condition or disability. These lone mothers also had concerns about low confidence and a lack of qualifications and experience, but were distinct in their attitudes towards work and parenting and did not tend to express a strong desire to care for their children at home themselves. In fact, their attitudes suggested that they would like to work, and saw work as a positive influence.

Non-working lone mothers' future plans

According to the Families and Children Study, over three-quarters of non-working lone mothers claiming Income Support were not actively seeking work. We now go on to look at non-working lone mothers' plans for the future in terms of what they *think* will happen to them over the next few years and what they *would like* to happen to them.

Table 9.13 shows that, despite the majority not actively looking for work, in 2007 over half of non-working lone mothers said they would *like* to get a job in the next few years, with the vast majority of these thinking this would actually happen. Of course, this survey was carried out before the recession and lone mothers may be less optimistic now. A significant proportion, three in ten, had a focus on staying at home to look after children – again suggesting that there are quite distinct groups of lone mothers in terms of their views and expectations of work and family responsibilities.

Table 9.13 Non-working lone mothers' plans for the future, 2007

	What mother would like to happen in next few years	What mother thinks will happen in next few years
	%	%
Get a paid job/become self-employed	63	54
Stay at home and look after children	27	29
Move home	26	18
Go to college/study	21	18
Settle down with a partner	16	9
Do some voluntary work	9	5
Have another child	6	3
None of these	1	6
Base	*237*	*237*

Base: Non-working lone mothers claiming Income Support with youngest child aged 7+
Source: Families and Children Study

Non-working lone mothers are well aware of the expectations being put on them to look for work. At the time of the Families and Children Study interviews, towards the end of 2007, the government was suggesting that lone parents who refuse to seek work might face cuts in their benefits. However, at that time lone parents were still able to claim Income Support simply for being a lone parent – there was no obligation to look for work. Despite this, 51 per cent of working lone mothers agreed with the statement that the government expected all lone parents to work, with only 22 per cent disagreeing.

Conclusions

Over the last decade public opinion on government spending on lone parents has been fairly consistent. In general the public does not think spending on lone parents is a priority compared to spending on other groups, but, at the same time, most feel that the level of spending on lone parents is about right or should even be increased slightly.

   Public opinion does suggest reasonable levels of support for conditionality rules placed on lone parents, with the majority of people thinking that benefits should be reduced a little, or even stopped, if a lone parent failed, when asked, to visit a job centre to help them find work. The duty for lone mothers to work is seen as higher when they have a school-age rather than pre-school-age child.

Indeed, most people think that lone parents should work at some stage, with younger people particularly likely to place more value on work – a view also favoured by working lone parents.

While non-working lone parents themselves appear more dubious about conditionality, only a few oppose it outright. However, the Families and Children Study shows non-working lone mothers are more likely to have a range of circumstances that may restrict their ability to find work – they are younger, have poor health and have children with poor health, have low education and worse living standards. Evidence from our analysis thus suggests there are a number of challenges to the success of the government's new approach, most notably the barriers lone parents face from having lower levels of human capital. Coupled with this is the wealth of existing research on the childcare needs of working parents. The government's Childcare Strategy has played a key role in increasing the employment of lone parents, yet there is now added pressure for lone parents to overcome the practical difficulties of finding, and being able to afford, suitable childcare.

Moreover, their attitudes to work are mixed: some do not feel confident about their abilities to find work, partly based on their circumstances described above, and some feel looking after children is more important than working. However, many want to work and expect to do so in the near future. In 2007, that would certainly have suggested that the government's strategy was on the road to success, but the onset of the recession must have put some of this in jeopardy if lone parents are unable to find work.

The next few years will determine the success of the new conditionality rules on the employment rates of lone parents. However, just as much interest will be on the impact on children in these newly working families. Although the government see work as the best route to well-being, not all working lone-parent families avoid poverty. Coupled with this is the potential disruption work schedules may do to families' home life. Without appropriate, well-timed childcare, children may have an increased possibility of spending time alone or of participating in risky behaviours, particularly in the hours after school and before their parents return from work. The government expects lone parents to look after themselves; the next few years will show us how well they fare.

Notes

1. The surveys reported in this chapter were conducted before the current recession which will undoubtedly have affected attitudes in a variety of ways. This is not necessarily a disadvantage: one way of looking at it is that the data from these surveys are a reflection of underlying, long-term attitudes.
2. The government's policy refers to lone *parents*. Many of the survey questions deal only with lone or single *mothers*. However, 96 per cent of lone parents are mothers and, the difference in wording is unlikely to have a substantial impact on attitudes.
3. The amount of money given is for the 2008 question. This is adjusted each time the question is asked to approximate the current level of benefits. In 2000 it was £95 and in 2004 £101.

4. This wording was used in 2003 and 2007. Prior to that the answer options were read out rather than presented on a card.
5. In 2000 and 2001, the question about what should happen to the benefits of a lone parent who did not attend an interview at the job centre was asked with the response options being read out by the interviewer. In 2002, a variant of this question using a showcard was asked, alongside the existing version. Data from the two question versions asked in 2002 were used to estimate the effect of using the showcard. This exercise showed that the results between the two versions were significantly different; consequently, the results for 2003 and 2007, presented in Table 9.5, were corrected to account for the difference in the data collection method and make the results comparable over time. The correction factor (ratio) was calculated by dividing the (weighted) percentages of answers collected without the showcard by the corresponding percentages for the version with the showcard. The resulting ratios for the relevant answers are shown below.

What should happen to the benefits of lone parents who fail to attend an interview at the job centre, by question version, 2002

What should happen to lone parents' benefits	Question without showcard	Question with showcard	Ratio (without showcard/with showcard)
	%	%	
Not affected	16.4	18.9	0.87
Reduced a little	44.2	37.4	1.18
Reduced a lot	14.7	16.1	0.91
Stopped	21.3	24.7	0.86
Base	*2271*	*1164*	

The values of the correcting factor were then used to calculate adjusted ratios for the years 2003 and 2007, when only the version with the showcard was used. The adjustment was done by multiplying the (weighted) percentages of answers to the question by corresponding values of the correcting factor. The table below shows both unadjusted and adjusted percentages, as well as the ratio of the two, recalculated to verify the results.

What should happen to the benefits of lone parents who fail to attend an interview at the job centre, by question version (unadjusted and adjusted), 2003 and 2007

What should happen to lone parents' benefits	2003			2007		
	Unad-justed	Adjusted	Ratio	Unad-justed	Adjusted	Ratio
	%	%		%	%	
Not affected	16.8	14.5	0.87	19.4	16.8	0.87
Reduced a little	38.2	45.2	1.18	33.8	39.9	1.18
Reduced a lot	14.2	13.0	0.91	15.2	13.9	0.91
Stopped	27.3	23.6	0.86	28.7	24.8	0.86
Base	*3272*			*3094*		

6. The question depicts only that the lone-parent family has a one year old child and not the other circumstances of the family – whether there are other children, the family's living standards or the personal characteristics of the child and the lone parent. Hence the findings should be interpreted with this in mind and the acknowledgement that views may differ given a more detailed family scenario.

7. The multivariate technique used was logistic regression. A description of this technique can be found in Appendix 1 to this report.

8. The Families and Children Study is a series of annual surveys that investigate the circumstances of British families with dependent children. The study began in 1999 with a survey of lone parent families and low income couple families. In 2001 the study was enlarged to be representative of all families with dependent children. One of the main objectives of the Families and Children Study is to provide information on general family welfare issues, including the government's long-term targets to eradicate child poverty. The survey therefore covers a number of themes related to work, income and living standards, including employment and self-employment, unemployment and job search, receipt of social security benefits and tax credits and expenditure and hardship. The survey also collects a range of socio-demographic and economic information from the parents and children, including family composition, educational qualifications, health and disability status, and social activities and relationships. The Families and Children Study is also a panel study, which means that it returns to interview the same families year after year. It can therefore be used to observe dynamic behaviour and experiences. For more information see the Families and Children Study website research.dwp.gov.uk/asd/asd5/facs.

9. We exclude lone fathers from our analysis as they are a distinct group of lone parents. Unfortunately there are too few lone fathers in the Families and Children Study data to allow separate analysis. There are also too few lone parents with youngest child aged 10 and over, or 12 and over, to allow separate analysis of the first group of lone parents to experience the new policy.

10. Non-working lone mothers who were not claiming Income Support may have received income from other sources, such as an absent parent, chosen not to or failed to claim the benefit, or could be a result of measurement error in the Families and Children Study data.

11. Clearly we can not replicate the other criteria that means a lone mother would be moved onto Jobseeker's Allowance. However, there were very few lone mothers in the Families and Children Study data that were claiming disability-related benefits for their children (a group that would be exempt from the obligations).

12. The measure of income used takes account of whether the respondent was part of an individual or multi-adult household. Otherwise, this difference for lone mothers would be expected.

References

Barnes, M., Conolly, A. and Tomaszewski, W. (2008a), *The circumstances of persistently poor families with children: Evidence from the Families and Children Study (FACS)*, DWP Research Report No. 487, Leeds: Corporate Document Services

Barnes, M., Lyon, N. and Millar, J. (2008b), *Employment transitions and the changes in economic circumstances of families with children: Evidence from the Families and Children Study (FACS)*, DWP Research Report no. 506, Leeds: Corporate Document Services

Crompton, R., Brockmann, M. and Wiggins, R.D. (2003), 'A woman's place ... Employment and family life for men and women', in Park, A., Curtice, J., Thomson, K., Jarvis, L. and Bromley, C. (eds.) *British Social Attitudes: the 20th Report – Continuity and change over two decades*, London: Sage

Daycare Trust (2007), *Childcare nation? Progress on the childcare strategy and priorities for the future*, London: Daycare Trust

Dench, G. (2008), 'Exploring parents' views', in Park, A., Curtice, J., Thomson, K., Phillips, M. and Clery, E.(eds.), *British Social Attitudes: the 25 Report*, London: Sage

Department for Work and Pensions (2008), *Raising expectations and increasing support: reforming welfare for the future*, Leeds: Corporate Document Services

Department for Work and Pensions (2009), *Households Below Average Income 1994/95–2007/08*, Leeds: Corporate Document Services

D'Souza, J., Conolly, A. and Purdon, S. (2008), *Analysis of the choices and constraints questions on the families and children study*, Department for Work and Pensions, Research report 481, Leeds: Corporate Document Services

Harker, L. (2006), *Delivering on Child Poverty: what would it take?*, A report for the Department for Work and Pensions, Norwich: The Stationery Office

Kent, K. (2009) 'Households, families and work', *Economic and Labour Market Review*, **17(22)**

Millar, J. (2008a), 'Making work pay, making tax credits work: An assessment with specific reference to lone-parent employment', *International Social Security Review*, **61(2):** 21–38

Millar, J., Ridge, T., (2001) *Families, poverty, work and care: A review of the literature on lone parents and low-income couple families with children*, Discussion Paper, Department for Work and Pensions, Leeds: Corporate Document Services

Philo, D., Maplethorpe, N., Conolly, A. and Toomse, M. (2009), *Families with children in Britain: findings from the 2007 Families and Children Study (FACS)*, Department for Work and Pensions Research Report No. 578, Norwich: The Stationery Office

Ridge, T. and Millar, J. (2008), Work and well-being over time: lone mothers and their children, DWP Research Report No. 536, Leeds: Corporate Document Services

Acknowledgements

The *National Centre for Social Research* is grateful to the Department for Work and Pensions for their financial support which enabled us to ask some of the questions in this chapter. The views expressed are those of the author alone.

The Families and Children Study (FACS) is commissioned by the Department for Work and Pensions and sponsored by Her Majesty's Revenue and Customs, the Department for Children, Schools and Families, the Department for Communities and Local Government and the Department for Transport.

Appendix

Table A.1 Socio-demographic background of working and non-working lone mothers with school-age children, 2007

	In work (for 16+ hours)	Not in work and claiming Income Support
Age of mother	%	%
Under 25	0	1
25–29	2	9
30–34	8	14
35–39	21	23
40–44	29	22
45 plus	39	30
Number of dependent children	%	%
1	64	51
2	30	31
3 or more	6	18
Age of youngest child	%	%
7–11 years	39	62
12–15 years	37	31
16–18 years	24	7
Ethnic group of mother	%	%
White	92	87
Non-white	8	13
Marital status	%	%
Single never married	32	46
Married	1	0
Separated	18	11
Divorced	45	41
Widowed	3	2
Base	*530*	*237*

Base: Lone mothers with youngest child aged 7+
Source: Families and Children Study

Table A.2 Economic characteristics of working and non-working lone mothers with school-age children, 2007

	In work (for 16+ hours)	Not in work and claiming Income Support
Family income	%	%
Highest quintile[+]	2	1
Fourth quintile	6	0
Third quintile	16	9
Second quintile	44	24
Lowest quintile	31	66
Receives child support	%	%
Yes	45	13
No	55	87
Tenure	%	%
Owned outright	9	2
Mortgage	52	3
Shared ownership	1	1
Social tenant	24	76
Private tenant	13	18
Other arrangement	1	1
Lives in overcrowded accommodation[++]	%	%
No	94	83
Yes	6	17
Base	*530*	*237*

Base: Lone mothers with youngest child aged 7+

Source: Families and Children Study

[+] Quintiles based on families with children

[++] 1+ rooms below bedroom standard

Table A.3 Levels of human capital of working and non-working lone mothers with school-age children, 2007

	In work (for 16+ hours)	Not in work and claiming Income Support
Long-standing illness	%	%
No	76	54
Yes	24	46
Family disability status	%	%
No one	63	37
Child/ren only	13	17
Mother only	13	26
Both mother and child/ren	11	20
Highest academic qualification	%	%
Degree	18	2
A level	11	7
GCSE grade A–C	41	27
GCSE grade D–G	9	21
Other	4	2
None	16	40
Highest vocational qualification	%	%
Level 5 NVQ	0	0
Level 4 NVQ	11	1
Level 3 NVQ	13	7
Level 2 NVQ	14	11
Level 1 NVQ	12	13
Other	10	7
None	39	61
Car access and licence	%	%
Licence and access	76	30
Licence no access	3	8
No licence	21	62
Base	*530*	*237*

Base: Lone mothers with youngest child aged 7+
Source: Families and Children Study

10 Food for thought: attitudes to innovative food technologies

*Elizabeth Clery**

The processes and technologies involved in food production in Britain and the resulting range of food products are constantly evolving and expanding. Innovative approaches to the selection, development, presentation, preservation and storage of food products are by no means a new phenomenon. For centuries people have been finding ways to modify the natural properties of food, a famous early example being pasteurisation, which prevented spoilage and increased the shelf-life of foods and drinks. Technological interventions have generally sought to maximise the benefits and minimise the limitations associated with particular types of food, for instance by making a food product healthier or less costly to produce, or increasing its shelf-life. Many food technologies (or the products resulting from them) which were once considered innovative are now commonplace: Quorn, a little-known product prior to the 1990s, is now a well-known meat substitute; while microwave ovens, which were rare in the 1970s, are now widespread in Britain.[1] Meanwhile, other innovative technologies and processes have been developed. While a number of these, such as techniques for the production and packaging of shelf-stable foods, have seamlessly entered the food chain and have attracted little discussion or opposition, this has not universally been the case. A particularly prominent example, in terms of the levels of public discussion it has generated, was the introduction of genetically modified (GM) foods in the 1990s. More recently, the actual and potential applications of nanotechnology and cloning to food production have attracted considerable debate.

Yet public attitudes, knowledge and concerns about developments in this area remain poorly understood. As the potential purchasers and consumers of the food products created using innovative technologies, the British public has a key role to play in determining their long-term impact and success. A recent review commissioned by the Food Standards Agency highlighted the existence of little robust nationally representative quantitative data in Britain on public attitudes in this area, with the majority of studies being highly localised and

* Elizabeth Clery is a Research Director at the *National Centre for Social Research* and is Co-Director of the *British Social Attitudes* survey series.

dealing with very specific products or technologies (Brook Lyndhurst, 2009). Moreover, those technologies or products that have attracted the most vocal public discussion, most recently GM foods, have received disproportionate attention from researchers, though, even in these areas, substantial gaps in the evidence base remain. The patchy nature of the evidence base in relation to innovative food technologies means it is difficult to draw empirical conclusions about this area as a whole. There are a number of questions of interest: what types of innovation are more likely to be acceptable to the British public; do innovative food products have to offer particular benefits to make them popular; are all new food technologies initially unpopular until they attain a degree of familiarity; and so on.

To address these limitations in the existing evidence base, this chapter will begin by reviewing public concern about developments in food technology, considering a range of existing food products that have been developed using innovative technologies. We will consider whether people tend to support or oppose innovation in food technology across the board, or if attitudes vary towards individual products. We then consider what it is about certain products that make them more and less acceptable to the public – is it particular benefits or the absence of certain drawbacks that make them more attractive; is public support for a particular food technology simply a function of the level of familiarity with its terminology and usage; is knowledge about food technology a relevant factor? We then explore whether attitudes to innovative food technologies vary between different groups in society, taking into account demographic characteristics, and a range of different attitudes and behaviours. Finally, the chapter will look towards the future to consider if and how public attitudes to future developments in food technology can best be anticipated and understood.

Views about innovation in food technology

We start by examining attitudes to foods developed using innovative technologies. First, we assess respondents' concerns about five innovative food products and processes, before going on to consider public attitudes towards GM foods.

Concern about using innovative technologies

To assess public views about innovative food technologies, we presented respondents with detailed descriptions of five processes or ingredients and asked how concerned they would be, either if the process described was part of the production of a product that they ate regularly, or about eating a food that contained that particular ingredient. The five processes and products asked about were the use of gases in the production of bags of salad leaves, high pressure treatment of fresh fruit juice, radiation exposure in microwave ovens, Benecol and Quorn. We described these to respondents as follows:

A process is used to produce bags containing ready-to-eat salad leaves. This involves filling the bags with gases that control the growth of bacteria and keep leaves fresher for longer

It is possible to increase the shelf-life of products such as fresh fruit juice by putting them under high pressure. Some people think using high pressure retains the flavour of the food more than pasteurisation using heat

A microwave is a device in which food can be exposed to radiation to heat it and kill bacteria before eating

A range of products including Benecol have been developed that contain a concentrated variety of an ingredient found in vegetable oil that lowers levels of cholesterol found in the blood

There is an ingredient called Quorn available that provides a non-meat source of protein grown in large tanks using a processed edible fungus and added to a variety of products

As shown in Table 10.1, in each case, a substantial majority, at least seven in ten, express at least some level of concern about eating food products resulting from the different ingredients and processes. However, the most common answer to four of the five items is "not very concerned", meaning that we should not overstate this. Minorities of a quarter (26 per cent) or less say they are not at all concerned about each of the products and processes.

As well as finding some overall similarity in levels of concern across the different items, the data also indicate that attitudes vary substantially depending on the process or ingredient being considered. The process used in the production of bags of ready-to-eat salad leaves attracts most concern, with six in ten saying they are very or fairly concerned about this, while the ingredient used to develop products such as Benecol causes least concern, with just over two in ten expressing this view. The low level of concern about the process used in the production of Benecol reflects the finding of previous research that such 'functional' foods, developed in order to provide a specific health benefit to the public, generally attract less concern than those produced in order to yield non-health-related benefits (Brook Lyndhurst, 2009).

Table 10.1 Concern about eating foods produced using innovative food products/processes

Product or process		Very concerned	Fairly concerned	Not very concerned	Not at all concerned	Base
Use of gases in bags of ready-to-eat salad leaves	%	22	37	29	10	2250
High pressure treatment of fresh fruit juice	%	10	27	45	16	2250
Radiation in microwaves	%	11	20	43	26	1121
Addition of concentrated variety of ingredient found in vegetable oil (e.g. to Benecol)	%	6	17	49	26	1119
Addition of ingredient grown in large tanks using a processed edible fungus (Quorn)	%	17	18	36	26	1104

The fact that clear majorities express some level of concern in relation to each of the different food products may be considered surprising because, with the exception of high pressure treatment in the production of fruit juices, they are all either relatively well known or have been available in Britain for more than a decade.[2] This might suggest that public consumption of food products cannot be assumed to reflect a lack of concerns about the technologies involved in their production. To test this theory, we asked respondents the following question, which we then compared with their answers to the question above asking about levels of concern about eating bags of ready-to-eat salad leaves[3]:

Do you buy bags containing ready-to-eat salad leaves?

Fifty-one per cent of those who buy bags of ready-to-eat salad leaves are very or fairly concerned about the process used in their production, compared with 67 per cent of those who do not purchase this product and 72 per cent of those who once did so, but for whom this is no longer the case. Clearly, these data do imply, at least in the case of bags of salad leaves, a relationship between individual concern about innovative technologies and the consumption of products where these technologies have been used. Nevertheless, the fact remains that half of those who buy bags of ready-to-eat salad leaves express a considerable degree of concern about the process involved in their production. It may be that the public is willing to consume food products even when it is concerned about the processes involved in their production, because it considers them to have significant advantages that outweigh any concerns. Alternatively, this, together with the finding that public concern about other familiar food products is relatively widespread, may suggest a lack of awareness about the processes involved in the production of particular products. Indeed, the relationship between public knowledge of food technologies and levels of concern about innovative products is something that we return to in greater detail later in the chapter.

Attitudes to GM foods

We also explored attitudes towards one type of technological innovation in food that has attracted particular attention in recent years – genetic modification. We first asked questions on this topic on the *British Social Attitudes* survey in 1999 and they have been fielded on a number of occasions since. GM foods are (still) not widely available for purchase in Britain; for this reason and to facilitate time-series analysis, rather than asking about concerns about purchasing or consuming GM foods, the questions focus on the potential benefits and drawbacks of GM foods being produced in Britain. We asked respondents how far they agreed or disagreed with these statements:

On balance the advantages of GM foods outweigh any dangers

In order to compete with the rest of the world, Britain should grow GM foods

GM foods should be banned, even if food prices suffer as a result

The responses, presented in Table 10.2, reveal a considerable degree of ambivalence about the benefits and drawbacks of GM foods. Four in ten (39 per cent) neither agree nor disagree that the advantages of GM foods outweigh any dangers, while a further one in ten are unable to select an answer to this question. Among those who do have a view, the balance of public opinion is in opposition to the idea of producing and selling GM foods in Britain. Two in ten (18 per cent) agree that the advantages of GM foods outweigh any dangers, while three in ten disagree. And around twice as many respondents disagree than agree with the view that Britain should grow GM foods to compete with the rest of the world (four in ten – 41 per cent – compared with two in ten). On the other hand, similar proportions agree and disagree with the proposition that GM foods should be banned, even if food prices suffer as a result – 26 per cent compared with 30 per cent. It may be that these data encapsulate public attitudes to issues other than GM foods, including the importance of food prices or the extent to which competing economically with the rest of the world should be a priority. Nevertheless, overall, it is clear that public attitudes to GM foods can be characterised by a strong degree of ambivalence, with views on this issue tending to oppose their production or widespread availability in Britain. These conclusions reflect those drawn from attitudinal research on GM foods generally (Brook Lyndhurst, 2009).

Table 10.2 Attitudes to GM foods

	The advantages of GM foods outweigh dangers	To compete with rest of the world, Britain should grow GM foods	GM foods should be banned, even if food prices suffer
	%	%	%
Agree	18	19	26
Neither agree nor disagree	39	31	33
Disagree	31	41	30
Can't choose	10	7	7
Base	*1975*	*1975*	*1975*

Do views about GM foods correlate with the attitudes towards innovative food products and technologies that we explored earlier in the chapter? To facilitate this analysis we used a summary measure of the five questions shown in Table 10.1. A score for each respondent was calculated, representing the number of products which they would be very or fairly concerned about eating. For three of these questions, there were two different versions, in each case asked of random halves of respondents (one version named the food product and the other did not).[4] The questions are reported in full in the next section (see Table 10.4). The range of scores reflects the diversity in views on this issue; 24 per cent are not concerned about any of the five processes or ingredients, while 19 per cent express concern about just one of the products. Similar proportions are concerned about two (18 per cent), three (16 per cent), four (12 per cent) or all of the five (11 per cent) of the products described.

Those who express support for GM foods are less likely to express concern about eating food products developed using alternative innovative technologies; 30 per cent of those who agree the advantages of GM foods outweigh its dangers were very or fairly concerned about three or more of the products considered, compared with 48 per cent of those who felt that the dangers of GM foods were greater. This suggests that the same factors that generate concern about GM foods may also foster concern about alternative food technologies. However, the evidence overall does not conclusively show that people hold a coherent set of attitudes and values in relation to innovation in food technology, as we also know that there are wide variations in attitudes towards the different food products and processes asked about.

Variations in public concern about different food products

We turn now to examine these variations in more detail, asking whether there are any underlying explanations that allow us to move beyond specific contexts in our understanding of public attitudes in this area. A number of different factors might be relevant here. First, we have already pointed out that the different products varied in terms of both the benefits they offer to consumers, and the potential risks they might pose. We start by considering the extent to which perceived advantages and disadvantages of products relate to decisions about whether to purchase and consume them. Second, we explore the issue of familiarity – asking whether public acceptance of a new process or product is, to some extent, a function of how well known it is. Third, we have already noted that knowledge of different processes may be one explanation for the finding that a sizeable proportion of the public buys bags of ready-to-eat salad leaves – produced by a process that it claims to have considerable concerns about. The role of knowledge is considered in more detail here, as we ask whether a respondent's level of knowledge about innovative technologies relates to their feelings of concern about this area.

Benefits and drawbacks of individual products

One factor that might influence levels of concern about particular innovative technologies in food production is the benefits that the resulting food products provide. In the descriptions of the five food products discussed previously, clear benefits to the consumer are stated explicitly or are implied in each case: for the processes involved in producing fresh fruit juice and bags of ready-to-eat salad leaves, a longer shelf-life; for microwaves, the convenience of being able to heat food quickly; for Quorn, convenience in terms of providing an alternative protein substitute to meat; and for Benecol, health benefits in terms of the reduction of cholesterol. Previous research has shown that levels of concern about particular food products are partly formed as the result of a risk–benefit assessment by the consumer, which tends to prioritise possible positive and negative impacts on health (Brook Lyndhurst, 2009). It therefore may not be coincidental that Benecol, the only one of our five products to yield a health benefit to consumers, attracts the lowest levels of concern.

To determine more precisely the impacts of particular benefits and drawbacks on public concerns about specific products, we described to respondents two hypothetical food products that could be developed using innovative processes and ingredients, each of which would yield a particular benefit to the consumer. Respondents were first asked whether or not they would buy the food products, described as follows:

Imagine an extremely low calorie cake. It tastes the same and looks the same as conventional cake sold in the supermarket but has had an extra ingredient added to reduce the number of calories it contains

Imagine a sausage that helps reduce the risk of high blood pressure, which tastes the same and looks the same as normal sausages sold in the supermarket. It would be available in meat and vegetarian varieties. The sausage could be produced by adding ingredients which have been medically proven to reduce the risk of high blood pressure

As shown in the first and fourth rows of Table 10.3, enthusiasm for the hypothetical products is by no means universal. Fifty-three per cent say they would buy the extremely low calorie cake rather than traditional cake, while 63 per cent would buy the sausage that helps reduce the risk to blood pressure, rather than a traditional sausage. Therefore, sizeable minorities would not buy each product even when a risk–benefit assessment would suggest its impact to be positive, or at least neutral (if they were not interested in the health advantage yielded). It may be that a lack of familiarity with the products and the ways in which they are produced would put substantial numbers off purchasing them, rather than the more familiar alternative; this is something we will explore in the next section.

Table 10.3 Whether would buy hypothetical food products with particular benefits and drawbacks

		Definitely would	Probably would	Probably would not	Definitely would not[5]	Base
Would buy extremely low calorie cake ...						
... rather than traditional cake	%	23	30	23	24	2250
... even if it were more expensive	%	12	27	24	35	2250
... even if it had a shorter shelf-life	%	13	28	24	35	2250
Would buy sausage that helps reduce the risk to blood pressure ...						
... rather than traditional sausage	%	26	37	20	15	2250
... even if it were more expensive	%	14	38	24	23	2250
... even if it had a shorter shelf-life	%	14	36	23	25	2250

To examine how people weigh up benefits and drawbacks, we then asked all respondents, with the exception of those who initially indicated that they would "definitely not" buy the product, whether they would buy the product if, in addition to the stated benefit, it also had associated disadvantages, in terms of cost and shelf-life. If a respondent had stated that they would "definitely not" buy the product as originally described, it was assumed that this would remain the case, when its potential disadvantages were highlighted. Perhaps, unsurprisingly, the proportions willing to buy the products decreased in each case. Around four in ten said they would still buy the extremely low calorie cake if it were more expensive than traditional cake (39 per cent) or had a shorter shelf-life (41 per cent). The equivalent figures for the sausage were 52 per cent and 50 per cent respectively. The similar levels found when either cost or shelf-life drawbacks are highlighted suggests that neither one of these aspects stands out as a particularly important consideration for the public.

It is notable that the proportions who would *definitely* buy the products almost halve when disadvantages are mentioned. However, in both cases, the group who would either definitely or probably buy the innovative product only declines by around 10 percentage points, suggesting that, for many, the perceived health benefits which initially encouraged interest outweigh the negative impacts of higher cost or reduced shelf-life.

Familiarity with innovative products

The fact that sizeable groups of respondents would not buy each hypothetical food product, even when an overall assessment of its benefits and risks could be regarded as neutral or positive, implies many may have innate concerns – unrelated to these benefits and drawbacks – about purchasing and consuming unknown food products. It might be that the public is unsure about food products about which it knows little, and thus that levels of concern about particular products are, to some extent, a function of their familiarity with the products, in terms of both terminology and usage.

To explore this, respondents were randomly assigned to two groups for each of the questions asking about levels of concern in relation to microwaves, Quorn and Benecol. We asked one half the version of the question which stated the name of the product or process (shown in full on p.219), while the other half was asked a question which was identical apart from omitting the product's name. In the case of the question about the "microwave", this term was replaced with the word "magnetron" (a little-known technical term for a microwave). Table 10.4 presents the levels of concern expressed about eating the foods created using the three different processes or ingredients, with results shown separately for those who were told the commonly known name of the product or process and those who were not.

What is clear is that, regardless of the description of an innovative process or ingredient, when this is attached to the name of a familiar product or process, levels of expressed concern are often much reduced. Most markedly, 57 per cent of respondents are very or fairly concerned about eating a food prepared using a magnetron, whereas this was the case for just 31 per cent of those who were asked about a microwave. Similarly, 52 per cent of respondents are concerned about eating a product such as Quorn when this was not named, compared with 35 per cent of those whose question explicitly referred to Quorn. It is interesting to note that for Benecol, being told the name of the product made little difference to levels of concern; 27 per cent of those given the description without Benecol being mentioned are very or fairly concerned, compared with 23 per cent of those whose question included the product's name. This may be a consequence of the fact that public concern about Benecol is much lower overall, meaning the minority who do express concern have more entrenched reasons for this stance that will not simply be eliminated by mentioning the product name.

Table 10.4 Levels of concern about different innovations in food, by whether name of product/process included in question text

		Level of concern		
		Very/ fairly	Not very/ not at all	*Base*
Device in which food can be exposed to radiation to heat it and kill bacteria before eating				
Referred to as microwave	%	31	69	*1121*
Referred to as magnetron[6]	%	57	38	*1157*
Products containing concentrated variety of ingredient found in vegetable oil that lowers levels of cholesterol in the blood				
Referred to as Benecol	%	23	75	*1119*
Not referred to as Benecol	%	27	72	*1131*
Ingredient that provides non-meat source of protein grown in large tanks using a processed edible fungus and added to variety of products				
Referred to as Quorn	%	35	62	*1104*
Not referred to as Quorn	%	52	44	*1129*

In addition to this explicit test of the impact of familiarity on public attitudes, we also sought to understand the importance of this factor by examining how attitudes to new food technologies change over time. *British Social Attitudes* has included questions on GM foods on a number of occasions. By comparing responses to questions asked in 1999, 2003 and 2008, we can explore how increasing public familiarity with the idea of the application of GM technology to food links with levels of public support.

As shown in Table 10.5, attitudes to GM foods changed dramatically between 1999 and 2003, and have continued to move in a similar direction in the last five years, but at a much slower pace. Writing in *The 21st Report*, Sturgis *et al.* (2004) noted that, while the strong opposition to GM foods evident in the 1990s had reduced considerably by 2003, this was due to an increasing ambivalence among the public, with greater proportions neither agreeing nor disagreeing with the three statements detailed below, rather than any significant increase in public support. Since 2003, although the changes only just attain statistical significance, we see small increases in the proportions expressing positive attitudes towards GM foods, while the level of ambivalent responses remains relatively unchanged. However, for each of the three statements, the negative attitude is held by a larger group than the positive attitude. For example, the percentage that agrees the advantages of GM foods outweigh any dangers has increased by four points, to 18 per cent (while 31 per cent disagree).

Table 10.5 Attitudes towards GM foods, 1999, 2003 and 2008

		Agree	Neither	Disagree	Base
In order to compete with the rest of the world, Britain should grow GM foods					
1999	%	10	18	65	833
2003	%	15	30	45	2649
2008	%	19	31	41	1975
GM foods should be banned, even if food prices suffer as a result					
1999	%	52	22	20	833
2003	%	29	33	26	2649
2008	%	26	33	30	1975
On balance, the advantag⌐⌐ of GM foods outweigh any dangers					
1999	%	12	22	57	833
2003	%	14	38	33	2649
2008	%	18	39	31	1975

It may be that attitudes to GM foods have changed little in recent years compared with the major shifts in public opinion witnessed between 1999 and 2003, because the availability of GM products in 2008 is very similar to the situation in 2003, meaning public familiarity is likely to be influenced by media and popular debate rather than by widespread usage. Indeed, analysis of the marked changes in public attitudes between 1999 and 2003 pointed towards the unprecedented quantity of media coverage at the end of that period, which may have made the subject of GM foods much more familiar, and thus less fearful to the British public (Sturgis *et al.*, 2004). Looking to the future, it seems possible that public attitudes may change to reflect the situation with regard to the production and availability of GM foods or the level of debate of this issue in Britain. Overall, these data do lend support to our findings in relation to alternative innovative food products, in suggesting that increasing public familiarity with an innovative technology tends to be associated with a reduction in opposition.

The role of knowledge

We turn now to examine whether levels of knowledge about innovation in food technology relate to levels of concern about eating products developed using these methods. We have already found that concerns about specific innovations in food technology are strongly linked to the extent to which the public is familiar with the products that are developed as a result. While familiarity could come simply from knowing the name of an innovative technology or through purchasing or consuming the food product, it could also result from an individual's level of knowledge about innovation in food technology. We would anticipate that those with a greater knowledge would have fewer concerns about eating innovative food products, as the inherent fear of the unknown which appears to foster concerns in this area would be limited.

To gain a measure of knowledge about innovation in food technology, each respondent completed a short knowledge test which included seven statements, as follows[7]:

GM, that is, genetically modified food is never sold in Britain (false)

Using microwave ovens to heat food involves radiation (true)

Organic crops are frequently grown using pesticides (false)

Pasteurised foods like orange juice have a longer shelf-life because they don't contain as much bacteria as fresh orange juice (true)

Some foods have extra ingredients added to them to make them healthier (true)

Bags containing ready-to-eat salad leaves are usually filled with gases to slow the growth of bacteria and ensure the leaves stay fresh for longer (true)

Omega-3 oils, which are usually obtained from fish, can also be manufactured from plant-like organisms called algae (true)

We asked respondents to say whether they thought each was "true" or "false" or if they were unsure.[8] The correct answer is shown in brackets after each statement. The proportions of respondents who answered each item correctly varied considerably, with 73 per cent answering the question about GM food correctly, more than double the proportion who gave an accurate answer in response to the question about Omega-3 oils (30 per cent). The remaining five items were each answered correctly by between five and seven in ten of the public (microwave ovens: 68 per cent; extra ingredients: 61 per cent; pasteurised foods: 54 per cent; organic food crops: 53 per cent; ready-to-eat salad leaves: 48 per cent). There was a tendency for items where only a minority identified the correct answer, for large proportions of the public to state they were unsure about the answer; this was the case for 42 per cent for the item about bags of ready-to-eat salad leaves and 57 per cent for the item about Omega-3 oils. In other words, the majority of those who did not know about a particular issue in food technology were aware that this was the case.

We then created a knowledge score for each respondent, ranging from zero (no correct answers) to seven (all seven items answered correctly). Overall, 19 per cent answered fewer than three questions correctly, 45 per cent answered three or four items correctly and 36 per cent answered five or more of the seven items correctly; the average score was 3.9.

As a number of the items included in the quiz were concerned with the specific innovative products for which levels of concern were measured, we can directly assess whether those with knowledge of the particular technology are less likely to be concerned about it by comparing the two sets of questions. As shown in Table 10.6, those who had knowledge of a particular innovative food technology tended to be less concerned than those without such knowledge about eating the related food product. The most marked gap is found for using gases in the preparation of bags of ready-to-eat salad leaves: 56 per cent of those who answered the knowledge question correctly were concerned about this product, compared with 72 per cent who answered incorrectly. Differences of around 10 percentage points were found for the questions on high pressure pasteurisation (of fresh fruit juice) and radiation in microwave ovens.

Table 10.6 Levels of concern about individual food products, by knowledge of technology used in development

	% very/fairly concerned	Base
Use of gases in bags of ready-to-eat salad leaves		
Knowledge question answered correctly	56	1043
Unsure	59	940
Answered incorrectly	72	262
High pressure treatment of fresh fruit juice		
Knowledge question answered correctly	32	1199
Unsure	43	721
Answered incorrectly	43	304
Radiation in microwaves		
Knowledge question answered correctly	27	730
Unsure	38	167
Answered incorrectly	37	206

We can also compare levels of knowledge and concern about innovative food technologies more generally, by analysing our summary measure of concern by the knowledge test scores. This suggests that levels of knowledge about innovation in food technology and levels of concern about eating products developed as a result are strongly linked. Just 30 per cent of those who answered five or more of the test items correctly were concerned about three or more of the products, compared with 43 per cent of those who answered three or four items correctly and 50 per cent of those who answered fewer than three items correctly. Clearly, then, levels of concern about innovation in food technology are strongly associated with knowledge of this area, just as they are strongly linked to product or process familiarity. In other words, levels of concern about innovative food products or processes can be explained to a substantial degree on the basis of the public's fear or misunderstanding of the unknown.

Who supports and opposes innovation?

To understand attitudes to innovative technologies fully, we must also consider whether different sections of the public hold particular views. The remainder of the chapter seeks to address a number of key questions. Are there certain personal characteristics, behaviours and attitudes that link with high levels of concern about innovative food technologies? How do these factors relate to each other and are there particular characteristics that ultimately predict attitudes in this area?

The existing literature on public attitudes to innovation in food technology suggests that there are few links with demographic characteristics, with the exception that women and the elderly generally express greater levels of concern. Instead, values and beliefs, including general ones such as attitudes to science, and more specific ones including attitudes to food, are seen as better predictors of attitudes in this area (Brook Lyndhurst, 2009). However, as noted previously, research on this topic has tended to focus on specific products and technologies, rather than attitudes to technological innovation across the board. In this final section, we examine whether these patterns in the distribution of attitudes to innovation in food technology hold true in relation to our summary measure of levels of concern about eating products developed using innovative technologies. We focus on the substantial minority of the public (39 per cent) who are either very or fairly concerned about three or more of the five products asked about.

Demographic characteristics

Analysis of our summary measure of concern confirms what has been found elsewhere, that age and sex are related, with older age groups and women being substantially more likely to be concerned about innovation in food technology. As Table 10.7 shows, more than half of those aged 65 years and over are concerned about three or more of the products asked about, compared with just one third of those aged between 18 and 34. Meanwhile, around five in ten women and three in ten men express concern about three or more of the innovative food products. This reflects the tendency, generally, for women to be more risk averse in relation to a wide range of scientific and technological developments (National Science Foundation, 2002).

Despite previous research findings suggesting other demographic characteristics are not relevant to this topic area, we envisaged that a number of other factors might logically be related to attitudes – namely educational levels, income, religion, ethnicity, location and the presence of dependent children. Data for those characteristics which were significantly linked to levels of concern about innovative food technologies are presented, alongside those for age and sex, in Table 10.7.

Table 10.7 Levels of concern about innovation in food technology, by demographic characteristics

	% very/fairly concerned about 3–5 innovative products or processes	Base
All	39	2250
Age		
18–34	31	485
35–49	35	819
50–64	48	375
65+	51	562
Sex		
Male	30	966
Female	48	1284
Highest educational qualification		
Degree or equivalent	30	615
A levels	32	312
GCSEs	39	546
No qualifications	55	549
Income		
More than £44,000	28	408
£23,000–£43,999	33	538
£12,000–£22,999	46	427
Less than £12,000	54	517
Ethnicity		
White	38	2074
Non-white	51	172
Religion		
Has a religion	43	1271
Does not have a religion	35	970

As noted previously, knowledge of innovation in food technology is strongly linked with levels of concern about this area. It therefore seemed plausible that those with higher educational qualifications would be less concerned about eating foods produced using innovative technologies, as they would either be more likely to acquire such knowledge, or would be more able to understand the technical concepts and language used. This relationship between education levels and levels of concern about innovation in food technology is confirmed by the data, with 30 per cent of those with degree-level qualifications expressing concern about three or more of the food products, compared with 55 per cent of those with no qualifications. Education levels are known to be strongly related to socio-economic status, which we measure in terms of household income, with those in low income groups tending to have fewer qualifications. It therefore comes as no surprise that those in the lowest income quartile are almost twice as likely as those in the highest to express concern about three or more of the food products described. This variation is notable, as previous research in this area has not produced conclusive results in terms of the presence of a link between socio-economic status and attitudes (Brook Lyndhurst, 2009).

In addition to age, sex, income and education, religion and ethnicity were the only other demographic characteristics examined that were significantly linked with levels of concern about innovative food technologies.[9]

Adherence to a religion is associated with levels of concern in this area: 43 per cent of those who have a religion are concerned about three or more of the food products, compared with 35 per cent of those who do not. Many religions preach against human interference in natural processes and respondents who adhere to these faiths may have considered the innovative processes used in the development of the different food products in this light.

As non-white groups tend to have higher levels of religiosity, it was also anticipated that ethnicity might be related to levels of concern about innovative food technologies. This was indeed the case, with around four in ten of those from a white ethnic group concerned about three or more of the food products, compared with five in ten of those from a non-white ethnic group.

To understand further the reasons for this, and for the greater levels of concern expressed by older age groups and women, it is necessary to consider other factors, namely attitudes and behaviour that might link to concerns and explain such demographic variation.

Related attitudes and behaviours

The existing literature suggests that attitudes and values, rather than demographic characteristics, tend to be more effective in predicting public attitudes to innovation in food technology – including attitudes to science and levels of social trust.[10] In addition, we might also expect levels of concern about innovation in food technology to relate to specifically food-related attitudes and behaviours. In particular, it seems plausible that attitudes to innovative food technologies would relate to attitudes to food safety, particularly if the main reason for public concern about the products described is uncertainty as to whether they are sufficiently safe. We were also interested in whether this was the case for individuals' dietary habits, their willingness to try new foods and their household role in relation to purchasing food. We asked respondents the following questions to assess these related attitudes and behaviours:

Thinking only of the food you eat at home, how much of the shopping for this food do you do? (all or most, about half, less than half, none)

Which, if any of the statements on this card apply to you?
I am a vegetarian or vegan
I avoid certain foods as I react badly to them
I am on a diet trying to lose weight
I avoid certain food for religious reasons
I avoid certain food because of medical advice
None of these

Which of the following statements comes closest to your view:
I am happy to eat foods that I have never tried before without knowing too much about them, OR
I wouldn't eat a food that I had never tried before unless I knew exactly what was in it

Generally speaking, which of these best describes your level of concern about food safety in Britain. By food safety, we mean things like food allergies and hygiene when storing and preparing food? [very concerned, fairly concerned, not very concerned, not at all concerned]

Please consider the following statements and tell me whether you agree or disagree? Overall, modern science does more harm than good [strongly agree, agree, neither agree nor disagree, disagree, strongly disagree]

Attitudes and behaviour in relation to food in particular and science more generally are diverse. Six-tenths of the respondents report doing all or most of the food shopping (58 per cent), with similar proportions indicating that they undertake about half (16 per cent), less than half (14 per cent) or none of this role (12 per cent). In terms of specific dietary behaviours, half of the public indicated they had one or more of these (50 per cent), with the most common behaviours being avoiding certain foods due to reacting badly to them or avoiding certain foods on medical advice (both of which were identified by 15 per cent of respondents). The public is evenly split in its attitudes to trying new types of food, with 48 per cent indicating they are happy to eat new foods without knowing too much about them and 47 per cent stating they would not try a new food unless they knew exactly what was in it. One of the factors that might determine attitudes to trying new types of food is concern about food safety. We found surprisingly high levels of public concern about this issue, with one third of respondents indicating they are very concerned (33 per cent), 43 per cent stating that they are fairly concerned and just 24 per cent indicating that they are either not very concerned or not at all concerned. By comparison, attitudes to science in general are, on balance, positive, though views are again mixed; 17 per cent agree with the notion that, overall, modern science does more harm than good, with 27 per cent neither agreeing nor disagreeing and half disagreeing with this view (50 per cent).

Table 10.8 presents the various attitudes and behaviours which are significantly associated with concerns about three or more of the products asked about. The difference in the levels of concern about innovation in food technology between those with different degrees of concern about food safety in general is stark: 55 per cent of those who are very concerned about food safety express concern about three or more of the food products asked about, compared with 17 per cent of those who are not very or not at all concerned about food safety. The latter group expresses the lowest level of concern about innovative food technologies of all the groups examined, whether defined by demographic, attitudinal or behavioural characteristics. This clearly indicates that concerns about innovation in food technology are very strongly linked to, and potentially informed by, concerns about food safety.

We might anticipate that those with a positive attitude towards scientific developments would be less likely to be concerned about the innovative food technologies which are one of the by-products of scientific activity. However, the relationship presented below appears to be more complicated. Those who express a positive attitude towards science, by disagreeing with the statement that modern science does more harm than good, are the least likely to express concern about three or more of the innovative products. Yet it is those who neither agree nor disagree with this statement (and who can thus be regarded as most ambivalent towards modern science) who are more likely to be concerned about innovation in food technology. This may reflect the fact that those who know least about scientific developments are least likely to have a strong view about them but, as we have seen, are also more likely to be concerned about the actual products developed as a result of such development activity.

Three of the dietary behaviours also emerged as significantly related to concerns about innovative foods. First, those who avoid certain foods because they react badly to them are more likely to be concerned about the innovative products described, possibly because they have a heightened level of concern about selecting food products in general, particularly those about which they know little; this might also explain why those who avoid certain food because of medical advice are also more likely to be concerned. Finally, although a comparatively small group, meaning some caution around the findings is required, those respondents who avoid certain foods for religious reasons are more likely than those who do not do so to be concerned about the products described. This ties in with the earlier finding that respondents belonging to a religion have higher levels of concern than their non-religious counterparts.

Levels of concern about innovative food technologies are also associated with individual propensity to try new types of food. Three in ten of those who would be happy to eat a new food even without knowing much about it are concerned about three or more of the innovative food products, compared with almost five in ten of those who would not be happy to try a new food unless they knew exactly what it contained. This measure clearly captures the extent to which the public is wary of the unknown, which we have identified previously as being strongly linked to attitudes to innovation in food.

Table 10.8 Levels of concern about innovation in food technology, by significant food-related attitudes and behaviours

	% very/fairly concerned about 3–5 innovative products or processes	Base
All	40	2247
Concern about food safety		
Very concerned	55	761
Fairly concerned	40	961
Not very/not at all concerned	17	523
Agreement with view that modern science does more harm than good		
Agree	42	330
Neither agree nor disagree	49	535
Disagree	32	996
Motivations for avoiding certain foods		
Avoids certain foods as reacts badly to them	46	287
Does not avoid certain foods for this reason	39	1962
Avoids certain foods for religious reasons	52	73
Does not avoid certain foods for this reason	39	2176
Avoids certain food because of medical advice	45	354
Does not avoid certain food because of medical advice	39	1895
Attitudes to trying new types of food		
Happy to eat foods not tried before without knowing too much about them	30	1062
Wouldn't eat a food that had never tried before unless knew exactly what was in it	48	1077
Involvement in food shopping		
Does all/most of shopping	43	1491
Does some shopping	35	554
Does no shopping	36	203

Finally, we envisaged that involvement in the purchasing and preparation of food might be linked with concerns about innovative technologies, as those undertaking these roles might have a greater understanding of the potential benefits and drawbacks of different food products, including those developed using innovative technologies. This was, in fact, the case, with those with a greater involvement with food, measured in terms of individual contribution to the household's food shopping, being more likely to express concern. In some ways the direction of this relationship could be considered counter-intuitive in the light of the findings on familiarity – if we assume that those who do more of the shopping will have a greater awareness of different food products, then we would have expected the reverse to be true. In fact, the link is likely to partly result from the fact that this group over-represents certain demographic characteristics – particularly being female and being older (themselves linked with higher levels of concern about innovative food technologies). Most notably, 70 per cent of women reported undertaking all or most of the food shopping, compared with 45 per cent of men, with 46 per cent of those aged between 18 and 34 doing this (compared with more than six-tenths of each of the older age groups).

What is clear is that public attitudes to innovation in food technology are strongly inter-meshed with, and cannot be easily separated from, other attitudes and behaviours in relation to science and food.

We have seen that attitudes to innovative food technologies vary substantially across the public, with a large number of demographic, attitudinal and behavioural factors being significantly linked. Inevitably, many of these factors will themselves be related to each other; for instance, it is known that those who have a religion are more likely to be older and from a non-white ethnic group. To identify the factors that relate to levels of concern about innovative food technologies, even when their links with each other are controlled for, multivariate analysis (logistic regression) was undertaken, the results of which are presented in the appendix to this chapter. While they were found to link with levels of concern about innovative food technologies, household income and ethnicity have not been included in this model as, unlike the other characteristics, the primary theoretical explanations for this related to their relationship with other significant characteristics, namely education and religion. Seven characteristics remain significantly linked to levels of concern about innovation in food technology once the other factors have been taken into account. Three of these are demographic characteristics – sex, age and education – while the remaining four are knowledge about innovation in food technology, levels of concern about food safety,[11] attitudes to science and willingness to try new types of food. This importance of demographic characteristics in linking with attitudes to innovation in food technology contradicts the assumptions of the existing literature, which identify general values and beliefs as having the key role to play. There is also a contradiction in terms of the precise demographic variables which are significant: once other factors are controlled for, age is no longer related to concerns, despite that being one of only two significant demographic characteristics identified by previous research. On the other hand, the importance of food-related attitudes and knowledge, and attitudes to science, highlight the fact that attitudes to innovation in food technology do not develop or operate in a vacuum, but form part of a set of beliefs and understandings of food, technology and science. In reducing levels of concern about innovative food technologies, it is likely that policy makers would need to focus on attitudes in relation to much broader areas than this specific topic alone.

Conclusions

What are the implications of our exploration of public attitudes to innovation in food technology for future developments in this area? The variation we have found in attitudes towards different food technologies makes it clear that it is impossible to predict attitudes to any future innovation simply on the basis of public reactions to existing products. Nevertheless, the evidence presented does suggest a number of ways in which attitudes to future developments in innovative food technologies could be anticipated. Public attitudes are characterised by a wariness about new technologies, particularly prevalent among those with less familiarity with their terminology or usage. This is illustrated by the notable differences in attitudes towards eating food prepared in a device using radiation: 57 per cent are concerned about this when the device is called a magnetron, whereas this was the case for just 31 per cent of those who were asked about a microwave. A strong link between concerns about innovative food products and knowledge of this area was also evident. Just 30 per cent of those who answered five or more of the test items correctly were concerned about three or more of the products, compared with 43 per cent of those who answered three or four items correctly and 50 per cent of those who answered less then three items correctly. A public that is better informed in relation to innovation in food technologies is thus also likely to be one that has fewer concerns about future developments. Nevertheless, to some extent, attitudes to any emerging food technology seem destined to be initially wary, before levels of familiarity and knowledge increase through public debate and more widespread use of the resulting products.

Moreover, it is clear that public concern cannot simply be eliminated by the existence of a particular benefit in an innovative food product; even if a risk–benefit assessment of an innovative product is positive, it seems likely that this inherent wariness will dissuade a considerable proportion of the public from considering purchasing or consuming it. This was the case for the hypothetical low calorie cake and cholesterol-reducing sausages we described to respondents: around half said they would not buy the cake, while a third (35 per cent) would not buy the sausages, even when it was explicitly stated that both offered particular benefits, and when no particular drawback had been mentioned.

It seems that there are particular issues that mean women, those in older age groups and those with fewer educational qualifications, express higher levels of concern about innovative food technologies. Further investigation of the factors underpinning these issues would be helpful if these concerns and negative attitudes to this area as a whole are to be reduced. However, any attempt to do so must also focus on attitudes that extend beyond this specific subject area – addressing, for instance, the negative attitudes, held by a substantial minority, towards scientific developments as a whole. In these ways, those involved in policy making and development in relation to innovative food technologies may be able to maximise the chances that the impact of these activities are more positive.

Notes

1. A survey by Mintel in 2006 estimated that 82.7 per cent of households in Great Britain owned a microwave oven.
2. Modified Atmosphere Packaging, the technique used in bags containing ready-to-eat salad leaves has been increasingly applied to a diverse range of food products. Microwaves became increasingly common within British households in the mid-1980s. Widespread distribution of Quorn, the leading brand of myco-protein food in Britain, began in the 1990s, while Benecol has been sold in Britain since the mid-1990s. High pressure pasteurisation, the most recent technological innovation, has been used in the production of food products in Britain since the beginning of this decade.
3. Respondents were asked whether they buy bags containing ready-to-eat salad leaves before being asked the question about their level of concern about the process used in the production of this product, with the two questions being separated by questions on other aspects of food. This order was used to ensure that respondents did not feel compelled to provide an answer in relation to their purchasing behaviour that reflected their previous stated levels of concern.
4. While respondents expressed greater levels of concern in response to the question versions where the name of the food product or process was not identified, this was not felt to be problematic for the calculation of a summary measure; the fact that each respondent was randomly assigned to a version of each of the three questions means that any differences in scores on the summary measure as a result of the use of two different question versions are unlikely to be systematic.
5. Although those respondents who indicated that they "definitely would not" buy the innovative product in response to the initial questions were not asked the follow-up questions, they were allocated to the "definitely would not" category in Table 10.3 above, to enable us to consider what proportion of the public in each instance would buy the innovative product.
6. In each case, those respondents who were asked about each process or ingredient without the commonly known name of a food product or process being included had the option of identifying this spontaneously themselves. This was done by two per cent in relation to microwaves, two per cent in relation to Quorn and less than 0.5 per cent in relation to Benecol.
7. Respondents were asked the knowledge test questions before the questions asking about levels of concern about different innovative products, to ensure that they had not been provided with any additional information about each product to that which they had prior to undertaking the survey.

8. Respondents who provided an "unsure" response for a particular item were assumed to have answered it incorrectly, with this option being included on the showcard to discourage uninformed guessing.

9. It was anticipated that individuals living in rural locations, who may be more likely to have direct contact with traditional methods of food production and agricultural farming, might be expected to have particular attitudes to the newer non-agricultural processes being introduced into food production. However, contrary to these expectations, those living in rural and urban locations expressed almost identical levels of concern about innovative food technologies. The experience of bringing up young children might increase levels of interest about the types of food being consumed by the family, which might heighten levels of concern about any innovative processes involved. In fact, those with dependent children were actually less likely to be concerned, which may be a consequence of their younger age profile. However, this difference narrowly missed attaining the relevant level of statistical significance.

10. Unfortunately our data do not allow us to examine the link between concerns and social trust.

11. It seemed possible that levels of public concern about food safety and about innovative food products might both stem from a general concern in relation to food, and that the two measures of specific concern might be correlated for this reason. A model excluding concern about food safety was also run, and produced very similar results to the one including this factor, reported in the text.

References

Brook Lyndhurst (2009), *An evidence review of public attitudes to emerging food technologies*, London: Food Standards Agency, available at http://www.food.gov.uk/multimedia/pdfs/emergingfoodteches.pdf

National Science Foundation (2002), *Science and Engineering Indicators – 2002*, Va., available at www.nsf.gov/statistics/seind02

Sturgis, P., Cooper, H., Fife-Schaw, C. and Shepherd, R. (2004), 'Genomic science: emerging public opinion', in Park, A., Curtice, J., Thomson, K., Bromley, C. and Phillips, M. (eds.), *British Social Attitudes – the 21st Report*, London: Sage

Acknowledgements

The *National Centre for Social Research* is grateful to the Food Standards Agency for their financial support which enabled us to ask the questions reported in this chapter, although the views expressed are those of the author alone.

Appendix

The following table shows the results of the logistic regression analysis which was referenced in the text of this chapter. Positive coefficients indicate that a group is more likely than the reference category (shown in brackets) to be concerned about three or more innovative food technologies, whilst a negative coefficient indicates that the group is less likely to be concerned.

Table A.1 Respondent concerned about three or more innovative food technologies *vs.* concerned with two or fewer logistic regression

Predictor variables	Co-efficient	Standard error	p value
Nagelkerke R2			
Age (65+)			
18–34	**-0.55	0.20	0.005
35–49	-0.31	0.18	0.076
50–64	-0.02	0.19	0.928
Sex (male)			
Female	**0.71	0.13	0.000
Highest educational qualification (no qualifications)			
Degree	*-0.41	0.18	0.023
A levels	-0.30	0.20	0.141
GCSEs	-0.20	0.17	0.236
Religion (has a religion)			
Does not have a religion	-0.08	0.12	0.487
Knowledge of innovation in food technology (5–7 items answered correctly)			
0–2 items answered correctly	**0.57	0.17	0.001
3–4 items answered correctly	**0.34	0.13	0.008
Modern science does more harm than good (disagrees with view)			
Agrees	**0.46	0.16	0.003
Neither agrees nor disagrees	**0.48	0.13	0.000
Concern about food safety (not very/not at all concerned)			
Very concerned	**1.27	0.17	0.000
Fairly concerned	**0.77	0.16	0.000
Attitude to trying new types of food (happy to eat food not tried before)			
Wouldn't eat food never tried before unless knew exactly what was in it	**0.36	0.12	0.002
Dietary habits (does not avoid foods as reacts badly to them)			
Avoids foods as reacts badly to them	0.29	0.17	0.088
Dietary habits (does not avoid foods for religious reasons)			
Avoids foods for religious reasons	0.31	0.28	0.262
Dietary habits (does not avoid food due to medical advice)			
Avoids food due to medical advice	-0.21	0.17	0.211
Involvement in food shopping (does no shopping)			
Does all shopping	-0.12	0.19	0.523
Does some shopping	-0.07	0.20	0.717
Base	*2250*		

* = significant at 95% level; ** = significant at 99% level

11 Smoking, drinking and drugs: reactions to reform

Rossy Bailey, Elizabeth Fuller & Rachel Ormston[*]

The use of legal or illegal substances which are associated with pleasure, but also with potential harm to health, is by no means a new phenomenon. These behaviours have long been accompanied by concerns about the potential impact on the individual, and on society. Public health research over the last few decades has paid close attention to mapping the prevalence of drug use, and assessing its impact on health. However, there has been less of a focus on finding out what the public thinks about such matters.

In this chapter we focus on attitudes towards three particular drugs: tobacco, alcohol, and cannabis. Of the three, cannabis use is least common: in England and Wales in 2006/7, eight per cent of 16–59 year olds had used the drug in the last year (five per cent in the last month); in Scotland in 2006, 11 per cent reported taking cannabis in the last year (seven per cent in the last month). Smoking cigarettes is more common: in 2007, 21 per cent of adults in England and Wales were smokers, while in Scotland the figure was 24 per cent. In contrast, drinking alcohol is widespread: in 2007, 65 per cent of adults in England and Wales and 57 per cent of adults in Scotland had done so in the last week (NHS Information Centre, 2008a, 2009a, 2009b).

The interest in surveying public attitudes towards these drugs might be unclear, especially considering the fact that two of them are used only by minorities of the British public. However, drug use has, historically, been a matter of public concern and debate, not least in relation to governmental measures to restrict the use of substances. This is a particularly apt time to consider public opinion towards such legislation, as the last five years have seen major shifts in UK policies relating to tobacco, alcohol and cannabis. The approaches have differed, but each has involved more interventionist methods of discouraging consumption. The bans on smoking in enclosed public places introduced in Scotland in 2006 and in England and Wales in 2007 are the most

---

[*] Rossy Bailey is a Senior Researcher at the *National Centre for Social Research* and co-director of the *British Social Attitudes* survey series. Rachel Ormston is a Research Director at the *Scottish Centre for Social Research*. Elizabeth Fuller is a Research Director at the *National Centre for Social Research*.

obvious indicators of this trend. Recent debates about setting a minimum price for alcohol follow a similar line. Such a policy is already being advocated by the Scottish government – though (at the time of writing) not by the UK government. Meanwhile, cannabis, the most commonly used illegal drug, has quite a different policy context, but legislation has moved in a similar direction: the 2009 reclassification of cannabis to Class B, following its downgrading to Class C just five years earlier, represented a return towards a stricter policy approach.

All three of these policies have been the subject of widespread public and media debate, much of which has focused on the morality of restricting people's choices in these ways. For example, while supporters of the smoking bans pointed to the major public health benefits that might accrue, those opposed argued that the bans infringed individual freedom. Indeed, one campaign group appealed for a judicial review of the English legislation, arguing it breached the Human Rights Act by failing to respect the right to privacy of people who wish to smoke in pubs and social clubs.[1] A similar debate about alcohol pricing has recently emerged. Responding to arguments made by England's Chief Medical Officer in support of a 50p minimum price per unit of alcohol (Donaldson, 2009), the Portman Group (who represent the drinks industry) have argued the policy "would have a marginal effect on harmful drinkers but force hard-working families to pay more for a drink".[2] Finally, the reclassification of cannabis in 2009 was contrary to advice from the government's own expert consultants, the Advisory Council on the Misuse of Drugs, who recommended (2008) that the potential health harms associated with cannabis use were better addressed as a public health issue than via the criminal justice system. The Liberal Democrat Home Affairs spokesperson at the time, Chris Huhne, concurred, saying "we need public education, not public flagellation".[3]

These policy shifts, and the debates which have accompanied them, focus attention on questions about what the role of the state should be with respect to substances which have potentially damaging effects on health. Policies that seek to control individual behaviour frequently provoke media accusations that we are living in a 'nanny state'. Equally, policy makers may be criticised for approaches seen as too soft or sympathetic. But what does the public think? This chapter assesses how far the public supports or opposes 'restrictive' policies in relation to tobacco, alcohol and cannabis. In doing so, it also seeks to identify which different social groups are more or less supportive of these policies. Lastly, in relation to tobacco and cannabis, it examines how public views have changed over time – considering, in particular, the question of whether policies have led, or followed, public opinion. This analysis aims to provide important clues as to the likely acceptability of future state action along similar lines.

This chapter draws on data from three surveys: the *British Social Attitudes* survey; its sister survey, *Scottish Social Attitudes*[4]; and the Health Survey for England (HSE).[5] Where possible, in addition to presenting data for Britain, we also compare data for Scotland and England.

Public views on restrictive policies

There are obviously significant differences between tobacco, alcohol and cannabis. Some caveats are therefore required around the extent to which we are able to compare public attitudes towards the three policy areas under consideration. First, the policy approaches differ substantially in the ways in which they aim to restrict behaviour. The smoking ban limits *where* people can smoke, proposals for a minimum price for alcohol aim to increase the financial *cost* of excessive drinking, and the reclassification of cannabis significantly increases the *legal penalties* associated with consumption.

Second, while one aim of each of these policies is certainly to improve people's health, it is far from being the only aim. The smoking bans were presented as measures to protect the health of *non*-smokers, rather than that of smokers. If attitudes to the smoking ban reflect concerns about the health of non-smokers, perhaps some people who might otherwise be opposed to restrictions on 'personal choice' might make an exception in this area. Similarly, proposals for alcohol price increases are in part fuelled by concern about the social cost of excessive drinking. The reclassification of cannabis is, perhaps, the case which is most clearly a reaction to the perceived impact of a drug on users, coming as it did on the back of concern about apparent increases in the strength of cannabis and in its impact on mental health (Moore *et al.*, 2007).[6]

Third, our surveys did not field identical questions about the three drugs. In particular, the questions varied depending on which drug or policy was being asked about, the survey they were carried on, and whether or not they were time-series questions, meaning that they did not specifically refer to current policy.[7] The full questions are given in the sections below.

Finally, as we have seen, there are different prevalence rates for the three drugs; drinking alcohol is a widespread activity, while tobacco and cannabis are only used by minorities of the public. If public attitudes primarily reflect self-interest, we are more likely to find majority support for measures restricting smoking and cannabis use than for alcohol.

Tobacco

For many years health campaigns have told us that smoking is bad for our health and the health of those around us. In the past 20 years, the environment for smokers has become progressively harsher. For example, in the 1980s, many workplaces began restricting or banning smoking among employees, and smoking was banned on many forms of public transport. In the 1990s, government policy included raising the real price of tobacco by means of taxation (Department of Health, 1998). At the same time, the NHS promoted help for people to give up smoking. These measures were to some extent successful in reducing smoking among adults, though a significant minority continued to smoke.[8] In the light of this, as well as a growing consciousness of the health harms caused by inhaling second-hand smoke, UK administrations stopped simply recommending that people gave up smoking and moved to restrict smoking in enclosed public places, first in Scotland in 2006 and then in England and Wales in 2007. At the time the introduction of the smoking ban caused widespread debate among supporters and protestors. So how do people feel about the smoking ban after it has been implemented?

The *British* and *Scottish Social Attitudes* surveys have both included the following question about attitudes towards a ban on smoking in pubs and bars:

> *Here are some places where people might like to smoke. For each one please tick one box to show whether you think smoking should be allowed there, whether there should be restrictions, or whether smoking should be banned there entirely. Firstly, in pubs and bars.*

In Britain as a whole, the majority support a smoking ban, with just seven per cent saying that smoking should be freely allowed (Table 11.1). However, the level of restriction, whether a complete ban or simply restricted to certain areas, divides the public. While just under half (46 per cent) support a ban on smoking in pubs and bars altogether, a similar proportion (41 per cent) prefer limiting smoking to certain areas of pubs and bars.

When we compare levels of support towards the ban in England and Scotland in 2007 we see attitudes were different on either side of the border. While attitudes in England were very similar to those in Britain, Scotland was much more supportive of a complete ban on smoking. There, nearly six in ten supported a complete ban in 2007, while a much smaller proportion (35 per cent) thought that smoking should be allowed in certain restricted areas.

Table 11.1 Support for smoking ban, Britain 2008, England and Scotland 2007

	Britain 2008	England 2007	Scotland 2007[+]
Smoking in pubs should be ...	%	%	%
... freely allowed	7	6	4
... restricted to certain areas	41	44	35
... banned altogether	46	46	58
Base	*1012*	*779*	*1312*

[+] Source: *Scottish Social Attitudes*

As the smoking ban was implemented a year earlier in Scotland than in England, people living in Scotland had more time to get used to the policy than those in England and this could have accounted for their more positive views.

However, attitudes in England in 2008, a year after the ban, are virtually identical to the England 2007 figures[9] – so this explanation holds no weight.

Alcohol

Whereas smoking and cannabis use are restricted to minorities of British people, the majority drink alcohol. The widespread prevalence of drinking has resulted in a degree of ambivalence about alcohol's effects; on the one hand, in moderation, it is acknowledged as a positive part of social life (Strategy Unit, 2004), but there is also increasing public and state concern about the damage caused by excessive drinking on both individuals and society. In recent years, attention has focused on the relationship between the cost of alcohol and drinking behaviour (Strategy Unit, 2004; Department of Health et al., 2007; Scottish Government, 2009a). As households' disposable income has risen, alcohol has become more affordable; taking 1980 as a baseline, by 2007, the affordability of alcohol had increased by 69 per cent (NHS Information Centre, 2008b). In 2008, the Department of Health commissioned a review of the impact of price on alcohol consumption (University of Sheffield, 2008). The proposal that has received most attention is the introduction of a minimum price per unit of alcohol. This was seen as likely to have a significant impact on excessive drinkers, particularly young people; meanwhile, opposition, at least in England, was framed in terms of the impact on 'ordinary' drinkers. This policy has not yet been implemented, although the Scottish government has included proposals for this in its 2009 alcohol strategy (Scottish Government, 2009a). In England, the argument in favour of minimum price per unit has not yet been accepted by the government. [10][11]

In 2007 the Health Survey for England asked the following question to gauge how supportive people would be of a more restrictive policy on alcohol pricing:

> *Please indicate how strongly you agree or disagree with the statements…The government should tax alcohol more heavily to encourage people to drink less*

A higher tax on alcohol was supported by just over a quarter (27 per cent) of people in England, while nearly twice as many (50 per cent) disagreed. A substantial minority (23 per cent) neither agreed nor disagreed. In the same year, the *Scottish Social Attitudes* survey asked a similar question on attitudes towards alcohol pricing. However, they removed the references to "government" and "tax" in the question text to see whether people supported the general principle of a restrictive policy on alcohol. Respondents were asked how much they agreed or disagreed that:

> *The price of alcohol should be put up to encourage people to drink less*

Despite the difference in question wording, support for an alcohol price increase in Scotland was similar to that found in England. A third (33 per cent) agreed that prices should be increased, while nearly half (46 per cent) disagreed.[12]

In both cases the question referred to general, unspecified price increases, rather than the minimum pricing approach advocated by the Department of Health consultation paper and proposed by the Scottish government. Moreover, these data were collected in 2007, since when there has been further political debate about the issue, which may in turn have had an impact on public views. However, the findings do give us an indication of the potential challenges ahead in convincing the public of the merits of using the price of alcohol to discourage excessive drinking.

Cannabis

Cannabis, unlike the other two drugs in this chapter, is illegal, and has been since the 1920s. In 1971, The Misuse of Drugs Act classified it as a Class B drug.[13] Recent policy changes have not changed the legal status of cannabis, but rather have focused on the level of classification. In 2004, cannabis was downgraded to Class C, but just five years later, in 2009, it was reclassified to Class B (meaning that penalties for those caught consuming cannabis increased[14]), representing a return to a more restrictive policy.

The *British Social Attitudes* survey has not included any questions about the reclassification of cannabis directly. However, we have asked whether or not cannabis should be legalised – a debate that has surfaced on a number of occasions since the 1960s. We cannot infer that this necessarily reflects the public's feelings towards the reclassification of cannabis. However, it does give us an indicator of how the public feels about legal restrictions on the use of cannabis more generally. Of course, unlike our questions on tobacco and alcohol, here we are assessing public attitudes towards a policy that has been in place for many decades and is the *status quo*, which in itself is likely to influence public attitudes.

We asked respondents how much they agreed or disagreed that "smoking cannabis (marijuana) should be legalised". The last time the question was asked (in 2007), just over half (54 per cent) disagreed, thereby supporting a restrictive policy towards cannabis. Half as many (25 per cent) agreed that cannabis should be legalised – perhaps a surprisingly large group considering that this goes against the *status quo*. The high level of "neither" responses (at 19 per cent) shows that many were undecided or did not have a strong view.

We also asked a second, more nuanced, question. Rather than simply talking about legalisation (or not), respondents could choose a middle option – that cannabis should be legal *with restrictions*:

> *Which of these statements comes closest to your own view?*
> *Taking cannabis should be legal, without restrictions*

Taking cannabis should be legal, but it should only be available from licensed shops

Taking cannabis should remain illegal

Again a majority (58 per cent) supported cannabis remaining illegal – a similar proportion to that found for our first question. However, just four per cent thought that cannabis should be legalised without restrictions, while a third (34 per cent) said it should be legal but only available from licensed shops. Perhaps, then, public attitudes are more nuanced on this issue than our first question suggested.

Overall, while we do not have a measure of attitudes towards the re-classification of cannabis, a majority of the public does support the government's position on cannabis being illegal. The actual level of support is broadly similar to public attitudes about smoking bans (albeit closer to the support found in Scotland than in England). In contrast, we found far lower levels of support for increasing the price of alcohol. If, as has sometimes been argued, public opinion just as often follows as shapes policy change, then perhaps the fact that a minimum price per unit of alcohol remains a theoretical prospect at the moment explains the lower levels of public enthusiasm for this policy. This is something we explore later in the chapter, where we examine how attitudes have changed over time in relation to smoking and cannabis use.

Who supports and opposes these policies?

We have seen that these different restrictions of potentially harmful substances attract varying levels of public support. Are there also differences in the types of people who are most and least likely to support these policies, or are similar sorts of people for and against restrictive legislation, regardless of how this is enacted?

In comparing different groups in the population, we have a number of expectations about which factors are likely to be relevant. We would expect personal circumstances – and, in particular, personal use of these drugs – to relate to attitudes on this subject. While we are able to look at how the views of frequent and less frequent drinkers differ with respect to alcohol price rises, our data are limited in that we do not have direct information on individuals' cannabis use and smoking. However, we know from other sources that certain socio-demographic characteristics are related to these behaviours, so can treat these as a proxy. For example, age is associated with rates of smoking, binge drinking and drug use (younger age groups being more likely to engage in these behaviours than older age groups). Meanwhile, smoking can be characterised primarily as a habit of the working classes, while the relationship between drinking and class is less straightforward. In fact, there is evidence to suggest that, at least on certain measures, people in middle-class households or occupations drink more than their working–class counterparts.[15] The relationship between class and cannabis use is less clear, but is, roughly speaking, closer to the pattern for smoking (NHS Information Centre, 2008b, 2009a, 2009b). Of course, the low rates of cannabis use and smoking among the public as a whole mean that personal use alone cannot explain the level of opposition found towards restrictive measures on these drugs.

Personal characteristics are also likely to be relevant due to the different types of intervention involved. In the case of alcohol, those on lower incomes might be more opposed to price increases than those who could better afford them, while it has been suggested that the smoking bans unfairly penalise working-class people. We also consider the impact of education, as for most of these measures it is conceivable that higher levels of education may relate to higher levels of support if these respondents are better able to understand the reasons for such policies.

In addition to such social and demographic characteristics, we might also expect that views would relate to a person's underlying values about government intervention. We anticipate there might be a different pattern in relation to the smoking ban, as this policy can be seen as protecting the rights of non-smokers as much as it infringes the personal freedom of smokers.

Frequency of drinking

First, and, perhaps, unsurprisingly, attitudes to increasing the price of alcohol vary depending on how often a person actually drinks alcohol (Table 11.2).

Table 11.2 Support for increasing price of alcohol, by frequency of drinking alcohol, Scotland and England, 2007[16]

	% who agree with increasing price of alcohol[+++]	
	Scotland, 2007[+]	England, 2007[++]
All	33	27
Frequency of drinking		
Every day/five or six days a week	25	14
Three or four days a week	24	13
Once or twice a week	26	23
Once or twice a month/every two months	35	33
Once or twice a year or less	46	43
Does not drink	55	57

[+] Source: *Scottish Social Attitudes*

[++] Source: Health Survey for England

[+++] In Scotland, the statement read "The price of alcohol should be put up to encourage people to drink less". In England the wording was "The government should tax alcohol more heavily to encourage people to drink less".

While around three in ten overall supported this policy, in both England and Scotland, support increased among those who drink just once or twice a month or less, to over half of those who never drink (57 per cent in England, 55 per cent in Scotland). The lower overall level of support for price increases in England is accounted for by those who drink most often being far less supportive than their counterparts in Scotland (for example, 14 per cent of those who drink on at least five days a week in England supported the measure, compared to 25 per cent in Scotland).

Sex and age

We know that men are generally more likely than women to drink to excess and take drugs. The 2007 Health Survey for England showed that 26 per cent of men compared with 15 per cent of women had drunk more than twice the recommended daily maximum limit on at least one day in the previous week (Craig and Shelton, 2008a). In Scotland in 2008, the corresponding proportions were 27 per cent and 18 per cent (Bromley *et al.*, 2009). Meanwhile, the most recent data from the British Crime Survey shows that, in England and Wales, 13 per cent of men had used illegal drugs in the last year, compared with seven per cent of women (Hoare, 2009). Men are also slightly more likely than women to be heavy smokers; in 2007, six per cent of men and four per cent of women smoked 20 or more cigarettes a day in England; the corresponding figures for Scotland were nine per cent of men and seven per cent of women (NHS Information Centre, 2009b).

Given their higher levels of consumption, are men less likely to be in favour of policies which restrict them? In relation to alcohol pricing, the answer appears to be yes – in England, 23 per cent of men compared with 32 per cent of women supported increased tax on alcohol, while in Scotland, 26 per cent of men compared with 38 per cent of women supported alcohol price increases more generally (Table 11.3). Similarly, fewer men than women were in favour of cannabis remaining illegal (53 per cent compared with 64 per cent). However, on the smoking ban the difference between the views of men and women was negligible. This may reflect the fact that the difference between the proportion of men and women who smoke is much smaller than the differences between the proportions of men and women who drink alcohol or take drugs.

Younger people have often been a focus of policy and debate around drink, drugs and smoking. Survey evidence indicates that 'binge drinking' is most common among younger age groups – for example, the 2008 Scottish Health Survey shows that 37 per cent of men and 41 per cent of women aged 16–24 drank more than double the daily maximum recommended units of alcohol on their heaviest drinking day in the previous week, compared with just two per cent of men and one per cent of women aged over 75 (Bromley *et al.*, 2009). Similarly, both smoking and drug use are more common among younger age groups.

Given that they are more likely to (over) indulge in all these behaviours we might expect younger people to be more opposed to government attempts to restrict them. This is broadly the case, though the pattern by age is not quite as clear-cut as one might expect (Table 11.3). Support for the smoking ban in England was lowest among 18–29 year olds, while in Scotland those aged 65 plus were also relatively less supportive. Support for alcohol price rises in both England and Scotland was lowest among the youngest age group and, broadly speaking, increased with age. However, for cannabis, while younger people (those most likely to take the drug) were less likely than the oldest age group to support cannabis remaining illegal (56 per cent compared with 73 per cent), it was 30–39 year olds who were least supportive – just 43 per cent thought cannabis should remain illegal. Thus, while it is generally the case that young people are more likely than older groups to oppose policies to restrict access to drink, drugs and smoking, the relationships are not always linear.

Table 11.3 Support for restrictive drug policies, by sex and age, Scotland 2007, Britain 2007, England 2007 and 2008[17]

	% who think smoking in pubs & bars should be banned		% who think cannabis should remain illegal	% who agree with increasing price of alcohol[+++]	
	Scotland, 2007[+]	England, 2008	Britain, 2007	Scotland, 2007[+]	England, 2007[++]
All	58	46	58	33	27
Sex					
Men	57	46	53	26	23
Women	60	46	64	38	31
Age					
18–29	52	40	56	24	21
30–39	63	49	43	33	26
40–64	60	47	58	32	26
65+	56	48	73	42	36

[+] Source: *Scottish Social Attitudes*
[++] Source: Health Survey for England
[+++] In Scotland, the statement read "The price of alcohol should be put up to encourage people to drink less". In England the wording was "The government should tax alcohol more heavily to encourage people to drink less".

Class, income and education

Smoking can be characterised primarily as a habit of the working classes, lower income groups and those with no qualifications (NHS Information Centre, 2009b). This was, perhaps, one of the reasons that John Reid, then Health

Secretary for England and Wales, suggested that the smoking ban risked removing "one of the very few pleasures" that people from "lower socio-economic categories" have in life.[18] These prevalence patterns are reflected in differing levels of support for the ban between people from different socio-economic groups. For example, in England in 2008, 52 per cent of employers, managers and professionals supported the smoking ban, compared with 40 per cent of those in routine and semi-routine occupations. In Scotland in 2007, the gap was even wider at 70 per cent compared with 44 per cent. Similar patterns are apparent with respect to education and income in both countries.[19] However, it is worth noting that a significant proportion of people from 'working-class' occupations and on lower incomes did support the ban in both countries by 2007/8 (Table 11.4).

Table 11.4 Support for restrictive drug policies, by class, education and income, Scotland 2007, Britain 2007, England 2007 and 2008[20]

	% who think smoking in pubs & bars should be banned		% say cannabis should remain illegal	% who agree with increasing price of alcohol[+++]	
	Scotland, 2007[+]	England, 2008	Britain, 2007	Scotland, 2007[+]	England, 2007[++]
Class					
Routine/semi-routine	44	40	65	36	28
Employers/managers and professionals	70	52	55	35	25
Education					
No qualifications	44	38	68	34	35
Higher education/degree	72	56	49	34	25
Income					
Bottom quartile	41	43	66	37	37
Top quartile	74	56	53	30	22

[+] Source: *Scottish Social Attitudes*
[++] Source: Health Survey for England. For Health Survey for England data top and bottom income quintiles shown
[+++] In Scotland, the statement read "The price of alcohol should be put up to encourage people to drink less". In England the wording was "The government should tax alcohol more heavily to encourage people to drink less".

When it comes to alcohol, there is a similar argument that alcohol price increases would disproportionately penalise working-class people on lower incomes. However, we also know that drinking is less clearly patterned by social class, and that, in fact, on a number of measures, middle-class people on higher incomes drink more (Bromley *et al.*, 2009; NHS Information Centre, 2009a). And here, our evidence appears to favour the importance of drinking behaviour over socio-economic position. In England, it is those with the lowest incomes who are most supportive of alcohol price rises (37 per cent in the lowest quintile, compared with 22 per cent in the highest), while a similar pattern is found for social class (albeit with much smaller differences). Similarly, in Scotland those on lower incomes are slightly more supportive of higher prices than those with high incomes (though, in fact, this difference is not statistically significant). Moreover, in England it is those with *no* qualifications rather than those with degrees who are most likely to support higher alcohol taxes.[21]

The relationship between attitudes towards cannabis and class, education and income is, perhaps, less obvious, not least because the prevalence of cannabis use among these different groups is less easily summarised. On the whole, it is more prevalent among working-class and low income groups (NHS Information Centre, 2008b), and yet these respondents are more likely to say cannabis should remain illegal than those in middle-class and higher income groups. The relationship with education does follow the usual pattern – those with no qualifications are the least likely to use cannabis, and are most likely to say cannabis should remain illegal (68 per cent compared with 49 per cent of those with degrees). However, that may in part reflect the fact that higher levels of education are often associated with more liberal attitudes to issues like drug use.[22] We look at this in more detail in the next section.

Libertarian–authoritarian values

Leaving aside an individual's demographic characteristics and social circumstances, we might expect that their attitudes to these policies would be influenced by their general orientation towards government intervention to control individual behaviour. The *British* and *Scottish Social Attitudes* surveys each include a set of questions designed to measure whether respondents are more 'libertarian' or 'authoritarian'. Their answers are combined into an additive scale for use in analysis (further details are given in Appendix I of this report). We might expect that those with more authoritarian values in general would be more supportive of policies which restrict liberty to indulge in harmful substances, and that, conversely, those who are more libertarian would oppose these kinds of interventions.

This does indeed appear to be the case with respect to the policies on alcohol and cannabis – as shown in Table 11.5. In 2007, 71 per cent of those who were more authoritarian said cannabis should remain illegal, compared with just 45 per cent of those of a more libertarian bent. And although the level of support for alcohol price increases in Scotland among the most authoritarian was fairly modest, at 39 per cent in 2007, this was still higher than the 26 per cent of libertarians who supported such a measure. However, something different appears to be happening with respect to the smoking ban. Here, it is those who are most libertarian who are most supportive – in 2008, 54 per cent of libertarians in England support the ban, compared with 44 per cent of those who are more authoritarian (the equivalent figures in Scotland in 2007 are 66 and 53 per cent). This may reflect the fact that the smoking ban was not purely focused on improving the health of individual smokers, but also on protecting the health of non-smokers. In this context, perhaps the smoking ban is not viewed in terms of individual liberties *versus* state control, but as controlling the liberties of some individuals to protect those of others – something which most libertarians would accept as necessary. However, it may also reflect the fact that there are more libertarians among those who are more highly educated, in managerial or professional occupations, and so on – groups that are also more likely to be non-smokers and thus to benefit from the ban.[23]

Table 11.5 Support for restrictive drug policies, by position on libertarian–authoritarian scale, Scotland and Britain 2007, England 2008[24]

Position on libertarian–authoritarian scale[25]	% who think smoking in pubs & bars should be banned		% who think cannabis should remain illegal	% who agree with increasing price of alcohol
	Scotland, 2007[+]	England, 2008	Britain, 2007	Scotland, 2007[+]
Libertarian	66	54	45	26
Authoritarian	53	44	71	39

[+] Source: *Scottish Social Attitudes*

Overall, the subgroup analyses suggest there is no straightforward way to summarise the relationship between any one characteristic and all three drugs. Rather, two broad findings help to explain this level of variation between the different drugs. First, groups most likely to (over) indulge in the drug in question are generally least likely to support restrictive policies, suggesting that self-interest is playing a key role. The main example is that in some respects, smoking and drinking alcohol are more prevalent among different groups (smoking among working-class, lower income groups and those with no qualifications; drinking among men, middle-class and higher income groups) and it is these groups who are least likely to support the restrictive measures. This finding may also help to explain why assumptions that those on lower incomes or in more working-class occupations would be more opposed to policies that have a financial implication did not hold true for alcohol. However, personal use is clearly not the full story; it does not always hold true that those groups who are most likely to use a particular substance are most opposed to restrictions on it (the relationship between cannabis and class being one example). This may be partly because a person's underlying libertarian–authoritarian values also appear to make a difference to their attitudes. But, interestingly, the relationship between these values and attitudes to the smoking ban is the opposite to that found for restrictive policies on alcohol and cannabis, suggesting that such policies can appeal to libertarians – if, as in the case of the smoking ban, there is an argument that it protects freedoms or rights of non-users.

How and why have views changed over time?

So far we have been looking at our most recent data on levels of support for restrictive policies towards legal and illegal substances. This section examines how views have changed over time and explores some of the reasons why these changes may have occurred. Is it the case that views have changed in line with the move towards more restrictive policies? If so, have policy changes followed or led public opinion? Our data do not allow us to examine change over time in relation to alcohol policy, so in this section we focus on tobacco and cannabis.

Reactions to the smoking ban in Scotland and England

A ban on smoking in public places came into effect in 2006 in Scotland and then in England and Wales in 2007. Attitudes towards smoking in public places were measured on the *British Social Attitudes* survey and the *Scottish Social Attitudes* survey before the ban came into force, and again afterwards.

As shown in Table 11.6, two years before the ban came into effect in Scotland, support for a complete ban on smoking in pubs and bars was relatively low, at a quarter of the public. However, support increased rapidly year on year so that just over half of people in Scotland supported the ban in 2006, the year it was introduced. In England, one year before the ban was introduced support was already relatively high, at around a half of the public. However, this represented a near doubling in support since the previous reading – 15 years earlier – when just over a quarter of people supported such a move. Unfortunately, we do not have a measure between 1990 and 2006 for England, meaning we cannot pinpoint when this change happened. However, while we may be comparing very different timescales and potentially a different pace of change, the general pattern of a sizeable increase in support by the time the ban was implemented is found in both countries.[26]

One year after the respective bans had been enacted, the pattern diverges somewhat. In Scotland in 2007, support for the ban increased a little further to 58 per cent. Meanwhile, support in England over the equivalent period (2007 to 2008) remained static.

Despite the differences between the two countries, there is evidence here that legislative change influenced public attitudes, rather than the other way round. In 1990 (England) and 2004 (Scotland), just a quarter of the public supported a smoking ban – in both cases, the level of support had roughly doubled by the time the ban had been introduced. In Scotland, this change in attitudes occurred in just two years (2004 to 2006), possibly due to public debate about the legislation and its potential benefits. Although support increased in England before the smoking ban was introduced, attitudes may well have been influenced by the situation in Scotland – in that sense, our 'test' of the precise timing of attitude change in relation to legislative change in England could have been contaminated by England's proximity to Scotland.

Table 11.6 Trends in support for a smoking ban in pubs, England and Scotland, 1990–2008

% supporting a complete ban on smoking in pubs[27]	1990	2004	2005	2006	2007	2008
England	27	n/a	n/a	48	46	46
Base	*1068*			*831*	*779*	*860*
Scotland[+]	n/a	25	37	53	58	n/a
Base		*1514*	*1409*	*1437*	*1312*	

[+] Source: *Scottish Social Attitudes*
n/a = not asked

Support for the ban increased far more rapidly in Scotland around the time of the ban than in England, and reached a higher level. So why have attitudes shifted more in Scotland than in England? The differential increase in support for the ban between Scotland and England is apparent across most demographic and social groups. In Scotland, most groups became significantly more supportive of the principle of banning smoking in pubs and bars between 2005 and 2007, while in England, the views of most groups either changed very little or became slightly more negative between 2006 and 2008. However, there is some tentative evidence that the middle classes in particular have reacted differently to the bans in England and Scotland. We saw earlier that class was a significant factor in explaining attitudes to the smoking ban in Scotland and England. But there is also evidence of a widening gap in attitudes between the middle classes in Scotland and their English counterparts. Support among this group for the Scottish ban stood at 70 per cent by 2007 – an above 'average' rise from 2005 (up 23 percentage points). Meanwhile, in England there was a greater than average *fall* in support for the ban among those in professional and managerial occupations, to 52 per cent in 2008 (down seven percentage points from 2006).

A further possible explanation for the greater increase in support for the ban in Scotland may lie in the fact that the Scottish smoking ban was widely viewed as a 'flagship' policy of the new Scottish Parliament. Perhaps warmer views of the smoking ban in Scotland reflect pride in the new parliament? Again, there is some tentative evidence to suggest that this may be the case. In 2005, there was little difference in support for the Scottish smoking ban between people who favoured devolution compared with those who favoured independence or Westminster rule. However, by 2007, 62 per cent of people in Scotland who supported Scotland having its own parliament within the UK agreed smoking should be banned altogether, compared with 52 per cent of those who supported Scottish independence and 53 per cent of those who would prefer Scotland to be run wholly from Westminster.[28] Further, among those who felt having a Scottish Parliament was "giving ordinary people more say in how Scotland is governed", 65 per cent supported an outright ban, compared with 53 per cent of those who felt it was "making no difference". Thus, in Scotland, attitudes to the smoking ban do in part appear to be related to attitudes to the institution that enacted it there.

Changing attitudes to cannabis

We have data on attitudes to cannabis going back to the very start of the *British Social Attitudes* survey series in 1983. Figure 11.1 shows that over a period of almost 20 years there was a liberalisation in attitudes towards the statement "smoking cannabis (marijuana) should be legalised".

Figure 11.1 Views on cannabis legalisation, 1983–2007

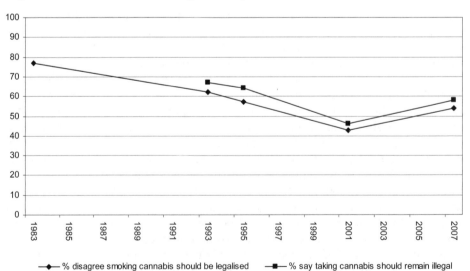

The data on which Figure 11.1 is based can be found in the appendix to this chapter

Nearly eight in ten disagreed that cannabis should be legalised in 1983; by 2001 the proportion had virtually halved to around four in ten. However, between 2001 and 2007 this trend appeared to reverse, with support for cannabis remaining illegal increasing to 54 per cent. A second question (shown earlier in the chapter) displays a similar pattern. We should exercise a little caution in describing the difference between two points in time as a change in a long-term trend. However, for both questions the change is marked – a gap of over ten percentage points between 2001 and 2007.

Although our questions ask about the legal status of cannabis, rather than its level of classification, the changes in attitudes seem to precede legislative changes. In 2004, following two decades of increasingly liberal public views, cannabis was downgraded from Class B to Class C. By 2007, the trend in opinion had reversed, meaning the subsequent 2009 reclassification to Class B (with harsher penalties) was, again, in line with the direction of public opinion.

What explains the liberalisation in attitudes to cannabis in the late 1990s and the partial reversal suggested by the 2007 figures? Unlike the smoking ban, which appears to have led to a change in public opinion, attitudes to cannabis shifted a long time in advance of the first change in legislation in 2004. Gould and Stratford (2002), writing in *The 19th Report*, found that views about the effects of cannabis were strongly related to overall attitudes towards legalisation. We repeated this analysis by asking respondents how much they agreed or disagreed with the following statements:

Cannabis is a cause of crime and violence

If you legalise cannabis, many more people will become addicts

Cannabis isn't nearly as damaging as some people think

Our analysis confirms that attitudes to the legal status of cannabis are strongly linked with responses to these questions. In 2007, among those who agreed that cannabis "isn't nearly as damaging as some people think", just 26 per cent said cannabis should remain illegal, compared with 81 per cent of those who disagreed with this statement. Virtually identical levels of support for cannabis remaining illegal were found for those taking the more restrictive view on the other two statements here.

Can we explain *changing* attitudes to the legal status of cannabis by changing perceptions of the harm caused by cannabis? Table 11.7 suggests we can, at least to some extent. For all three statements, attitudes became more liberal between 1995 and 2001, followed by a return to a more restrictive position by 2007 – a pattern which mirrors public attitudes towards legalising cannabis.

It seems likely that external factors have influenced attitudes towards cannabis on all of these measures. Perhaps the changes in attitudes seen between 2001 and 2007 were, in part, a reaction by the public to the reclassification in 2004. It certainly seems plausible that increased media coverage about the mental health implications of cannabis use, and greater addictiveness of new strains of cannabis, may have influenced perceptions about the consequences of cannabis use. The weight of expert evidence was less clear-cut, however, and the Advisory Council for the Misuse of Drugs (2008), set up by the government to provide the evidence base to support drug policy, recommended that the classification of cannabis should remain unchanged. In returning cannabis to Class B in 2009, the government seemed more in tune with media and public opinion than with the evidence presented by its own expert advisors.

Table 11.7 Attitudes to the impact of cannabis, Britain, 1995, 2001 and 2007

	1995	2001	2007
% agree cannabis is a cause of crime and violence	51	45	55
% agree legalising cannabis means more people will become addicts	60	51	58
% disagree cannabis not as damaging as some people think	43	34	52
Base	*1227*	*1081*	*1056*

Conclusions

This chapter set out to address three main questions. First, we asked whether or not the public supports various 'restrictive' policies in relation to tobacco, alcohol and cannabis. In doing so, we recognised that there are important differences in the way current and proposed government policies in these areas attempt to 'restrict' behaviour. Thus it is perhaps unsurprising that there were differences in the levels of support for the three policy areas. A majority of the public supported the principle of cannabis remaining illegal, while around half support the ban on smoking in pubs and bars (a measure that is a little more popular in Scotland than in England). However, proposals for increasing the price of alcohol, as of 2007 at least, attracted only minority support.

Our second question sought to explore whether there are also differences in the types of people who are most or least likely to support these policies. There are, but these patterns vary for the three drugs in question – suggesting that attitudes reflect a number of different factors. Our data on alcohol pricing shows that those who use substances themselves are less supportive of measures to restrict such behaviour. We also found that patterns of use by age, sex, class and income were generally reflected in attitudes towards restrictive policies. However, this was not always the case – most notably in relation to cannabis, where, in spite of their higher levels of use of cannabis, working-class respondents were more likely to think it should remain illegal. This may, in part, be due to the fact that holding more liberal values in general is both associated with opposition to drug restrictions, and is less common among people in routine and semi-routine occupations. But liberal opposition to restrictions on the freedom to consume potentially harmful substances does not seem to hold for the smoking bans, of which libertarians appear to be more supportive than their more authoritarian counterparts.

It seems, then, that the appeal or otherwise of these policies is not simply a reflection of some general underlying attitude to government interventions to restrict consumption of potentially harmful substances. Rather, our evidence suggests that attitudes in each area reflect a complex range of issues, including own use of the substance, broader social attitudes, including perceptions of the impact of the drug, and a person's libertarian–authoritarian stance.

Our final question asked how views on the legal status of cannabis and on smoking bans had changed over time. Support for banning smoking in pubs and bars in Scotland increased just before and after the introduction of such a ban, suggesting that in this case public opinion may have followed rather than led policy change. In England, support had already increased by the time the ban was implemented, though attitudes here may well have been influenced by the situation in Scotland (the ban was implemented one year earlier there).

Those who are in favour of policies on alcohol pricing might take comfort from this: the level of support found before the smoking bans (around 25 per cent) is similar to the 2007 level of support for an alcohol pricing policy. It seems at least plausible that public attitudes towards this policy could become more supportive in future if it were to become law, and if benefits in terms of health and public order were seen to follow from this legislative change.

Interestingly, attitudes to the smoking ban have shifted significantly more in Scotland than in England. Our data suggests that this may, in part, reflect the greater popularity of the Scottish smoking ban with the Scottish middle-classes compared with their English counterparts. We have also seen that warmer views of the smoking ban in Scotland seem to relate to positive attitudes towards the Scottish Parliament. Meanwhile, public views about cannabis indicate that trends in public opinion on the restriction of harmful substances are reversible, and can precede legislative change, rather than follow it. After 20 years, during which opinion became more liberal, recent years have seen a return to a more restrictive view of cannabis. The recent reclassification of cannabis back to Class B appears to be in tune with this hardening of public opinion.

Notes

1. Discussed in 'Legal challenge to ban on smoking', BBC news website, 29th June 2007, http://news.bbc.co.uk/1/hi/uk/6252016.stm, accessed 21st June 2009.
2. Quoted in 'Plans for a minimum alcohol price', BBC news website, 15th March 2009, http://news.bbc.co.uk/1/hi/health/7944334.stm, accessed 21st June 2009.
3. Quoted in *The Guardian*, 7th May 2008.
4. The *Scottish Social Attitudes* survey (SSA) was established in 1999, with the explicit remit of providing more robust attitudinal data at the Scotland level. Almost identical in design to the *British Social Attitudes* survey, it involves around 1,500 face-to-face interviews each year with a probability sample of the Scottish population aged 18 and above. Respondents also complete a short pen and paper self-completion questionnaire. For further technical details of the 2007 survey, see Annex B of Ormston and Webster (2008).

5. The Health Survey for England is an annual survey commissioned by the NHS Information Centre. It collects data from a probability sample of individuals in private households; in 2007, around 7,000 adults aged 16 or over took part. See Craig and Shelton (2008b).

6. The most dramatic if not the most influential media argument in favour of reclassification was outlined by the *Independent on Sunday* newspaper, which had previously campaigned in favour of decriminalising cannabis. On 18th March 2007, its front page headline read 'Cannabis: an apology' and the paper devoted considerable space to arguing that cannabis presented a real danger to the mental health of users, due largely to the increase in strength of the forms of the drug most commonly on sale, specifically sensimilla, also known as skunk.

7. The main difference between the questions is how closely they reflect current or proposed legislative measures. Our smoking question asks specifically about restricting smoking in pubs and bars, but offers two different options for how those restrictions should be applied. In contrast, our question on cannabis is very general, asking simply whether the drug should be legalised or not. Similarly, the questions on alcohol refer to general, unspecified price increases and not plans for a minimum price per unit of alcohol as proposed by the Scottish government.

8. Trend data for England presented in the NHS Information Centre (2008a).

9. The figures are: six per cent say "freely allowed", 42 per cent "restricted to certain areas" and 46 per cent "banned altogether".

10. See 'Brown lukewarm on alcohol pricing', BBC news website http://news.bbc.co.uk/go/pr/fr/-/1/hi/health/7945357.stm

11. The Welsh Assembly government has considered increasing the price of alcohol via taxation to limit misuse. See Welsh Assembly Government (2008).

12. There was a small difference in the *strength* of feeling: the proportion who said "strongly disagree" was higher in England than in Scotland (17 per cent compared to 10 per cent).

13. Cannabis policy history from Transform: Drugs Policy Foundation website, http://www.tdpf.org.uk/Policy_Timeline.htm accessed 18th September 2009

14. Further details on penalties are available at http://drugs.homeoffice.gov.uk/drugs-l aws/cannabis-reclassifications/

15. NHS Information Centre (2009a) found that households in England where the reference person had a managerial/professional occupation had the highest proportions of men and women who had drunk at all in the last seven days, the highest proportion who had drunk on five or more days in the previous week, and slightly higher proportions who had drunk more than eight (for men) or six (for women) units on their heaviest drinking day. The most recent Scottish Health Survey data (Bromley *et al.*, 2009) suggest differences by socio-economic class in 'binge drinking' (exceeding 8/6 units) are marginal, though those in managerial/professional occupations were more likely to have drunk at all in the last week and women (but not men) in managerial and professional occupations were more likely than women in routine and semi-routine occupations to have exceeded 14 units per week.

16. Bases for Table 11.2 are as follows:

	% who agree with increasing price of alcohol	
	Base Scotland, 2007	Base England, 2007
All	1312	6362
Frequency of drinking		
Every day/five or six days a week	120	1079
three or four days a week	163	961
Once or twice a week	395	1627
Once or twice a month/every couple of months	343	1206
Once or twice a year or less	136	480
Does not drink	143	713

17. Bases for Table 11.3 are as follows:

	% who think smoking in pubs & bars should be banned		% who think cannabis should remain illegal	% who agree with increasing price of alcohol	
	Base Scotland, 2007	Base England, 2008	Base Britain, 2007	Base Scotland, 2007	Base England, 2007
All	1312	860	1056	1312	6362
Sex					
Men	550	365	487	550	2825
Women	762	495	569	762	3537
Age					
18–29	155	127	155	155	1075
30–39	214	148	189	214	1079
40–64	634	385	426	634	2722
65+	306	193	283	306	1486

18. Quoted in 'Smoking 'working class pleasure'', BBC website, 9th June 2004, http://news.bbc.co.uk/1/hi/uk_politics/3789591.stm accessed 20/06/2009

19. Further analyses (regressions) were also carried out (see Appendix I to this report for more details on this type of analysis); results are available from the authors on request. The findings from this analysis (England only) show that income was not significantly related to views on the smoking ban.

20. Bases for Table 11.4 are as follows:

	% who think smoking in pubs & bars should be banned		% who think cannabis should remain illegal	% who agree with increasing price of alcohol	
	Base Scotland, 2007	Base England, 2008	Base Britain, 2007	Base Scotland, 2007	Base England, 2007
Class					
Routine/semi-routine	362	262	303	362	2499
Employers/managers and professionals	501	313	380	501	2119
Education					
No qualifications	299	198	280	299	1677
Higher education/degree	444	245	290	444	1884
Income					
Bottom quartile	237	175	227	237	780
Top quartile	293	179	245	293	1208

21. Note also that regression analysis suggests that class, education and income are not consistent predictors of views on alcohol pricing after other factors have been taken into account. Perhaps the most we can conclude here is that those on low incomes, in working-class professions or with lower levels of education are no more likely than their wealthier middle-class counterparts to feel aggrieved by alcohol price increases.
22. Regression analysis suggests that this is indeed primarily a reflection of more liberal attitudes of university graduates – education and class are not significant predictors of attitudes to the legality of cannabis once respondents' positions on the libertarian–authoritarian scale are taken into account.
23. Indeed, further (regression) analysis of which factors are most significant in predicting attitudes to the smoking ban suggests that how libertarian or authoritarian a person is, is not significant after other factors, like education, age and class, are taken into account. This supports the view that the greater level of support among libertarians primarily reflects the fact that there are more libertarians among those who are more highly educated, in managerial or professional occupations, and so on.

24. Bases for Table 11.5 are as follows:

Position on lib–auth scale	% who think smoking in pubs & bars should be banned		% who think cannabis should remain illegal	% who agree with increasing price of alcohol
	Scotland, 2007	England, 2008	Britain, 2007	Scotland, 2007
Libertarian	405	240	307	405
Authoritarian	475	339	298	475

25. Respondents were given an additive score between 1 and 5 (with 1 being the most liberal and 5 being the most authoritarian), based on their responses to a number of questions measuring how liberal or authoritarian they are on different issues (see Appendix I of this report). Respondents were then grouped, with the lowest third of scores classed as the most 'liberal', the top third the most 'authoritarian' and the middle third classed as 'centre'.

26. Bearing in mind the links we found in the previous section between those most likely to smoke and attitudes towards the smoking ban, it seems possible that changes in the prevalence of smoking might be connected to these shifts in opinion. However, while smoking levels have decreased over the last decade or so, the changes have been fairly small, and cannot explain large shifts in attitudes to smoking bans over a very short period, seen particularly in Scotland. For example, the 2008 Scottish Health Survey found that 29 per cent per cent of men and 28 per cent of women aged 16–64 were current smokers – only slightly lower than the 32 per cent of men and 31 per cent of women in the same age group who smoked in 2003 (Bromley et al., 2009).

27. Question wording was slightly different in 1990 and 2006 on the *British Social Attitudes* survey. It was: 'Please tick one box on each line to show what you think about allowing people to smoke in each of the following places. g) ... in pubs?', whereas in later years the answer options have been stated explicitly in the question stem, as outlined previously.

28. The *Scottish Social Attitudes* survey asks people how they would prefer Scotland to be governed, and offers five options:

Scotland should become independent, separate from the UK and the European Union;

Scotland should become independent, separate from the UK but part of the European Union;

Scotland should remain part of the UK, with its own elected parliament which has some taxation powers;

Scotland should remain part of the UK, with its own elected parliament
which has no taxation powers; or
Scotland should remain part of the UK without an elected parliament
Respondents who pick either of the first two options are classed as supporting
independence; those who pick the third or fourth options are classed as supporting
devolution (Scotland having its own parliament within the UK); while those who
pick the final option are classed as supporting Scotland returning to being run
wholly from Westminster.

References

Advisory Council for the Misuse of Drugs (2008), *Cannabis classification and public
health,* London: Home Office

Bromley, C., Bradshaw, P. and Given, L. (2009), *The Scottish Health Survey 2008:
Volume 1 – main report,* Edinburgh: The Scottish Government

Craig, R. and Shelton, N. (eds.) (2008a), *Health Survey for England 2007: Volume 1 –
Healthy Lifestyles: knowledge, attitudes and behaviour*, Leeds: NHS Information
Centre

Craig, R. and Shelton, N. (eds.) (2008b), *Health Survey for England 2007: Volume 2 –
Methodology and documentation*, Leeds: NHS Information Centre

Department of Health (1998), *Smoking Kills: a White Paper on Tobacco* Cm 4177,
London: The Stationery Office, available at
http://www.archive.official-documents.co.uk/document/cm41/4177/4177.htm

Department of Health, Home Office, Department for Education and Skills, Department
for Culture, Media and Sport (2007), *Safe. Sensible. Social. The next steps in the
national alcohol strategy*, available at
http://www.homeoffice.gov.uk/documents/Alcohol-strategy.pdf

Donaldson, Sir Liam (2009), *150 years of the Annual Report of the Chief Medical
Officer: On the state of public health 2008*, London: Department of Health

Gould, A. and Stratford, N. (2002), 'Illegal drugs: highs and lows', in Park, A., Curtice,
J., Thomson, K., Jarvis, L. and Bromley, C. (eds.), *British Social Attitudes – the 19th
Report*, London: Sage

Hoare, J (2009), *Drug misuse declared: Findings from the 2008/2009 British Crime
Survey*, London: Home Office

Moore, T.H.M., Zammit, S., Langford-Hughes, A., Barnes, T., Jones, P., Burke, M. and
Lewis, G. (2007), 'Cannabis use and risk of psychotic or affective mental health
outcomes: a systematic review', *The Lancet, 370*: 319–328

NHS Information Centre (2008a), *Statistics on Smoking: England 2008*, London: NHS
Information Centre

NHS Information Centre (2008b), *Statistics on Drug Misuse: England 2008*, London:
NHS Information Centre

NHS Information Centre (2009a), *Statistics on Alcohol: England 2009*, London: NHS
Information Centre

NHS Information Centre (2009b), *Statistics on Smoking: England 2009*, London: NHS
Information Centre

Ormston, R. and Webster, C. (2008), *Scottish Social Attitudes Survey 2007: Something To Be Ashamed Of Or Part Of Our Way of Life? Attitudes Towards Alcohol in Scotland*, Edinburgh: Scottish Government, available at http://www.scotland.gov.uk/Publications/2008/08/01112359/0

The Scottish Government (2009a), *Changing Scotland's relationship with alcohol: a framework for action,* Edinburgh: The Scottish Government

The Scottish Government (2009b) *Scotland's People: Annual Report – results from the 2007/8 Scottish Household Survey*, Edinburgh: Scottish Government National Statistics

Strategy Unit (2004), *Alcohol Harm Reduction Strategy for England* Cabinet Office, London, available at. http://www.cabinetoffice.gov.uk/strategy/work_areas/alcohol_misuse.aspx

University of Sheffield (2008), *Modelling the Potential Impact of Pricing and Promotion Policies for Alcohol in England: Results from the Sheffield Alcohol Policy Model*, Sheffield: University of Sheffield

Welsh Assembly Government (2008), *Working together to reduce harm – the substance misuse strategy for Wales 2008–2018*, available at http://wales.gov.uk/consultations/housingcommunity/workingtogether/?lang=en

Acknowledgements

The *National Centre for Social Research* is grateful to the NHS Information Centre for use of Health Survey for England data and to the Scottish Government for use of *Scottish Social Attitudes* data.

Appendix

The data for Figure 11.1 are shown below.

Table A.1 Views on cannabis legalisation, 1983–2007

	1983	1993	1995	2001	2007
% disagree smoking cannabis should be legalised	77	62	57	43	54
Base	*1650*	*1261*	*1058*	*942*	*912*
% say taking cannabis should remain illegal	n/a	67	64	46	58
Base		*1484*	*1227*	*1081*	*1056*

n/a = not asked

Appendix I
Technical details of the survey

In 2008, the sample for the *British Social Attitudes* survey was split into four sections: versions A, B C and D, each made up a quarter of the sample. Depending on the number of versions in which it was included, each 'module' of questions was thus asked either of the full sample (4,486 respondents) or of a random quarter, half or three-quarters of the sample. The structure of the questionnaire can be found at www.natcen.ac.uk/bsaquestionnaires.

Sample design

The *British Social Attitudes* survey is designed to yield a representative sample of adults aged 18 or over. Since 1993, the sampling frame for the survey has been the Postcode Address File (PAF), a list of addresses (or postal delivery points) compiled by the Post Office.[1]

For practical reasons, the sample is confined to those living in private households. People living in institutions (though not in private households at such institutions) are excluded, as are households whose addresses were not on the PAF.

The sampling method involved a multi-stage design, with three separate stages of selection.

Selection of sectors

At the first stage, postcode sectors were selected systematically from a list of all postal sectors in Great Britain. Before selection, any sectors with fewer than 500 addresses were identified and grouped together with an adjacent sector; in Scotland all sectors north of the Caledonian Canal were excluded (because of the prohibitive costs of interviewing there). Sectors were then stratified on the basis of:

- 37 sub-regions;
- population density with variable banding used, in order to create three equal-sized strata per sub-region; and
- ranking by percentage of homes that were owner-occupied.

Three hundred and two postcode sectors were selected, with probability proportional to the number of addresses in each sector.

Selection of addresses

Thirty addresses were selected in each of the 302 sectors. The issued sample was therefore 302 x 30 = 9,060 addresses, selected by starting from a random point on the list of addresses for each sector, and choosing each address at a fixed interval. The fixed interval was calculated for each sector in order to generate the correct number of addresses.

The Multiple-Occupancy Indicator (MOI) available through PAF was used when selecting addresses in Scotland. The MOI shows the number of accommodation spaces sharing one address. Thus, if the MOI indicates more than one accommodation space at a given address, the chances of the given address being selected from the list of addresses would increase so that it matched the total number of accommodation spaces. The MOI is largely irrelevant in England and Wales, as separate dwelling units (DU) generally appear as separate entries on PAF. In Scotland, tenements with many flats tend to appear as one entry on PAF. However, even in Scotland, the vast majority of MOIs had a value of one. The remainder were incorporated into the weighting procedures (described below).

Selection of individuals

Interviewers called at each address selected from PAF and listed all those eligible for inclusion in the *British Social Attitudes* sample – that is, all persons currently aged 18 or over and resident at the selected address. The interviewer then selected one respondent using a computer-generated random selection procedure. Where there were two or more DUs at the selected address, interviewers first had to select one DU using the same random procedure. They then followed the same procedure to select a person for interview within the selected DU.

Weighting

The weights for the *British Social Attitudes* survey correct for the unequal selection of addresses, DUs and individuals and for biases caused by differential non-response. The different stages of the weighting scheme are outlined in detail below.

Selection weights

Selection weights are required because not all the units covered in the survey had the same probability of selection. The weighting reflects the relative selection probabilities of the individual at the three main stages of selection: address, DU and individual. First, because addresses in Scotland were selected using the MOI, weights were needed to compensate for the greater probability of an address with an MOI of more than one being selected, compared to an address with an MOI of one. (This stage was omitted for the English and Welsh data.) Secondly, data were weighted to compensate for the fact that a DU at an address that contained a large number of DUs was less likely to be selected for inclusion in the survey than a DU at an address that contained fewer DUs. (We use this procedure because in most cases where the MOI is greater than one, the two stages will cancel each other out, resulting in more efficient weights.) Thirdly, data were weighted to compensate for the lower selection probabilities of adults living in large households, compared with those in small households.

At each stage the selection weights were trimmed to avoid a small number of very high or very low weights in the sample; such weights would inflate standard errors, reducing the precision of the survey estimates and causing the weighted sample to be less efficient. Less than one per cent of the sample was trimmed at each stage.

Non-response model

It is known that certain subgroups in the population are more likely to respond to surveys than others. These groups can end up over-represented in the sample, which can bias the survey estimates. Where information is available about non-responding households, the response behaviour of the sample members can be modelled and the results used to generate a non-response weight. This non-response weight is intended to reduce bias in the sample resulting from differential response to the survey.

The data was modelled using logistic regression, with the dependent variable indicating whether or not the selected individual responded to the survey. Ineligible households[2] were not included in the non-response modelling. A number of area-level and interviewer observation variables were used to model response. Not all the variables examined were retained for the final model: variables not strongly related to a household's propensity to respond were dropped from the analysis.

The variables found to be related to response were; Government Office Region (GOR), dwelling type, condition of the local area, relative condition of the address and whether there were entry barriers to the selected address. The model shows that response increases if there are no barriers to entry (for instance, if there are no locked gates around the address and no entry phone) and if the general condition of the address and area is good. Response is also higher for addresses in the North East and East Midlands, but lower for semi-detached and terraced houses as well as for purpose-built flats and maisonettes. The full model is given in Table A.1.

Table A.1 The final non-response model

Variable	B	S.E.	Wald	df	Sig.	Odds
Govt Office Region			30.38	10	0.00	
North East	0.22	0.10	4.50	1	0.03	1.25
North West	0.12	0.08	2.15	1	0.14	1.12
Yorks. and Humber	0.00	0.08	0.00	1	0.98	1.00
East Midlands	0.36	0.09	16.51	1	0.00	1.43
West Midlands	0.09	0.08	1.17	1	0.28	1.09
East of England	-0.01	0.08	0.01	1	0.91	0.99
London	0.13	0.08	2.86	1	0.09	1.14
South East	0.03	0.07	0.14	1	0.71	1.03
South West	0.07	0.08	0.61	1	0.43	1.07
Wales	0.17	0.10	2.59	1	0.11	1.18
Scotland	(baseline)					
Barriers to address			7.61	1	0.01	
No barriers	0.21	0.08	7.61	1	0.01	1.24
One or more	(baseline)					
Condition of the area			21.57	2	0.00	
Mainly good	0.24	0.13	3.46	1	0.06	1.27
Mainly fair	0.06	0.13	0.25	1	0.62	1.07
Mainly bad	(baseline)					
Relative condition of the address			57.52	2	0.00	
Better	0.73	0.10	52.29	1	0.00	2.07
About the same	0.31	0.08	15.12	1	0.00	1.36
Worse	(baseline)					
Dwelling type			15.43	5	0.01	
Semi-detached house	-0.12	0.05	6.24	1	0.01	0.88
Terraced house	-0.13	0.05	6.47	1	0.01	0.87
Flat – purpose built	-0.28	0.08	11.70	1	0.00	0.76
Flat – conversion	-0.03	0.13	0.06	1	0.80	0.97
Other	-0.14	0.21	0.43	1	0.51	0.87
Detached house	(baseline)					
Constant	-0.24	0.18	1.77	1	0.18	0.79

Notes:
The response is 1 = individual responding to the survey, 0 = non-response
Only variables that are significant at the 0.05 level are included in the model
The model R^2 is 0.01 (Cox and Snell)
B is the estimate coefficient with standard error **S.E.**
The **Wald**-test measures the impact of the categorical variable on the model with the appropriate number of degrees of freedom **df**. If the test is significant (**sig.** < 0.05), then the categorical variable is considered to be 'significantly associated' with the response variable and therefore included in the model

The non-response weight is calculated as the inverse of the predicted response probabilities saved from the logistic regression model. The non-response weight was then combined with the selection weights to create the final non-response weight. The top one per cent of the weight were trimmed before the weight was scaled to the achieved sample size (resulting in the weight being standardised around an average of one).

Calibration weighting

The final stage of weighting was to adjust the final non-response weight so that the weighted sample matched the population in terms of age, sex and region.

Table A.2 Weighted and unweighted sample distribution, by GOR, age and sex

	Population	Unweighted respondents	Respondents weighted by selection weight only	Respondents weighted by un-calibrated non-response weight	Respondents weighted by final weight
Govt Office Region	%	%	%	%	%
North East	4.4	4.8	4.3	4.4	4.4
North West	11.5	11.9	6.5	11.7	11.5
Yorks. and Humber	8.7	8.7	8.5	8.9	8.7
East Midlands	7.4	8.9	8.2	7.9	7.4
West Midlands	9.0	9.3	3.1	9.2	9.0
East of England	9.5	8.3	4.5	8.5	9.5
London	12.7	10.9	9.9	11.7	12.7
South East	14.0	15.0	5.1	15.4	14.0
South West	8.9	8.8	8.8	8.8	8.9
Wales	5.0	4.8	10.8	4.6	5.0
Scotland	8.8	8.7	10.3	9.0	8.8
Age & sex	%	%	%	%	%
M 18–24	6.2	2.9	4.3	4.3	6.2
M 25–34	8.2	5.9	6.5	6.7	8.2
M 35–44	9.6	8.5	8.5	8.5	9.6
M 45–54	8.2	7.7	8.2	8.1	8.2
M 55–59	3.9	3.0	3.1	3.1	3.9
M 60–64	3.6	4.4	4.5	4.5	3.6
M 65+	8.9	10.6	9.9	9.8	8.9
F 18–24	5.8	4.1	5.1	5.2	5.8
F 25–34	8.2	8.8	8.8	8.9	8.2
F 35–44	9.8	11.3	10.8	10.8	9.8
F 45–54	8.4	9.5	10.3	10.2	8.4
F 55–59	4.0	4.5	4.7	4.6	4.0
F 60–64	3.7	4.8	4.6	4.5	3.7
F 65+	11.6	14.0	10.9	10.8	11.6
Base	46,537,051	4486	4486	4486	4486

Only adults aged 18 and over are eligible to take part in the survey, therefore the data have been weighted to the British population aged 18+ based on the 2007 mid-year population estimates from the Office for National Statistics/General Register Office for Scotland.

The survey data were weighted to the marginal age/sex and GOR distributions using raking-ratio (or rim) weighting. As a result, the weighted data should exactly match the population across these three dimensions. This is shown in Table A.2.

The calibration weight is the final non-response weight to be used in the analysis of the 2008 survey; this weight has been scaled to the responding sample size. The range of the weights is given in Table A.3.

Table A.3 Range of weights

	N	Minimum	Mean	Maximum
DU and person selection weight	4486	0.55	1.00	2.20
Un-calibrated non-response weight	4486	0.42	1.00	2.39
Final calibrated non-response weight	4486	0.34	1.00	3.82

Effective sample size

The effect of the sample design on the precision of survey estimates is indicated by the effective sample size (neff). The effective sample size measures the size of an (unweighted) simple random sample that would achieve the same precision (standard error) as the design being implemented. If the effective sample size is close to the actual sample size, then we have an efficient design with a good level of precision. The lower the effective sample size is, the lower the level of precision. The efficiency of a sample is given by the ratio of the effective sample size to the actual sample size. Samples that select one person per household tend to have lower efficiency than samples that select all household members. The final calibrated non-response weights have an effective sample size (neff) of 3,651 and efficiency of 81 per cent.

All the percentages presented in this report are based on weighted data.

Questionnaire versions

Each address in each sector (sampling point) was allocated to either the A, B, C or D portion of the sample. If one serial number was version A, the next was version B, the third version C and the fourth version D. Thus, each interviewer was allocated seven or eight cases from each of versions A, B, C and D. There were 2,265 issued addresses for each version.

Fieldwork

Interviewing was mainly carried out between June and September 2008, with a small number of interviews taking place in October and November.

Fieldwork was conducted by interviewers drawn from the *National Centre for Social Research*'s regular panel and conducted using face-to-face computer-assisted interviewing.[3] Interviewers attended a one-day briefing conference to familiarise them with the selection procedures and questionnaires.

The mean interview length was 66 minutes for versions A and B of the questionnaire, 72 minutes for version B and 68 minutes for version D.[4] Interviewers achieved an overall response rate of between 54.8 and 55.9 per cent. Details are shown in Table A.4.

Table A.4 Response rate[1] on *British Social Attitudes*, 2008

	Number	Lower limit of response (%)	Upper limit of response (%)
Addresses issued	9060		
Out of scope	870		
Upper limit of eligible cases	8190	100.0	
Uncertain eligibility	166	2.0	
Lower limit of eligible cases	8024		100.0
Interview achieved	4486	54.8	55.9
Interview not achieved	3538	43.2	44.1
Refused[2]	2763	33.7	34.4
Non-contacted[3]	357	4.4	4.4
Other non-response	418	5.1	5.2

1 Response is calculated as a range from a lower limit where all unknown eligibility cases (for example, address inaccessible, or unknown whether address is residential) are assumed to be eligible and therefore included in the unproductive outcomes, to an upper limit where all these cases are assumed to be ineligible (and are therefore excluded from the response calculation)

2 'Refused' comprises refusals before selection of an individual at the address, refusals to the office, refusal by the selected person, 'proxy' refusals (on behalf of the selected respondent) and broken appointments after which the selected person could not be recontacted

3 'Non-contacted' comprises households where no one was contacted and those where the selected person could not be contacted

As in earlier rounds of the series, the respondent was asked to fill in a self-completion questionnaire which, whenever possible, was collected by the interviewer. Otherwise, the respondent was asked to post it to the *National*

Centre for Social Research. If necessary, up to three postal reminders were sent to obtain the self-completion supplement.

A total of 496 respondents (11 per cent of those interviewed) did not return their self-completion questionnaire. Version A of the self-completion questionnaire was returned by 88 per cent of respondents to the face-to-face interview, version B by 89 per cent and versions C and D by 90 per cent. As in previous rounds, we judged that it was not necessary to apply additional weights to correct for non-response to the self-completion questionnaire.

Advance letter

Interviewers were supplied with letters describing the purpose of the survey and the coverage of the questionnaire, which they posted to sampled addresses before making any calls. [5]

Analysis variables

A number of standard analyses have been used in the tables that appear in this report. The analysis groups requiring further definition are set out below. For further details see Stafford and Thomson (2006). Where there are references to specific question numbers, the full question text, including frequencies, can be found at www.natcen.ac.uk/bsaquestionnaires.

Region

The dataset is classified by the 12 Government Office Regions.

Standard Occupational Classification

Respondents are classified according to their own occupation, not that of the 'head of household'. Each respondent was asked about their current or last job, so that all respondents except those who had never worked were coded. Additionally, all job details were collected for all spouses and partners in work.

With the 2001 survey, we began coding occupation to the new Standard Occupational Classification 2000 (SOC 2000) instead of the Standard Occupational Classification 1990 (SOC 90). The main socio-economic grouping based on SOC 2000 is the National Statistics Socio-Economic Classification (NS-SEC). However, to maintain time-series, some analysis has continued to use the older schemes based on SOC 90 – Registrar General's Social Class, Socio-Economic Group and the Goldthorpe schema.

National Statistics Socio-Economic Classification (NS-SEC)

The combination of SOC 2000 and employment status for current or last job generates the following NS-SEC analytic classes:

- Employers in large organisations, higher managerial and professional
- Lower professional and managerial; higher technical and supervisory
- Intermediate occupations
- Small employers and own account workers
- Lower supervisory and technical occupations
- Semi-routine occupations
- Routine occupations

The remaining respondents are grouped as "never had a job" or "not classifiable". For some analyses, it may be more appropriate to classify respondents according to their current socio-economic status, which takes into account only their present economic position. In this case, in addition to the seven classes listed above, the remaining respondents not currently in paid work fall into one of the following categories: "not classifiable", "retired", "looking after the home", "unemployed" or "others not in paid occupations".

Registrar General's Social Class

As with NS-SEC, each respondent's social class is based on his or her current or last occupation. The combination of SOC 90 with employment status for current or last job generates the following six social classes:

I	Professional etc. occupations	
II	Managerial and technical occupations	'Non-manual'
III (Non-manual)	Skilled occupations	
III (Manual)	Skilled occupations	
IV	Partly skilled occupations	'Manual'
V	Unskilled occupations	

They are usually collapsed into four groups: I & II, III Non-manual, III Manual, and IV & V.

Socio-Economic Group

As with NS-SEC, each respondent's Socio-Economic Group (SEG) is based on his or her current or last occupation. SEG aims to bring together people with jobs of similar social and economic status, and is derived from a combination of employment status and occupation. The full SEG classification identifies 18 categories, but these are usually condensed into six groups:

- Professionals, employers and managers
- Intermediate non-manual workers
- Junior non-manual workers
- Skilled manual workers
- Semi-skilled manual workers
- Unskilled manual workers

As with NS-SEC, the remaining respondents are grouped as "never had a job" or "not classifiable".

Goldthorpe schema

The Goldthorpe schema classifies occupations by their 'general comparability', considering such factors as sources and levels of income, economic security, promotion prospects, and level of job autonomy and authority. The Goldthorpe schema was derived from the SOC 90 codes combined with employment status. Two versions of the schema are coded: the full schema has 11 categories; the 'compressed schema' combines these into the five classes shown below.

- Salariat (professional and managerial)
- Routine non-manual workers (office and sales)
- Petty bourgeoisie (the self-employed, including farmers, with and without employees)
- Manual foremen and supervisors
- Working class (skilled, semi-skilled and unskilled manual workers, personal service and agricultural workers)

There is a residual category comprising those who have never had a job or who gave insufficient information for classification purposes.

Industry

All respondents whose occupation could be coded were allocated a Standard Industrial Classification 2007 (SIC 07). Two-digit class codes are used. As with social class, SIC may be generated on the basis of the respondent's current occupation only, or on his or her most recently classifiable occupation. SIC 2003 was also generated in 2008 as it was the first year of SIC 2007 coding.

Party identification

Respondents can be classified as identifying with a particular political party on one of three counts: if they consider themselves supporters of that party, as closer to it than to others, or as more likely to support it in the event of a general election. The three groups are generally described respectively as *partisans*, *sympathisers* and *residual identifiers*. In combination, the three groups are referred to as 'identifiers'. Responses are derived from the following questions:

Generally speaking, do you think of yourself as a supporter of any one political party? [Yes/No]

[If "No"/"Don't know"]

Do you think of yourself as a little closer to one political party than to the others? [Yes/No]

[If "Yes" at either question or "No"/"Don't know" at 2nd question]
[Which one?/If there were a general election tomorrow, which political party do you think you would be most likely to support?]

[Conservative; Labour; Liberal Democrat; Scottish National Party; Plaid Cymru; Green Party; UK Independence Party (UKIP)/Veritas; British National Party (BNP)/National Front; RESPECT/Scottish Socialist Party (SSP)/Socialist Party; Other party; Other answer; None; Refused to say]

Income

Two variables classify the respondent's earnings (REarn) and household income (HHInc) on the questionnaire (see www.natcen.ac.uk/bsaquestionnaires). Two new derived variables were added to the *British Social Attitudes* 2008 dataset giving quartiles of these variables. They are [REarnQ] and [HHIncQ] and are calculated based on quartiles of all valid responses to the questions.

Attitude scales

Since 1986, the *British Social Attitudes* surveys have included two attitude scales which aim to measure where respondents stand on certain underlying value dimensions – left–right and libertarian–authoritarian.[6] Since 1987 (except 1990), a similar scale on 'welfarism' has been asked. Some of the items in the welfarism scale were changed in 2000–2001. The current version of the scale is listed below.

A useful way of summarising the information from a number of questions of this sort is to construct an additive index (Spector, 1992; DeVellis, 2003). This approach rests on the assumption that there is an underlying – 'latent' – attitudinal dimension which characterises the answers to all the questions within each scale. If so, scores on the index are likely to be a more reliable indication of the underlying attitude than the answers to any one question.

Each of these scales consists of a number of statements to which the respondent is invited to "agree strongly", "agree", "neither agree nor disagree", "disagree" or "disagree strongly".

The items are:

Left–right scale

Government should redistribute income from the better off to those who are less well off. *[Redistrb]*

Big business benefits owners at the expense of workers. *[BigBusnN]*

Ordinary working people do not get their fair share of the nation's wealth. *[Wealth]*[7]

There is one law for the rich and one for the poor. *[RichLaw]*

Management will always try to get the better of employees if it gets the chance. *[Indust4]*

Libertarian–authoritarian scale

Young people today don't have enough respect for traditional British values. *[TradVals]*

People who break the law should be given stiffer sentences. *[StifSent]*

For some crimes, the death penalty is the most appropriate sentence. *[DeathApp]*

Schools should teach children to obey authority. *[Obey]*

The law should always be obeyed, even if a particular law is wrong. *[WrongLaw]*

Censorship of films and magazines is necessary to uphold moral standards. *[Censor]*

Welfarism scale

The welfare state encourages people to stop helping each other. *[WelfHelp]*

The government should spend more money on welfare benefits for the poor, even if it leads to higher taxes. *[MoreWelf]*

Around here, most unemployed people could find a job if they really wanted one. *[UnempJob]*

Many people who get social security don't really deserve any help. *[SocHelp]*

Most people on the dole are fiddling in one way or another. *[DoleFidl]*

If welfare benefits weren't so generous, people would learn to stand on their own two feet. *[WelfFeet]*

Cutting welfare benefits would damage too many people's lives. *[DamLives]*

The creation of the welfare state is one of Britain's proudest achievements. *[ProudWlf]*

The indices for the three scales are formed by scoring the leftmost, most libertarian or most pro-welfare position, as 1 and the rightmost, most authoritarian or most anti-welfarist position, as 5. The "neither agree nor disagree" option is scored as 3. The scores to all the questions in each scale are added and then divided by the number of items in the scale, giving indices ranging from 1 (leftmost, most libertarian, most pro-welfare) to 5 (rightmost, most authoritarian, most anti-welfare). The scores on the three indices have been placed on the dataset.[8]

The scales have been tested for reliability (as measured by Cronbach's alpha). The Cronbach's alpha (unstandardised items) for the scales in 2008 are 0.82 for the left–right scale, 0.71 for the welfarism scale and 0.81 for the libertarian–authoritarian scale. This level of reliability can be considered "very good" for the left–right and libertarian–authoritarian scales and "respectable" for the welfarism scale (DeVellis, 2003: 95–96).

Other analysis variables

These are taken directly from the questionnaire and to that extent are self-explanatory (see www.natcen.ac.uk/bsaquestionnaires). The principal ones are:

Sex (Q. 41)
Age (Q. 42)
Household income (Q. 1353)
Economic position (Q. 977)
Religion (Q. 1111)
Highest educational qualification obtained (Qs. 1232–1233)
Marital status (Qs. 140–146)
Benefits received (Qs. 1309–1346)

Sampling errors

No sample precisely reflects the characteristics of the population it represents, because of both sampling and non-sampling errors. If a sample were designed as a random sample (if every adult had an equal and independent chance of inclusion in the sample), then we could calculate the sampling error of any percentage, p, using the formula:

$$s.e. \ (p) = \sqrt{\frac{p(100 - p)}{n}}$$

where n is the number of respondents on which the percentage is based. Once the sampling error had been calculated, it would be a straightforward exercise to calculate a confidence interval for the true population percentage. For example, a 95 per cent confidence interval would be given by the formula:

$$p \pm 1.96 \times s.e.\ (p)$$

Clearly, for a simple random sample (srs), the sampling error depends only on the values of p and n. However, simple random sampling is almost never used in practice, because of its inefficiency in terms of time and cost.

As noted above, the *British Social Attitudes* sample, like that drawn for most large-scale surveys, was clustered according to a stratified multi-stage design into 302 postcode sectors (or combinations of sectors). With a complex design like this, the sampling error of a percentage giving a particular response is not simply a function of the number of respondents in the sample and the size of the percentage; it also depends on how that percentage response is spread within and between sample points.

The complex design may be assessed relative to simple random sampling by calculating a range of design factors (DEFTs) associated with it, where:

$$\text{DEFT} = \sqrt{\frac{\text{Variance of estimator with complex design, sample size n}}{\text{Variance of estimator with srs design, sample size n}}}$$

and represents the multiplying factor to be applied to the simple random sampling error to produce its complex equivalent. A design factor of one means that the complex sample has achieved the same precision as a simple random sample of the same size. A design factor greater than one means the complex sample is less precise than its simple random sample equivalent. If the DEFT for a particular characteristic is known, a 95 per cent confidence interval for a percentage may be calculated using the formula:

$$p \pm 1.96 \times complex\ sampling\ error\ (p)$$

$$= p \pm 1.96 \times \text{DEFT} \times \sqrt{\frac{p(100 - p)}{n}}$$

Calculations of sampling errors and design effects were made using the statistical analysis package STATA.

Table A.5 gives examples of the confidence intervals and DEFTs calculated for a range of different questions. Most background variables were fielded on the whole sample, whereas many attitudinal variables were asked only of a half or quarter of the sample; some were asked on the interview questionnaire and some on the self-completion supplement.

Table A.5 Complex standard errors and confidence intervals of selected variables

	% (p)	Complex standard error of p	95% confidence interval	DEFT	Base
Classification variables					
Q. 275 Party identification (full sample)					
Conservative	31.9	1.0	29.8–34.0	1.49	4486
Labour	27.4	0.8	25.8-29.0	1.20	4486
Liberal Democrat	9.0	0.6	7.9-10.1	1.33	4486
Q. 1099 Housing tenure (full sample)					
Owns	70.2	1.2	67.8-72.5	1.76	4486
Rents from local authority	10.7	0.8	9.3-12.3	1.64	4486
Rents privately/HA	17.0	0.9	15.3-18.9	1.64	4486
Q. 1111 Religion (full sample)					
No religion	43.2	0.9	41.4-45.0	1.23	4486
Church of England	22.5	0.6	20.9-24.1	1.30	4486
Roman Catholic	9.3	0.5	8.4-10.2	1.06	4486
Q. 1167 Age of completing continuous full-time education (full sample)					
16 or under	53.2	1.0	51.3-55.2	1.30	4486
17 or 18	19.5	0.7	18.2-20.9	1.17	4486
19 or over	23.1	1.0	21.3-25.1	1.52	4486
Q. 228 Home internet access (full sample)					
Yes	72.5	0.8	70.9-74.0	1.18	4486
No	27.5	0.8	26.0-29.1	1.18	4486
Q. 1100 Urban or rural residence (3/4 sample)					
A big city	10.4	1.3	8.1-13.3	2.50	3364
The suburbs or outskirts of a big city	24.0	1.6	20.9-27.4	2.23	3364
A small city/town	43.5	2.1	39.4-47.7	2.47	3364
Country village	19.1	1.5	16.3-22.3	2.24	3364
Farm/home in the country	2.3	0.4	1.6-3.3	1.29	3364
Attitudinal variables (face-to-face interview)					
Q. 296 Benefits for the unemployed are ... (3/4 sample)					
... too low	21.1	0.9	19.4-23.0	1.30	3358
... too high	61.0	1.2	58.7-63.3	1.39	3358
Q. 578 Level of concern about food safety in Britain (3/4 sample)					
Very concerned	33.0	1.2	30.7-35.4	1.21	2250
Fairly concerned	42.8	1.3	40.2-45.4	1.25	2250
Not very concerned	20.5	1.0	18.5-22.6	1.20	2250
Not at all concerned	3.5	0.5	2.7-4.6	1.21	2250

Table continued on next page

	% (p)	Complex standard error of p	95% confidence interval	DEFT	Base

Q. 388 How serious a problem is traffic congestion in towns, cities (3/4 sample)

A very serious problem	16.6	0.9	14.9-18.5	1.42	3094
A serious problem	33.7	1.0	31.9-35.7	1.17	3094
Not a very serious problem	31.3	1.1	29.2-33.5	1.34	3094
Not a problem at all	18.1	1.0	16.3-20.0	1.44	3094

Q. 1078 How important or unimportant is it for Britain to continue to have a monarchy (1/4 sample)

Very important	32.7	1.6	29.7-35.9	1.13	1128
Quite important	29.6	1.5	26.8-32.6	1.08	1128
Not very important	18.7	1.2	16.4-21.3	1.06	1128
Not at all important	8.5	1.0	6.8-10.6	1.17	1128
Monarchy should be abolished	7.7	0.9	6.1-9.8	1.18	1128

Q. 1103 In a year from now, do you expect house prices in your area to have gone up, to have stayed the same, or to have gone down (1/4 sample)

Gone up by a little	22.4	1.4	19.7-25.4	1.16	1129
Stayed the same	29.2	1.4	26.6-32.0	1.02	1129
Gone down by a little	44.1	1.7	40.8-47.4	1.13	1129

Attitudinal variables (self-completion)

A58a Government should redistribute income from the better off to those who
B55a are less well off (full sample)

C37a Agree strongly	8.3	0.6	7.2-9.6	1.38	3990
D49a Agree	29.6	0.8	28.0-31.3	1.16	3990
Neither agree nor disagree	25.2	0.8	23.7-26.8	1.12	3990
Disagree	27.6	0.8	26.1-29.1	1.10	3990
Disagree strongly	7.3	0.5	6.3-8.3	1.24	3990

B36 Opinion of person who does not report change of circumstances to
C2   benefit office – so is £500 better off (3/4 sample)

D2 Not wrong	1.2	0.2	0.8-1.7	1.17	3000
A bit wrong	11.6	0.7	10.3-13.1	1.21	3000
Wrong	50.1	1.1	47.9-52.3	1.22	3000
Seriously wrong	34.9	1.1	32.8-37.0	1.22	3000

A7 Generally speaking, would you say that people can be trusted or that you
B7 can't be too careful in dealing with people? (1/2 sample)

People can almost always be trusted	2.4	0.4	1.8-3.2	1.07	1986
People can usually be trusted	42.8	1.1	40.6-45.1	1.03	1986
You usually can't be too careful	41.6	1.3	39.1-44.1	1.16	1986
You almost always can't be too careful	9.8	0.7	8.4-11.4	1.12	1986

A38a People should be able to travel by plane as much as they like (1/4 sample)

Agree	66.2	1.8	62.6-69.7	1.18	990
Neither agree nor disagree	18.1	1.3	15.6-20.9	1.09	990
Disagree	11.7	1.2	9.5-14.3	1.18	990

The table shows that most of the questions asked of all sample members have a confidence interval of around plus or minus two to three per cent of the survey percentage. This means that we can be 95 per cent certain that the true population percentage is within two to three per cent (in either direction) of the percentage we report.

Variables with much larger variation are, as might be expected, those closely related to the geographic location of the respondent (for example, whether they live in a big city, a small town or a village). Here, the variation may be as large as six or seven per cent either way around the percentage found on the survey. Consequently, the design effects calculated for these variables in a clustered sample will be greater than the design effects calculated for variables less strongly associated with area. Also, sampling errors for percentages based only on respondents to just one of the versions of the questionnaire, or on subgroups within the sample, are larger than they would have been had the questions been asked of everyone.

Analysis techniques

Regression

Regression analysis aims to summarise the relationship between a 'dependent' variable and one or more 'independent' variables. It shows how well we can estimate a respondent's score on the dependent variable from knowledge of their scores on the independent variables. It is often undertaken to support a claim that the phenomena measured by the independent variables *cause* the phenomenon measured by the dependent variable. However, the causal ordering, if any, between the variables cannot be verified or falsified by the technique. Causality can only be inferred through special experimental designs or through assumptions made by the analyst.

All regression analysis assumes that the relationship between the dependent and each of the independent variables takes a particular form. In *linear regression*, it is assumed that the relationship can be adequately summarised by a straight line. This means that a one percentage point increase in the value of an independent variable is assumed to have the same impact on the value of the dependent variable on average, irrespective of the previous values of those variables.

Strictly speaking the technique assumes that both the dependent and the independent variables are measured on an interval-level scale, although it may sometimes still be applied even where this is not the case. For example, one can use an ordinal variable (e.g. a Likert scale) as a *dependent* variable if one is willing to assume that there is an underlying interval-level scale and the difference between the observed ordinal scale and the underlying interval scale is due to random measurement error. Often the answers to a number of Likert-type questions are averaged to give a dependent variable that is more like a continuous variable. Categorical or nominal data can be used as *independent* variables by converting them into dummy or binary variables; these are variables where the only valid scores are 0 and 1, with 1 signifying membership of a particular category and 0 otherwise.

The assumptions of linear regression cause particular difficulties where the *dependent* variable is binary. The assumption that the relationship between the dependent and the independent variables is a straight line means that it can produce estimated values for the dependent variable of less than 0 or greater than 1. In this case it may be more appropriate to assume that the relationship between the dependent and the independent variables takes the form of an S-curve, where the impact on the dependent variable of a one-point increase in an independent variable becomes progressively less the closer the value of the dependent variable approaches 0 or 1. *Logistic regression* is an alternative form of regression which fits such an S-curve rather than a straight line. The technique can also be adapted to analyse multinomial non-interval-level dependent variables, that is, variables which classify respondents into more than two categories.

The two statistical scores most commonly reported from the results of regression analyses are:

A measure of variance explained: This summarises how well all the independent variables combined can account for the variation in respondents' scores in the dependent variable. The higher the measure, the more accurately we are able in general to estimate the correct value of each respondent's score on the dependent variable from knowledge of their scores on the independent variables.

A parameter estimate: This shows how much the dependent variable will change on average, given a one-unit change in the independent variable (while holding all other independent variables in the model constant). The parameter estimate has a positive sign if an increase in the value of the independent variable results in an increase in the value of the dependent variable. It has a negative sign if an increase in the value of the independent variable results in a decrease in the value of the dependent variable. If the parameter estimates are standardised, it is possible to compare the relative impact of different independent variables; those variables with the largest standardised estimates can be said to have the biggest impact on the value of the dependent variable.

Regression also tests for the statistical significance of parameter estimates. A parameter estimate is said to be significant at the five per cent level if the range of the values encompassed by its 95 per cent confidence interval (see also section on sampling errors) are either all positive or all negative. This means that there is less than a five per cent chance that the association we have found between the dependent variable and the independent variable is simply the result of sampling error and does not reflect a relationship that actually exists in the general population.

Factor analysis

Factor analysis is a statistical technique which aims to identify whether there are one or more apparent sources of commonality to the answers given by respondents to a set of questions. It ascertains the smallest number of *factors* (or dimensions) which can most economically summarise all of the variation found in the set of questions being analysed. Factors are established where respondents who give a particular answer to one question in the set, tend to give the same answer as each other to one or more of the other questions in the set. The technique is most useful when a relatively small number of factors are able to account for a relatively large proportion of the variance in all of the questions in the set.

The technique produces a *factor loading* for each question (or variable) on each factor. Where questions have a high loading on the same factor, then it will be the case that respondents who give a particular answer to one of these questions tend to give a similar answer to the other questions. The technique is most commonly used in attitudinal research to try to identify the underlying ideological dimensions which apparently structure attitudes towards the subject in question.

International Social Survey Programme

The *International Social Survey Programme* (ISSP) is run by a group of research organisations, each of which undertakes to field annually an agreed module of questions on a chosen topic area. Since 1985, an *International Social Survey Programme* module has been included in one of the *British Social Attitudes* self-completion questionnaires. Each module is chosen for repetition at intervals to allow comparisons both between countries (membership is currently standing at over 40) and over time. In 2008, the chosen subject was Religion, and the module was carried on the A and B versions of the self-completion questionnaire (Qs. 1.1–1.34).[9]

Notes

1. Until 1991 all *British Social Attitudes* samples were drawn from the Electoral Register (ER). However, following concern that this sampling frame might be deficient in its coverage of certain population subgroups, a 'splicing' experiment was conducted in 1991. We are grateful to the Market Research Development Fund for contributing towards the costs of this experiment. Its purpose was to investigate whether a switch to PAF would disrupt the time-series – for instance, by lowering response rates or affecting the distribution of responses to particular questions. In the event, it was concluded that the change from ER to PAF was unlikely to affect time trends in any noticeable ways, and that no adjustment factors were necessary. Since significant differences in efficiency exist between PAF and ER, and because we considered it untenable to continue to use a frame that is known to be biased, we decided to adopt PAF as the sampling frame for future *British Social Attitudes* surveys. For details of the PAF/ER 'splicing' experiment, see Lynn and Taylor (1995).

2. This includes households not containing any adults aged 18 and over, vacant dwelling units, derelict dwelling units, non-resident addresses and other deadwood.

3. In 1993 it was decided to mount a split-sample experiment designed to test the applicability of Computer-Assisted Personal Interviewing (CAPI) to the *British Social Attitudes* survey series. CAPI has been used increasingly over the past decade as an alternative to traditional interviewing techniques. As the name implies, CAPI involves the use of lap-top computers during the interview, with interviewers entering responses directly into the computer. One of the advantages of CAPI is that it significantly reduces both the amount of time spent on data processing and the number of coding and editing errors. There was, however, concern that a different interviewing technique might alter the distribution of responses and so affect the year-on-year consistency of *British Social Attitudes* data.

   Following the experiment, it was decided to change over to CAPI completely in 1994 (the self-completion questionnaire still being administered in the conventional way). The results of the experiment are discussed in *The 11th Report* (Lynn and Purdon, 1994).

4. Interview times recorded as less than 20 minutes were excluded, as these timings were likely to be errors.

5. An experiment was conducted on the 1991 *British Social Attitudes* survey (Jowell *et al.*, 1992) which showed that sending advance letters to sampled addresses before fieldwork begins has very little impact on response rates. However, interviewers do find that an advance letter helps them to introduce the survey on the doorstep, and a majority of respondents have said that they preferred some advance notice. For these reasons, advance letters have been used on the *British Social Attitudes* surveys since 1991.

6. Because of methodological experiments on scale development, the exact items detailed in this section have not been asked on all versions of the questionnaire each year.

7. In 1994 only, this item was replaced by: Ordinary people get their fair share of the nation's wealth. *[Wealth1]*

8. In constructing the scale, a decision had to be taken on how to treat missing values ("Don't knows", "Refused" and "Not answered"). Respondents who had more than two missing values on the left–right scale and more than three missing values on the libertarian–authoritarian and welfarism scales were excluded from that scale. For respondents with just a few missing values, 'Don't knows' were recoded to the midpoint of the scale and 'Refused' or 'Not answered' were recoded to the scale mean for that respondent on their valid items.

9. See www.natcen.ac.uk/bsaquestionnaires.

References

DeVellis, R.F. (2003), *Scale Development: Theory and Applications,* 2nd edition, Applied Social Research Methods Series, 26, Thousand Oaks, CA: Sage

Jowell, R., Brook, L., Prior, G. and Taylor, B. (1992), *British Social Attitudes: the 9th Report*, Aldershot: Dartmouth

Lynn, P. and Purdon, S. (1994), 'Time-series and lap-tops: the change to computer-assisted interviewing', in Jowell, R., Curtice, J., Brook, L. and Ahrendt, D. (eds.), *British Social Attitudes: the 11th Report*, Aldershot: Dartmouth

Lynn, P. and Taylor, B. (1995), 'On the bias and variance of samples of individuals: a comparison of the Electoral Registers and Postcode Address File as sampling frames', *The Statistician*, **44**: 173–194

Spector, P.E. (1992), *Summated Rating Scale Construction: An Introduction*, Quantitative Applications in the Social Sciences, 82, Newbury Park, CA: Sage

Stafford, R. and Thomson, K. (2006), *British Social Attitudes and Young People's Social Attitudes surveys 2003*: Technical Report, London: National Centre for Social Research

Subject index